French Determiners
In and Across Time

Edited by
Lucia M. Tovena

ISBN 978-1-84890-019-6

College Publications
Scientific Director: Dov Gabbay
Managing Director: Jane Spurr
Department of Computer Science
King's College London, Strand, London WC2R 2LS, UK

http://www.collegepublications.co.uk

Original cover design by orchid creative   www.orchidcreative.co.uk
Printed by Lightning Source, Milton Keynes, UK

Table of contents

Looking at French determiners across time

L.M.Tovena

1 Premisse

This joint volume originates from work done within the project ELICO *Evolution LInguistique et COrpus* (Linguistic evolution and corpora) as part of the action of the French Agence Nationale de Recherche (ANR) to foster the constitution and exploitation of corpora for the humanities. It includes a presentation of the database of occurrences of determiners in annotated contexts developed within the project, and seven contributions on a selection of determiners ranging from Latin counterparts of French items to their current instantiations. The authors came from different theoretical frameworks and entered the project without an a priori agreement on theoretical assumptions, but with the overt aim of sharing evidence and confronting views on the study of the evolution and the properties of determiners in French.

In the following, we start by recalling the goals of the ELICO project and then we present some aspects of its topic, which is the study of the system of determination in French and of its evolution. A brief presentation of the contributions contained in this volume concludes this introduction.

2 The theme and the goals of the project ELICO

The ELICO project has focussed on the evolution of determiners in French from the 13th to the 18th century. Language change has attracted much interest in the last twenty years, as witnessed by the ever growing amount of publications on grammaticalization, lexicalization, pragmaticalization, etc. ELICO tackled this (very general) question specifically in the area of determiners, which form a central category in languages and still exhibit a relatively reduced sensitivity to domain and content, like prepositions and pronouns and unlike verbs, adjectives or nouns, for instance. As for the methodology, ELICO has constituted and annotated a corpus of literary texts. ELICO's choice of indexing texts by means of different descriptors, including genres, is our answer to the concern expressed by many scholars about the validity and relevance of linguistic data examined in abstraction from textual genres or types.

The initial configuration of the project was determined by six factors:
– choosing an empirical domain where research had already been carried out both

by the members of the project and more generally by the community, in order to get down to work right away and rapidly be able to set up a collection of specific linguistic features to be used in the database,

– choosing weakly referential units, whose dependence from the specific domain[1] is reduced in comparison to nouns and verbs, for instance,

– contributing to the study of a topical issue in linguistics in the descriptive, cognitive and typologist communities[2], independently from the different frameworks and schools, in other words, to study the 'system' of determination,

– favouring meshing and cross-fertilisation among researchers from the communities of formal linguistics and corpus and descriptive linguistics,

– exploiting the expertise that some of the members had acquired for electronic corpora of Ancient French (namely BFM - Base de Français Médiéval, http://bfm.ens-lsh.fr/),

– producing a corpus that goes beyond the usual notion of linguistic resource and can be a actual tool of analysis. This goal was pursued by adopting a double set of descriptors, one for linguistic information and one for textual information. The end result is a database where occurrences of determiners are collected and the properties of their local environnments are made explicit. For instance, it is specified when a determiner occurs in a question, in a sentence containing a modal, in a noun phrase headed by a mass noun, etc.

3 Determination and linguistic evolution

In rallying the semantic descriptive tradition in linguistics to a position more characteristic of the formal tradition, the ELICO project has assumed that the term of determiner in general applies to simple articles and demonstratives, e.g. *le, la, un, cet* (the$_{masc}$, the$_{fem}$, a, this) and also to some units that are not classified as articles, e.g. *tout, certains, plusieurs*, etc. (all, certain, several) and to complex forms like *beaucoup de, un quelconque, un certain, tous les, n'importe quel*, etc. (much/many, any, a certain, all the$_{plu}$, whichever) in a language like French. Similarly, within ELICO and in full agreement with the tradition, the determiners of contemporary French have been understood as elementary expressions that compose with common nouns and result in a noun phrase (NP). The study of pronouns—namely of units that can replace an NP, e.g. *il, elle, celui-ci, le sien*, etc. (he, she, this one, hers)—has been included only

---

[1]Domain dependence corresponds to the fact that the domains of the various texts may strongly influence the frequency of nouns, verbs, adjectives, even of prepositions and grammatical constructions (Resnik, 1993).

[2]Typology is the area of linguistics where languages are studied comparatively and their analogies and differences are evaluated, cf. Greenberg (1974); Ramat (1987); Croft (2000); Son (2001) for some general introductions.

occasionally for forms that have double use.

The relevance of studies devoted to determiners in natural languages does not need to be established further in terms of quantity and variety of facets that have been discussed, see Bach et al. (1995); Diessel (1999a,b); Haspelmath (1997); Lyons (1999); Himmelmann (2001); Landman (2004); Chesterman (2005); Dobrovie-Sorin and Beyssade (2004); Stark et al. (2007); Müller and Klinge (2008); Gomeshi et al. (2009) for some recent references. Determiners are units that are referentially poor. They do not indicate objetcs, events or properties, and, as a consequence, they rank rather low on the scale that orders lexical and functional expressions. However, their conditions of use can be pretty sophisticated, because determiners touch upon several important dimensions of syntactic and discourse organisation. First of all, determiners are related to the general issue of quantification (Peters and Westerståhl, 2006), understood as the set of relations between the various domains of individuals introduced by the referential terms, in particular by nouns and verbs. The paper by Carlier in this volume contributes to this topic. For example, *beaucoup* (much/many) can quantify over individuals and events, thus behaving as an adnominal or adverbial modifier, as shown by its various uses and in particular by the phenomenon of quantification at a distance, e.g. *J'ai lu beaucoup de livres* (I read many books) vs. *J'ai beaucoup lu de livres* (I read books a lot/many books). The issue of its characterisation is still under discussion, as witnessed by a recent analysis in terms of binary generalised quantifier put forth by Burnett (2009). Second, determiners have anaphoric properties that constrain their insertion in the discourse and interfere with its organisation, see the paper by De Mulder et al. in this volume. From a diachronic point of view, the referential and textual facets of determiners represent an area hard to study, because a very general issue, to wit anaphora, meets the question of the evolution of the main determiners from Latin, see (Sabanééva, 2003) about their Latin origin. As it is known, for instance, indefinites signal that the new referent is ranked relatively low on the scale of possibility of identification, and, on the contrary, definite determiners, demonstratives and possessives signal that the referent *can* be identified, because it has already been introduced in the discourse or is one of the referents that are accessible. Here, one of the main questions is whether the textual properties are a reflect of the semantic profile specific to each determiner and for which texts provide a natural context of manifestation, hence semantic and textual properties are strongly independent from one another; or whether the textual function is part of the semantic profile, as proposed by Guillot (2003, 2004) for demonstratives. Similar questions can be asked for the indefinite article (Carlier, 2001) and for the definite article (Epstein, 1994, 1995; Carlier and De Mulder, 2006; Guillot et al., 2007). Finally, some determiners exploit modal and intersubjective properties, namely the properties that concern the way in which the agents in the discourse, i.e. the speaker and the hearer, view the entities that constitute the reference of the nouns that are determined. For

3

instance, these entities can be seen as known or unknown to the speaker, different from one another, equivalent with respect to some properties, included in her domain of influence or interest, etc. The papers by Bortolussi, Corblin, Jayez and Tovena, and Pescarini contained in this volume concern several aspects of this topic. Recall that the empirical class of indefinites is somewhat fuzzy. In linguistic work, the articles *un/des* (a, some) and the numerals are lined up within this category, but the status of other units, such as *certains* (certain) or *tout* (all) is by far less clear. This is due to a tension between a referential criterion and a criterion related to generalised quantification. Both *certains* and *tout* do not refer to specific individuals, and from this point of view they qualify as indefinites, see Gondret (1976); Kleiber and Martin (1977); Corblin (2001); Jayez and Tovena (2002, 2004, 2006, 2008); Corblin (2004); Corblin et al. (2010); Schnedecker (2005). However, *tout* is not symmetric[3], contrary to *certains* or *un*, and, in this respect, it does not side with the majority of indefinites (Keenan, 1987; Dobrovie-Sorin and Beyssade, 2004; Tovena and Jayez, 1999b). The group of indefinites partially overlaps with the two other groups of negative polarity items and of free choice items (FCI). On the one hand, determiners–and more generally elements including pronouns and idiomatic NP called minimisers (Bolinger, 1972)– that exhibit an affinity with environments such as negation, questions, etc., are said to be sensitive to the negative polarity of the context[4] in linguistics. As for FCI, the guiding line behind a number of essais is that they are expressions whose semantic function is fully expressed within a semantic structure that allows modal variation.[5] The origin and the behaviour of determiners sensitive to negative polarity, such as *le moindre, quelque ... que ce soit* and *un quelconque* have not yet been well explored, see (Tovena and Jayez, 1999a) on *le moindre*. On the other hand, some determiners are associated to epistemic states of the speaker or her affective states, which is what are called attitudes or modalities in semantics. For instance, *un quelconque* corresponds to a state of ignorance of the speaker, e.g. the sentence *Marie a eu un problème quelconque* (Mary had some problem or other) leads the hearer to think that the speaker does not know which problem Marie experienced. The articles

---

[3]The property of 'symmetry' corresponds to the possibility of permuting the order of the properties. The proposition *tout chat est un félin* (every cat is a feline), which is zoologically true, is not equivalent to the proposition *tout félin est un chat* (every feline is a cat), which is zoologically false. The same applies to *chaque* (each). *Tout* and *chaque* are still classified among the indefinites in some recent grammars, cf. Riegel et al. (1994).

[4]The reader is referred to (Baker, 1970; Ladusaw, 1979; Linebarger, 1980) for some classic contribution, (Giannakidou, 1998; Tovena, 1998, 2001) for some more recent syntheses, and (Tovena et al., 2004) specifically on French.

[5]The reader is referred to Dayal (1998); Giannakidou (2001); Jayez and Tovena (2005), but also LeGrand (1975). Although they diverge on specific points, these analyses have contributed to clarify several important common aspects of the class of FCIs, for instance the need that values be free to vary, which is also expressed in the litterature by the term 'alternatives', the issue of whether variation must exhaust the relevant domain, and the need of distinguishing between being an FCI and having existential or universal quantificational force.

by Jayez and Tovena and by Pescarini in this volume contribute to the study of these aspects. This type of study is fairly recent and is related to the issues of polarity sensitivity and of manifestations of subjectivity in a language.

This variety of possible perspectives on determiners has a match on the side of the expression of quantity. Some determiners, such as *beaucoup de, la plupart de* and *plusieurs*, express or seem to convey information on proportions. This is rather clear for *beaucoup*—see (Vogeleer, 2003) for a close scrutiny of its semantic content—, but it is less obvious in the case of *plusieurs* whose analysis is connected to the general problem of comparative structures, see (Combettes, 2006; Jayez, 2006). In more general terms, it is fruitful to compare the notion of quantity with the notions of measure and discourse orientation, in the sense of Ducrot.

One task pursued in the research component of the ELICO project has been to work on the general question of exploring the ways in which the handling of referential links and text cohesion by determiners has evolved in the centuries under study. In the literature, this general question has been subdivided into more specific issues such as the study of the distinction between definite and indefinite determiners, the range of anaphora covered by determiners, and the question of where to put demonstratives in this picture. Specialised diachronic studies were available on these topics, whereas questions concerning polarity sensitivity and attitudes, to our knowledge, had not been the topic of previous diachronic studies. The ELICO project contributed to fill this gap and to bring closer the study of the evolution of a language and the study of phenomena known as crucial from a typological perspective. Among the issues that were taken up, let us mention the nature of environments for polarity sensitive items (did they change over time?), the relation between polarity and sensitivity to attitudes (are they related, as claimed by some recent approaches?), and the relation between attitudes and non definiteness (are determiners sensitive to attitudes necessarily indefinite, again as suggested by current approaches?). In order to evaluate linguistic changes and to give explanations for them, we pay attention to both linguistic environments *and* text types. We take this second aspect into consideration because it can constitute a possible criterion of competition. For instance, if someone wants to express a general truth on a class, a group, etc., in contemporary French she can choose among several determiners, e.g. *le* (the$_{sg}$), *les* (the$_{pl}$), *un* (a), *tout* (all), etc. It is not at all obvious that these determiners spread evenly across types of texts. Similarly, in case of equality or inequality of distribution, it is not at all obvious that such equality or inequality carves out the same regions or is constant through time. Therefore, if one feels that there is a relation between a type of text and a given use or the evolution of a given use, it is useful to be able to point at possible alternative explanations and to compare them.

4 The papers in this volume

The construction of a diachronic database on determiners in French has been an important component of the research project ELICO. Its rationale and its specificity are presented in the first paper of this book. The ELICO database is a collection of about 20,000 occurrences of determiners presented with a citation context. It is the context that has been extensively annotated with linguistic information, not the determiners themselves, so that the database does not impose a specific analysis, can support advanced research carried out within different theoretical frameworks and can be used as a test bench for linguistic hypotheses. The occurrences have been extracted from a corpus of texts that are representative of various genres and that covers six centuries (13th–18th). The texts were divided into temporal categories and textual information is explicitly provided. This double type of annotation–i.e. linguistic and textual–is an innovative feature that makes it possible for the user to combine within a single query constraints on global properties of texts and constraints concerning relevant linguistic evidence. Hence, the database enables scholars to study the evolution of determiners through the analysis of their uses and the sensitivity of such uses to textual properties, and not just through classical quantitative information, e.g. the frequency of units.

The members of the project ELICO have focussed their research on three general issues, rather than aiming at a punctual cartography of determiners. The issues are the referential and textual properties of determiners, the quantifiers, and the interaction with polarity and with speaker attitudes, and the papers analyse them within the descriptive and formal linguistics traditions. The potential resulting from the interaction of these traditions shows in several contributions, for instance when the diachronic perspective meets the need for a compositional analysis of the meaning of complex expressions. This is the case in the paper by Walter De Mulder, Céline Guillot and Jesse Mortelmans, whose purpose is to describe the evolution of the semantic value of the complex demonstratives *ce N-ci* and *ce N-là* from their origin and in a diachronic perspective. The authors first focus on the value of the elements *-ci* and *-là*, under the hypothesis that the value of the initial shared simple demonstrative *ce* is as it is described in the literature and is preserved in the complex forms. They argue that French demonstratives are token-reflexive: it is always through the context of utterance of the demonstrative expression that the referent is identified, in one case on the basis of elements included in such a context (*ce N-ci*), in the other case on the basis of elements of a context other than the context of use (*ce N là*). Then they investigate whether these complex forms have taken over the semantic values of the Old French paradigms *cist* and *cil*. Finally, they briefly examine the semantic value of *ce N-ci* et *ce N-là* in Modern French. The diachronic perspective can also cast some light on the characterisation of some French quantifiers. In her paper, Anne Carlier addresses the question of the morphosyntactic status of the French quantifying expression *beaucoup* 'a lot / much, many', which can quantify over events and individuals. This question has extensively been discussed in the literature. Three hypotheses have been put forward: *beaucoup* has been categorized as an adverb, as having a double categorical status, both a determiner and an adverb, or as an expression which is underspecified as to its categorical status. Her paper, based on a diachronic study of the Classical Latin quantifier *multum* and of *beaucoup* when becoming a quantifying expression in Middle French, formulates a new hypothesis that allows a better understanding of the use of *beaucoup* in Modern French: i) from a distributional viewpoint, it explains why *beaucoup* used as an adverb can bear on a verb but not on an adjective or an adverb; ii) it offers a fine-grained account of the morphosyntactic categorization of *beaucoup* in its different uses in Modern French and clarifies its syntactic differences with respect to quantifying determiners like *plusieurs* (several); iii) from a semantic viewpoint, it explains in which contexts *beaucoup* behaves as an ordinary quantifier, having normal scope relations.

Finally, work on indefinites and modal determiners within ELICO has contributed in several ways to the ongoing debate on the topic. Three papers are about the determiner *quelque* and its ancestors. This determiner in the plural form is often used in opposition to *plusieurs* as the preferred way to express a modest quantity. Conversely, in the singular, it is perceived as old fashioned in most of its uses, yet, it recently captured much interest among linguists because it shows some peculiarities that exceed the behaviour of a simple indefinite and whose characterisation is a true challenge. The various Latin forms that cover the uses of modern French *quelque(s)* are discussed by Bernard Bortolussi. Bortolussi argues that there is no direct Latin etymon for French *quelque(s)* or Italian *qualche*, even though many indefinite pronouns performing the semantic functions of *quelque(s)* do exist, namely *aliquis, aliquot, quis, quisquam/ullus, quidam, quispiam,* etc. Bortolussi highlights their variety and their close dependence to syntactic and pragmatic contexts. The uses of *quelques* are shared out by the three plural forms *aliquot, aliqui* and *quidam*. Similarly, the three singular forms *quidam, aliquis* and *quis* cover the uses that Haspelmath has called [specific known], [specific unknown] and [non-specific, irrealis] respectively. *Quis* appears to be quite different from the others, in that it yields universal quantification when combined with *si* (if): *si quis* has the same meaning as *quicumque* (everyone). In Late Latin, the fine distribution of Classical Latin was lost, and the indefinite pronouns seem free to alternate; even the distributive pronoun (*quisque*) appears in the same collocations as *quis: si quis / si quisque, ut quis / ut quisque* and expresses universal quantification. Ultimately *qualis* and compound *qualis*-forms, such as *qualisqualis, qualiscumque* and *qualisque* (which does look like *quelque* at first sight), may have been able to compete with those indefinite pronouns that express universal quantification and free choiceness. Thus, Latin exhibits the full array of problematic issues associated with indefinites in modern French (and other languages), despite the fact that the whole set of lexical items is substituted by new forms in Romance languages. A special problem in this array of issues is represented by the interaction with negation, that could lead to characterising an indefinite as NPI or PPI, see proposals along this line by Szabolcsi (2004) for *some* and Iatridou and Zeijlstra (2009) for N-words, among others. In their paper, Jacques Jayez and Lucia M. Tovena offer a semantic characterisation of *quelque* as an indefinite that exploits inferences and ignorance. The form *quelque* N P, where P is a property, signals that the existence of an entity of type N satisfying P is information one gets via an inference (the evidential aspect of the item) and that the exact identity of such an entity remains unknown (the epistemic aspect). Jayez and Tovena show that the intuitive association of *quelque* with free choice (FC) determiners, e.g. *n'importe quel* (no matter which) or *quelconque*, is plausible as long as the evidential aspect is taken into consideration. The fact that *quelque* is marginal in the immediate scope of negation is interpreted as a manifestation of the semantic working of this determiner, i.e. due to the fact that *quelque* conveys the value of an existential indefinite as its main content and at the same time a conventional implicature contributing its inferential and epistemic values. Its behaviour is explicated by relating it to the more general problem of computing implicatures, instead of labelling it positive polarity sensitivity and scoping preferences. Finally, the paper lays the foundations for a diachronic study of *quelque*, which, in spite of their current limits, have already raised a number of important points, including the concessive origin of the item, the relatively early emergence of an anti-specific use and the difficult issue of the articulation/distinction between existential and universal interpretations. The attention paid to the affective 'colours' of sensitive items echoes the current debate on the range of interpretations of FC items.

Scope relations with respect to negation and colours are discussed also in the last two papers of the collection. The question raised by the fact that *quelque* is usually marginal in the immediate scope of negation is at the centre of Francis Corblin's paper. Corblin argues that the French indefinite pronouns *quelqu'un* (someone) and *quelque chose* (something) cannot be analysed as positive polarity items à la Baker (1970), nor as doubly sensitive to negative polarity à la Szabolcsi (2004). Restriction on scope relations with negation, according to him, and on the use in generic sentences, find a motivation only in the existential nature of the items. Such a claim is viewed as a partial coming back to Russell's initial approach to the semantics of English *some* in terms of existential quantification. In his paper, Corblin shows that such an intrinsic existential nature is a lexical property of the determiner *quelqu-* in French. The issue of the affective colours of FC items is discussed by Sandrine Pescarini. Pescarini aims at describing the creation and the development of indefinites formed on the verb *importer*, in particular *n'importe quel*. The members of this family of forms are regularly used since the beginning of the 19th century. They were built compositionally and nowadays, after a lexicalisation step, their meanings are no longer computed by putting together the contribution of each component. Pescarini ascribes to *n'importe quel* the three interpretative values of widening, indifference and low-level that are typical of FC items, and shows how they can be derived diachronically. Besides its intrinsic value, this paper is also relevant for it makes the reader aware of the existence of a form whose motivation is peculiar to French but that exhibits synchronic values very close to English *any*, which has been considered a sort of prototype for FC items in the semantic literature.

5 Acknowledgements

The project *Evolution LInguistique et COrpus* ELICO (Linguistic evolution and corpora) benefitted by the financial support of Agence Nationale de Recherche française, ANR project 06-CORP-028-01 (2007-2010), which is gratefully acknowledged. We express our gratitude to all the members of the project who worked for it, to the colleagues who contributed to the workshops and to all the people who made possible the practical organisation of various events and activity in various ways.

Our warm thanks go to all the precious hands that annotated the database, namely Margot Colinet, Audrey Fontaine, Julie Glickman, Rozenn Guérois, Vanessa Obry, Sandrine Pescarini, Dana Sleiman and Prescillia Vigneron; to Margot Colinet, Rozenn Guérois, Céline Guillot and Lucia M. Tovena for coordinating the annotation process; and to Jacques Jayez and Lucia M. Tovena for supervising it. We are also very grateful to Asma Ben Abacha and Clément Plancq for setting up the database and the annotation and query interfaces, and for providing much needed technical support. We wish to thank all the members of ELICO who worked on the definition of the attributes and values for the annotation of the database and who accepted to act as experts on specific issues.

Thanks to Rozenn Guérois and Lucia M. Tovena for the thematic bibliography available on the web site (http://elico.linguist.univ-paris-diderot.fr/index.php).

Last but not least, a first French version of the book that was distributed in electronic form, benefitted from the comments and advice of the following panel of reviewers: Bernard Bortolussi, Heather Burnett, Francis Corblin, Benjamin Fagard, Donka Farkas, Michèle Goyens, Céline Guillot, Christiane Marchello-Nizia, Walter De Moulder, Anna Orlandini, Sophie Prevost and Lucia M. Tovena. Many thanks to all of them. Subsequently, all the authors provided revised versions of their contributions in English, and Margot Colinet helped to read the proofs, all highly appreciated help that made it possible to publish the book in its current form.

Finally, thanks to Ruth Kempson and Jane Spurr at College Publications for their help and cooperation.

References

Bach, E., E. Jelinek, A. Kratzer, and B. Partee H. (1995). *Quantification in Natural Languages.* Dordrecht: Kluwer.

Baker, C. L. (1970). Double negatives. *Linguistic Inquiry 1*, 169–186.

Bolinger, D. (1972). *Degree Words.* The Hague: Mouton.

Burnett, H. (2009). Formal approaches to semantic microvariation: Adverbial quantifiers in European and Québec French. Master's thesis, University of California, Los Angeles.

Carlier, A. (2001). La genèse de l'article *un. Langue Française 130*, 65–88.

Carlier, A. and W. De Mulder (2006). Les premiers stades de développement de l'article défini. *Verbum 12*, 81–110.

Chesterman, A. (2005). *On Definiteness.* Cambridge: Cambridge University Press.

Combettes, B. (2006). *Plusieurs*: étude diachronique. *Scolia 20.*

Corblin, F. (2001). Où situer *certain* dans la typologie des groupes nominaux? In G. Kleiber, B. Laca, and L. Tasmowski (Eds.), *Typologie des groupes nominaux*, pp. 99–117. Rennes: Presses Universitaires de Rennes.

Corblin, F. (2004). Quelque. In F. Corblin and H. de Swart (Eds.), *The handbook of French semantics*, pp. 99–107. Stanford: CSLI.

Corblin, F., L. M. Tovena, and E. Vlachou (Eds.) (2010). *Les indéfinis de choix libre du français.* Langue française 166. Paris.

Croft, W. (2000). *Explaining linguistic change – an evolutionary approach.* London: Longman.

Dayal, V. (1998). ANY as inherently modal. *Linguistics and Philosophy 21*, 433–476.

Diessel, H. (1999a). *Demonstratives. Form, Function, and Grammaticalization.* Amsterdam: John Benjamins.

Diessel, H. (1999b). The morphosyntax of demonstratives in synchrony and diachrony. *Linguistic Typology 3*, 1–49.

Dobrovie-Sorin, C. and C. Beyssade (2004). *Définir les indéfinis.* Paris: CNRS Editions.

Epstein, R. (1994). The development of the definite article in French. In W. Pagliuca (Ed.), *Perspectives on Grammaticalization*, pp. 63–80. Amsterdam: John Benjamins.

Epstein, R. (1995). The later stages in the development of the definite article : evidence from French. In H. Andersen (Ed.), *Historical Linguistics 1993*, pp. 159–176. Amsterdam: John Benjamins.

Giannakidou, A. (1998). *Polarity sensitivity as (Non) Veridical Dependency.* Amsterdam: John Benjamins.

Giannakidou, A. (2001). The meaning of free choice. *Linguistics and Philosophy 24*, 659–735.

Gomeshi, J., I. Paul, and M. Wiltschko (Eds.) (2009). *Determiners.* Amsterdam:

John Benjamins.

Gondret, P. (1976). *Quelques, plusieurs, certains, divers*: une étude sémantique. *Le Français Moderne 2*, 143–152.

Greenberg, J. (1974). *Language typology: a historical and analythic overview.* Then Hague: Mouton.

Guillot, C. (2003). *Le rôle du démonstratif dans la cohésion textuelle au XVème siècle. Eléments de grammaire textuelle.* Ph. D. thesis, ENS-LSH, Lyon.

Guillot, C. (2004). *Ceste parole* et *ceste aventure* dans la Queste del Saint Graal, marques de structuration discursive et transitions narratives. *L'information Grammaticale 103*, 29–36.

Guillot, C., S. Heiden, and A. Lavrentev (2007). Typologie des textes et des phénomènes linguistiques pour l'analyse du changement linguistique avec la base de français médiéval. In D. Malrieu (Ed.), *Corpora et Questionnements du littéraire, Actes des Journées d'étude internationales*, Paris, pp. 125–139. LINX, numéro spécial.

Haspelmath, M. (1997). *Indefinite Pronouns.* Oxford: Oxford University Press.

Himmelmann, N. (2001). Articles. In M. Haspelmath, E. König, W. Oesterreicher, and W. Raible (Eds.), *Language Typology and Language Universals*, Volume 1. Berlin: Mouton de Gruyter.

Iatridou, S. and H. Zeijlstra (2009). On the scopal interaction of negation and deontic modals. In *Pre-proceedings of the Seventeenth Amsterdam Colloquium*, pp. 296–305.

Jayez, J. (2006). How many are 'several'? *Belgian Journal of Linguistics 19*, 187–209.

Jayez, J. and L. M. Tovena (2002). Determiners and (Un)certainty. In *Proceedings of Semantics and Linguistic Theory XII*, pp. 164–183.

Jayez, J. and L. M. Tovena (2004). *Tout* as a genuine free choice item. In F. Corblin and H. de Swart (Eds.), *The handbook of French semantics*, pp. 71–81. Stanford: CSLI.

Jayez, J. and L. M. Tovena (2005). Free–Choiceness and Non-Individuation. *Linguistics and Philosophy 28*, 1–71.

Jayez, J. and L. M. Tovena (2006). Epistemic determiners. *Journal of Semantics 23*, 217–250.

Jayez, J. and L. M. Tovena (2008). Evidentiality and determination. In *Proceedings of Sinn und Bedeutung 12*, pp. 271–286.

Keenan, E. L. (1987). A semantics definition of 'indefinite NP'. In E. J. Reuland and A. G. ter Meulen (Eds.), *The Representation of (In)definiteness*, pp. 286–317. MIT Press.

Kleiber, G. and R. Martin (1977). La quantification universelle en français. *Semantikos 2:1*, 19–36.

Ladusaw, W. A. (1979). *Polarity sensitivity as inherent scope relations.* published by Garland Publishing Inc., 1980, University of Texas at Austin.

Landman, F. (2004). *Indefinites and the Type of Sets.* Oxford: Blackwell Publishing.

LeGrand, J. E. (1975). *Or and Any: The Semantics and Syntax of Two Logical Operators.* Ph. D. thesis, University of Chicago.

Linebarger, M. C. (1980). *The grammar of negative polarity.* published by Indiana University Linguistics Club, 1981, Massachusetts Institute of Technology.

Lyons, C. (1999). *Definiteness.* Cambridge: Cambridge University Press.

Müller, H. H. and A. Klinge (Eds.) (2008). *Essays on nominal determination.* Amsterdam: John Benjamins.

Peters, S. and D. Westerståhl (2006). *Quantifiers in Language and Logic.* Oxford: Oxford University Press.

Ramat, P. (1987). *Linguistic typology.* Berlin: Mouton de Gruyter.

Resnik, P. (1993). *Selection and information: a class-based approach to lexical relationships.* Ph. D. thesis, University of Pennsylvania.

Riegel, M., J.-C. Pellat, and R. Rioul (1994). *Grammaire méthodique du français.* Paris: Presses Universitaires de France.

Sabanééva, M. (2003). Aux sources latines des articles français. *Le Français Moderne 61*, 167–178.

Schnedecker, C. (2005). *Certain* et ses avatars (*certain n/un certain n; certains n/de certains n; certains*): approche diachronique. *Travaux de Linguistique 50*, 131–150.

Son, J. J. (2001). *Linguistic Typology. Morphology and syntax.* Harlow: Pearson Education.

Stark, E., E. Leiss, and W. Abraham (Eds.) (2007). *Nominal determination.* Amsterdam: John Benjamins.

Szabolcsi, A. (2004). Positive polarity – negative polarity. *Natural Language and Linguistic Theory 22*, 409–452.

Tovena, L. M. (1998). *The fine structure of polarity sensitivity.* New York: Garland Publishing Inc.

Tovena, L. M. (2001). The phenomenon of polarity sensitivity: questions and answers. *Lingua e Stile XXXVI*, 131–167.

Tovena, L. M., V. Déprez, and J. Jayez (2004). Polarity sensitive items. In F. Corblin and H. de Swart (Eds.), *The handbook of French semantics*, pp. 391–415. Stanford: CSLI.

Tovena, L. M. and J. Jayez (1999a). *Any*: from scalarity to arbitrariness. In F. Corblin, J.-M. Marandin, and C. D.-Sorin (Eds.), *Empirical issues in formal syntax and semantics II*, pp. 39–57. The Hague: Holland Academic Graphic.

Tovena, L. M. and J. Jayez (1999b). Déterminants et irréférence. L'exemple de *tout*. In M.-J. Reichler-Béguelin (Ed.), *Référence temporelle et nominale*, pp. 235–268. Berne: Peter Lang.

Vogeleer, S. (2003). Les quatre lectures du quantificateur *beaucoup de*. *Languages 37*.

THE ELICO DATABASE OF LINGUISTIC EVIDENCE

FOR THE SYNCHRONIC AND DIACHRONIC STUDY OF FRENCH DETERMINERS

L.M.Tovena and Jacques Jayez

tovena@linguist.jussieu.fr, jjayez@ens-lsh.fr

Abstract

In this paper, we present the rationale behind the construction of the ELICO database of linguistic evidence that was built as part of the activity of the project *Evolution linguistique et corpus*, and we describe its main properties. The database—based on a collection of texts spanning over six centuries (13th – 18th) and containing pieces of literature from twelve literary genres-- is doubly annotated with linguistic information about the occurrences of determiners and the contexts that host them, and textual information about the excerpts from which such occurrences are taken. Thanks to this double annotation, the database opens the possibility to study the evolution of determiners through the analysis of their uses and the sensitivity of such uses to textual properties, and not just through standard quantitative information.

1 Introduction

Articulating linguistic research and corpora exploitation is by now a well known style of approach, which is linked to the consolidation[1] of 'corpus linguistics' as an independent field, see for example Aijmer and Altenberg (2004), Leistyna and Meyer (2003), Renouf and Kehoe (2005), Reppen et al. (2002), Wilson et al. (2006) for some recent references. Work illustrating this approach is distributed around two main poles. In the production clustered around one pole, attention focuses on the properties of texts, discourse or conversations, and researchers endeavour to detect various features, be they lexical, grammatical, thematic, stylistic, related to interaction or related to the textual structure, etc. Conversely, the relation between linguistic hypotheses and types of data are at the heart of work around the other pole, namely issues such as acceptability, actual occurrences,

---

1 We talk of consolidation of the field, not of its emerging. Indeed, many specialists of this discipline agree that this type of research more reasonably took off during the 50s, namely around the notion of *collocation* (Fries 1952).

experimental data, cf. Kepser and Reis (2005). The ELICO project belongs to this second group. The activity of the project consisted in studying the evolution of *determiners* in the French language from the 13th to the 18th century (included) through the creation and exploitation of an electronic database of occurrences annotated for this particular aim. The project targeted two types of results. We wanted to constitute an electronic corpus enriched with linguistic information, and we planned to use it to re-evaluate the major hypotheses about the evolution of the determiners and to produce analyses for less studied determiners.

In this paper, we present the database of linguistic evidence built by the ELICO project. The database consists of a double collection of records containing linguistic information about specific occurrences of determiners and textual information about the excerpts from which the occurrences are taken. We start by recalling the general goals of the project in section 2. We then present the rationale behind the construction of the database and some of the choices made in section 3. In section 4 we describe the main properties of the linguistic annotation and in section 5 we illustrate some querying possibilities. Finally, in section 6 we provide some elements for the evaluation of the database and mention some perspectives.

2   General themes of the ELICO project

The ELICO project has contributed to extend and refine our linguistic knowledge in a major area of language change research, namely determination in natural language[2]. It is not possible to recall all the actual components of the project, or to discuss all the scientific questions raised and proposals put forth, we will review only some of the most salient points.

From the theoretical point of view, the project addresses and is to be understood with respect to three main sets of problems in linguistics, which are i) the systems of determination used by natural languages, whose significance is crucial for all families of languages, ii) the factors that influence the evolution of languages, and iii) the relation between linguistic theories and linguistic evidence. The specific problems tackled by ELICO have been to foster synergies between an analytical style of linguistic study--which implies a constant attention to the linguistic culture, i.e. theories, hypotheses, key observations, representations--and the use of data from corpora, in the sense of taking into considerations occurrences from a corpus as well as more general properties such as genre, domain and style of a text.

The initial configuration of the project was determined by several factors. We selected a topic for which there was a sizeable amount of literature available in general and an initial

---

[2] For a glimpse of the many aspects of determination discussed in the literature in general and specifically about French, the reader is referred, among others, to Bach et al. (1995), Bosveld et al. (2000), Diessel (1999a,b), Carlier and Goyens (1998), Chesterman (2005), Coene and D'hulst (2003), Dobrovie-Sorin and Beyssade (2005), Haspelmath (1997), Lyons (1999), Himmelmann (2001), Jayez and Tovena (2006), Landman (2004), Stark et al. (2007), Müller et Klinge (2008), Gomeshi et al. (2009).

reasonable degree of expertise inside the project, so that we could define the collection of specific linguistic features to be used in the database in a relatively short time. We also exploited in house expertise with electronic corpora of Ancient French, in particular from the members of the group who had constituted the Base de Français Médiéval at Lyon (http://bfm.ens-lsh.fr/). Next, determiners are weakly referential units, whose frequency in a text is less likely to be affected by the domain of the text than in the case of nouns or verbs. As a consequence, it was possible to constitute a collection of texts with an even distribution of domains across time.[3] Furthermore, we intended to produce a database of occurrences of determiners that goes beyond the usual notion of linguistic resource and can be a actual tool of analysis. We intended to pursue this goal by adopting a double set of descriptors, for linguistic and for textual information.

The ELICO diachronic database is a collection of occurrences of determiners in French presented with a citation context. It is the context that has been extensively annotated with linguistic information, not so much the determiners themselves. For instance, we coded overtly that a given determiner occurs within a question, or in a sentence containing a modal verb, or in a noun phrase headed by a mass noun. This way of coding information can be used to collect linguistic evidence, since the occurrences of a determiner can be classified on the basis of linguistic features. Thus, the database does not impose a specific analysis, can support advanced research carried out within different theoretical frameworks and can be used as a test bench for linguistic hypotheses. The database also contains textual information, and this double type of annotation makes it possible for the user to combine constraints on global properties of texts and constraints concerning relevant linguistic evidence within a single query. The ELICO database enables scholars to study the evolution of determiners through the analysis of their uses and the sensitivity of such uses to textual properties. By offering the possibility of taking into account textual factors while looking at linguistic information, it provides the opportunity to evaluate whether the option of ignoring text types undermines the validity of linguistic hypotheses, as claimed by many practitioners of corpus linguistics.

3 Setting up the database

The database that ELICO had set out to constitute *and* to exploit is based on a corpus of texts classified according to their genre and where information on linguistic contexts is explicitly encoded and is therefore accessible to tools for searching a base. This type of goal can be organised in the three subtasks of, first, selecting the texts in a way that is as

---

[3] Representativeness is an issue very frequently raised about textual corpora. This term usually refers to the degree with which the corpus conveys a faithful image of a phenomenon. In a corpus intended for a linguistic exploitation, this means that no relevant linguistic phenomenon should be left out and no minor phenomenon should be made too salient. This would be the case if the corpus were to contain too many texts in which the phenomenon under examination is under- or over-represented. In a project for the study of the evolution of the language, the degree of temporal resolution is also an important issue. We defined slices of 50 years each, which seemed a reasonable compromise when one looks at existing studies on the evolution of determiners.

quantitatively balanced as possible with respect to given criteria, second, constituting the corpus and the collection of occurrences and annotating all the contexts with information that is a function of their syntactic-semantic properties, and third, exploit the resources produced.

3.1   The collection of texts

The initial corpus used to build the database of ELICO covers six centuries (13th--18th). Two different reasons justify the choice of these boundaries. On the one hand, the quantity of texts dated earlier than 13th century is limited, and it was too reduced to be integrated in the database in a satisfactory way. It is also particularly difficult to have access to these texts for a public domain use. On the other hand, the 18th century is considered to be a reliable frontier with respect to the major changes for determiners in French. By this time, the major classes of determiners have acquired most of their central features.

The corpus is constituted by texts representative of various genres. Variety in a database is often associated to the variety of the *type* of text, and it is obvious that there are dependencies between some linguistic characteristics and the types of texts, see for instance Sekine (1998) about the relation between syntactic structures and the fictional/non fictional character of texts. The terminology and the notions relating to the types of texts are complex and partly messy, as argued by Lee (2001, 2006), who insists on the difference between internal properties of the corpora and external ones, see Lehrberger (1982), Swales (1990) and Steen (1999) for some proposals of sets of attributes that allow one to constitute the intended types. Among the external properties one finds the topics or domains, such as political, religious, etc., the medium of communication and distribution, e.g. press, publishing, broadcasting, etc., the social and ritual context, e.g. fiction, official communication, etc., and the goal, e.g. persuasion, amusement. The internal properties primarily concern the elements defining the structure of the text, such as divisions, hierarchy and discourse relations, and its linguistic aspects.

The project did not have a collection of texts at its disposal nor the financial resources to acquire one, therefore we used primarily texts in public domain, already in digitalised form when possible. Our sources have been textual databases such as Gallica[4], Wikisource and Internet Archive. Around twenty texts were provided or digitalised by the Unité de Recherche sur l'Ancien français ('unit of research on Ancient French') of the Ecole Normale Supérieure in Lyon (see Base de Français Médiéval ('database of medieval French') at http://bfm.ens-lsh.fr/).

The corpus of texts is slightly more than one million words in total. We set out with the intention of associating each genre with an equal global volume of texts, but problems such as restrictions on legal rights to exploit many texts lead us to some adjustments. The threshold of a hundred and fifty thousand words for each half century was a target

---

[4] Gallica 2, which became publicly available only after the summer 2008, has been a major source of texts for the two intermediate centuries.

successfully reached for the last two centuries, but it had to be lowered to eighty thousand words per half a century for the first four centuries.

We worked on 361 texts that were divided into temporal categories. The texts are in prose or verse and are representative of the following twelve genres: biography, didactic texts, speeches, economy, letters, history, legal texts, arts, philosophy, politics, religion and theatre. From this collection we produced 435 excerpts of three thousand words each, taking care to vary the point of extraction from the text when the excerpts were smaller than complete texts. Each excerpt was checked with respect to a reference edition, whenever possible, in order to detect and correct possible typos.

In discussing the selection of texts, we were primarily concerned with the case where a *genre* could have an impact on what we could call *linguistic resources*, i.e. lexical and grammatical preferences. This type of influence can be observed in a given text on three points; i) some resources may violate a constraint of register, for instance when colloquial terms or constructions are used in religious texts written in a solemn style; ii) some resources may belong to a specific jargon, for instance legal or philosophical parlance; iii) some resources may be affected by the type of discourse structures specific of a genre, for instance rigid formulae, text schemata or custom, cf. Adam (1992, 1999). In an ideal world, it should be possible to predict which constellation of external properties, i.e. which of the elements used in a classification by genre, has an influence on the linguistic properties of a text, i.e. its internal properties. However, this is not a realistic goal, except if it is possible to carry out a preliminary study on a very large scale. To this type of limitation, one must add the two well known phenomena represented by the cultural variation of textual genres across time—see for instance the change of referent for a word such as *roman* ('novel'), the appearance of newspapers, etc.—and the actual difficulty in appreciating the weight[5] of each genre at a given time. All these considerations lead us to adopt a mixed approach. A future extension of the database can correct potential biases due to size that could affect the analysis of the least frequent units, for instance for lack of enough occurrences. In the current implementation, we did not aim at using complete texts[6], rather we gave priority to the criterion of balance, when the conditions made it possible. A first extension could be to compile a list with the numbers of occurrences for each determiner in each genre and to report all cases of over or under representation relative to the genres[7]. This would enable us to notice the dependencies between genre and occurrences. The example of the determiner

---

[5] We mean the proportion of the mass of texts associated to a genre.

[6] The very notion of 'complete text' is not crystal clear. A chapter in a book is a partial text with respect to the whole opus, but it is complete with respect to the division into chapters. It has also been frequently noticed that the same text may contain textual sequences of different nature that can be perceived as complete from the point of view of genre (cf. Adam 1992, 1999).

[7] Technically, a genre induces an over/under representation of a phenomenon with respect to a measure if the measure tells us that the distribution that was observed is significantly different from the distribution on which the measure is based.

ledit ('the aforementioned'), associated to legal texts (de Wolf 2003, Guillot et al. 2007, Mortelmans 2006) shows that this is a crucial piece of information in some cases.

3.2   Information about the excerpts

The excerpts are organised into temporal slices of 50 years and each of them is associated to a file that identifies it and contains a record that categorises it. The set of descriptors we adopted broadly corresponds to a subset of what was used for the BFM (http://bfm.ens-lsh.fr/), with little variations. The textual description contains at least information about the author of the text, specifying the date of birth, the title and the date of the text, the date of publication, the name of the publisher, the literary genre, the form (prose or verse) and the source of the text in the corpus. These files have been filled in by hand. Here is an example of a file relative to a text by Montesquieu.

```
identifiant : DialogueDeSyllaEtDEucrate_Montesquieu

auteur : Montesquieu, Charles-Louis de Secondat, baron
de

titre : Dialogue de Sylla et d'Eucrate

dates auteur : 18-01-1689 10-02-1755 (deb,fin)

#lieu.naissance : La Brède          champ facultatif

date manuscrit : 1722

date edition : 1745

editeur commercial : au Mercure de France

forme texte : prose

genre texte : philosophique littéraire

source : Wikisource
```

The collection of files matches the set of texts. This first collection of textual records forms part the ELICO database together with a second collection of files containing occurrences of determiners and linguistic features of their contexts, which is a specificity of ELICO and is described in section 4.

3.3   The annotation interface

The type of annotation: Annotating a determiner in the ELICO database means to associate all its occurrences, in their various morphological manifestations in each text of the corpus, with an overt representation of specific syntactic and semantic information organised in the form of a set of features, i.e. as attribute-value pairs. The task of annotating was done by hand, but the process of annotation was semi-automatized so that the task could be executed in the most rapid and most coherent and consistent way for the whole ELICO database. In particular, the interface automatically took care of two subtasks. The first one is locating the occurrences of each determiner in their various forms[8] and extracting a citation context used in the annotation. The second one is creating a file for each record, containing a unique identifier for the occurrence of the determiner, and filling in the values for the attributes that can be recognised automatically. Some of the features can be instantiated automatically. In general, these are syntactic features, for instance picking out the noun associated with the determiner, marking whether there is a modifier of the noun, and what type of modifier it is, e.g. an adjective, a relative clause or a participle. The excerpts are pure text, with no structure in it, so it was possible to use Natural Language Processing tools and techniques to extract information useful for the annotation. In particular, the interface exploited some customised extraction rules and applied them through the morpho-syntactic tagger TreeTagger (http://www.ims.uni-stuttgart.de/projekte/corplex/TreeTagger/). All automatically produced values can be modified manually by the annotator. As for the features that could not be detected automatically, in general all the semantic ones, the annotator filled in the information by hand. The annotator was also the only authority for deciding whether a form had to be annotated or not, since the interface proposes all the forms that match a given set of strings, but homographs and adverbs had be discarded. The status of each file was marked overtly, from provisional to final, and its content could be modified at any time during the annotation process. The interface was accessible via a server and this made it possible to annotate the occurrences by working at a distance. Several annotators were able to connect to the database and work at the same time.

Decision support: No text tagging was planned within the project for practical reasons, namely that conceiving and implementing a tagger would have represented a goal on its own, and that using a tagger available off the shelf would have required separate trainings for the various temporal slices, which is energy and time consuming[9] and rather risky. However, during the phase of annotation, TreeTagger was run by the interface and the output of its analysis was presented as support to the decision of the annotator, but was not saved somewhere in the final annotated corpus.

---

[8] For each determiner, the interface uses a list of forms that gathers together all the inflected forms and graphic variants relevant for the six centuries under examination, more on it at section 4.

[9] Leaving aside considerations on the intrinsic qualities of well known taggers such as CORDIAL or TREETAGGER, the training process is energy and time consuming because these taggers are not interactive, i.e. it is not possible to modify their vocabulary before starting the tagging. This is a drawback in a number of situations when working with texts from 6 centuries.

<u>Storing the annotations</u>: The option of storing information outside the texts offered a good compromise between the task of creating a database that realises our scientific goals and practical constraints such as complying to the current legal regulations on literary texts. More precisely, the database of occurrences ELICO is structured fully independent (in the physical sense) from the texts from which the occurrences have been extracted. The option of storing information outside the texts also meant that the latter remained untouched and that they can possibly be used for other future projects. Indeed, tasks like information extraction are much easier when performed on bare texts.

The annotating interface described above proved very useful in the first phase of annotation, but showed some limitations as the collection of files attached to each text grew, because it turned out to be too greedy in computing resources. During the phase of revision of the records, a lighter interface environment was used. As for editing the files content, the application XMLSpy was parametrised with an xml schema and a specific editing form. The Subversion version control system provided a way to retain the multi user option. The change from one environment to the other offered us the opportunity to modify the format of the records by adding a field for the citation context. This change fully implemented our choice of making the collection of records on the determiners really independent from the collection of excerpts, in agreement with the policy of the project.

4   The database of occurrences of determiners in citation contexts

It is clearly not possible to work on the totality of the determiners of a language, and it is actually not clear whether such a set can be identified. The project ELICO defined a list of determiners for which the annotation interface was pre-programmed, and then selected a subset of it as the actual goal, leaving the rest for a subsequent annotating phase. The selected subset of determiners is the following: *le moindre, chaque, chaque un* and *tout, ledit, quelque, quelques* and *quelque un, aucun* and *aucuns, plusieurs, maint* and *moult*. The output of the annotating work is a collection of over 20,000 linguistic records that constitute the ELICO database together with the records on textual information.

The various forms each determiner may have had in the six centuries under examination, including typographical variants, and the set of its inflected forms, all together constitute its 'manifestations' in diachrony and are targeted by the annotation. For each determiner, these forms were collected in a list that is associated with the contemporary masculine singular form, that we use as the lemma of the determiner. These lists were used by the annotation interface in searching the texts for prospective occurrences, and can also be exploited by the query interface when searching through the records.

The information contained in the linguistic records is the explicit representation of implicit information that can provide evidence relevant for a linguistic analysis. The type of knowledge targeted in the ELICO project is represented as a set of attribute-value pairs. The features are mainly about the syntactic structure of the context and the semantic interpretation. All information is in French.

Each record contains a field with the citation context and information that can be conceptually organised in three blocks as follows.

- First, there is a block of information about the occurrence itself. These are: 1. the form of occurrence, 2. its syntactic category (determiner or pronoun), 3. the presence of *de* in the form, and 4. its being part in a multi-determiner.
- Next, there are features about the noun or NP attached to the determiner. First of all, 5. the form of the noun. Then follows grammatical information such as 6. number, 7. gender and 8. the presence of a nominal coordination within the NP (det N1 coordination N2). Then properties with a strong semantic impact are delimited, such as 9. whether the noun is abstract (i.e. it names an event, an action, a feeling or a quality), or concrete, or a 'unit of time' or 'instanciation/measure', 10. mass vs count distinction, 11. the distinction between proper noun or common noun, 12. the presence of modifiers (e.g. adjective, participle, subordinate clause, complement of the noun), 13. the form of the modifiers and 14. their position with respect to the noun.
- Finally, there are some features relative to the context. Feature 15. is the grammatical status of the NP and is used to describe the function of the NP containing the determiner within the sentence. This is one of the features with the richest set of values and it codes syntactic and semantic information. Next, there are three features devoted to the verbal form of the clause that hosts the NP, namely 16. mode of the verb of the clause 17. tense, and 18. voice. Finally, there is coded information about the clause, 19. whether the main verb is a modal, 20. what is the nature of the sentence (i.e. polarity and grammatical form); then, mainly in order to compute effects of logical double negation, 21. the presence of *sans* ('without') taking the NP in its scope, and 22. the presence of a form of conditional structure.

In each record there also is a free-text field where annotators were encouraged to store comments and information not coded by the features. For instance, cases where the universal quantifier *tout* is floated are noted here.

5   Quering the database

Among the actions taken to disseminate the results and resources produced by the ELICO project, there is the effort to make the database accessible on line to the international community of researchers in an as open form as possible. This is not yet possible at the time of writing this paper, but this action is already under way. Access will be possible through the official site of the project (http://elico.linguist.univ-paris-diderot.fr/index.php).

The database can be queried to get all the cases that satisfy the criteria the user chose among the criteria proposed by the interface. It is possible to formulate a query about a specific form, for instance the feminine plural form of the universal quantifier, e.g. *toutes*, or to collect all the forms of a determiner across time by using a query on the whole group of forms, for instance by using the lemma 'tout'. It is also possible to formulate more complex queries by using specific criteria for searching the database. The sets of values for each feature are presented in pull down menus. The form of the determiner targeted by the query is the only field where the user has to type some text in. In the version of the database described in this section, all the criteria belong to the linguistic records associated with the determiners.

As an example, we have reproduced below a subset of the selection of criteria. In this example, the user asked for the forms of *quelque*[10] that occur in a sentence with the verb in the indicative mode and containing an expression of negation. The value of the other contextual features is left undefined. (test done in May 2010)

The query returned 7 answers, among which one is from the text *Le voyage de Gênes* by Marot. Let us look at this answer more closely. The properties of the occurrence of *quelque* that it contains are reproduced below.

---

[10] The reader is referred to (Corblin 2004, this volume), (Jayez and Tovena 2008, this volume), (Combettes 2004) i.a., for a discussion of some properties of this determiner.

```
quelque --- #LeVoyageDeGenes_Marot    V  A
```

Type : determinant
Forme avec "DE" : non
Multidéterminant : non

Traits relatifs au nom (ou GN) attaché au déterminant

Nom : macule
Genre : feminin
Nombre : singulier
Coordination nominale du GN : non

Marquage sémantique de l'occurrence du N

Nom abstrait | nom concret | unité de temps | instanciation | autres : autre
Nom massif | nom comptable : comptable
Nom propre | nom commun : commun
Présence d'un modifieur auprès du nom : non
Modifieur(s) : ....
Place du modifieur par rapport au nom : non

Traits relatifs au contexte

Statut grammatical du groupe nominal : CD
Mode : indicatif
Temps : passe
Voix : active
Verbe modal principal : non
Nature de la phrase : negative
Dans la portée de "SANS" : non
Présence d'une structure conditionnelle : non

The accessible textual environment of the form is of about 800 characters. In the example under discussion, the context available is the following.

> et banieres Povres souldars sortent de leurs tesnieres, Courent les rues comme demoniacles, Gastans des nobles tours, maisons et pinacles. Lors eussiez veu, contre murs et pallis, Où imprimées estoyent les fleurs de lis, Lascher leurs traitz ; les ungs les derompoyent Les aultres fange à l'encontre jettoyent, En tel façon qui n'en demoura nulle Qui fust entiere ou n'eust **quelque** macule. Durant ce trouble, ceste turbe maligne Va conspirer d'aller mettre en ruine Le Castellat et de bouter à mort Tous les Françoys, qui lors gardoyent le fort, Lesquelz, sachans la place estre non forte, Et d'aultre part voyans ceste cohorte Plus animez à faire leur emprinse Que juifz à faire de Jhesucrist la prinse, Delibererent de leur rendre la place En leur [11]

This quotation gives us the opportunity to discuss the problem of the interaction with negation in the frame of a contextual type of annotation. Some element, among which the determiner *quelque* (≈ 'some'), are known to have a much reduced compatibility with clausemate negation. This is shown, for instance, by the contrast between the marginal example ?? *Il n'a pas fait quelque effort* ('he did not make some effort') and the fully

---

[11] Approximate translation: 'The poor soldiers leave their den. They run through the streets like demons, damaging noble towers, houses and pinnacles. One could see them throw arrows against walls and hangings, where *fleurs de lys* were printed. Some of them tore them apart, others threw mud at them, so that none of them remained intact or clean. During theses troubles, this wicked mob decides on destroying the castle and killing all the Frenchmen who guarded the fort by throwing them down. The latter, as they knew that the place is not very strong and, moreover, realised that the crowd was more determined to catch them than the Jews to catch Jesus Christ, chose to surrender'

acceptable example *Il n'a fait aucun effort* ('he did not make any effort'). However, the presence of two negations usually strongly improves the perception of the examples, cf. *non sans quelque effort* ('not without some efforts'). This is the case exemplified in the quotation, where *quelque* occurs in a negative clause, *but* this clause is itself nested under the scope of another negation. It is essential to recall that the information coded in the database often is about the local context only. Features of the local context can raise the awareness of the user, but for a proper use of the database the user is always expected to take into consideration a broadened context before reaching any conclusions.

Since the date of the example discussed in the preceding paragraph, the answers have been extended by including textual information. The database has also been enriched by providing on-line documentation about all the features of the linguistic record. Each feature is associated with a double form of informational support, directly accessible from the page with the query form. For each attribute, a one sentence reminder of its meaning is presented graphically as a 'hint' attached to the attributes, and a longer presentation of the feature, including examples, is provided in a page text accessible through a hypertext link.

6   Summary and perspectives

In this paper, we have presented some of the motivations and processes that have resulted in the construction of the ELICO database of linguistic evidence for diachronic and synchronic study of French determiners. The database is doubly annotated with linguistic information about the occurrences of determiners and about the contexts that host them, and with textual information about the excerpts from which such occurrences are taken.[12]

We are currently extending the research facilities by allowing users to exploit features of both textual and grammatical sets in a query. Constructing such an extension is not trivial because it is not possible to just gather all the criteria in the same query form. This would clutter the graphical window and complicate the query workflow. The dependency between the two sets cannot be fixed once and for all. For instance, a sequence of queries can lead to modify the textual criteria, leaving the grammatical ones unchanged, or the reverse.

The main originality of the ELICO database is its content, not the technical details of the implementation, for which we partly resorted to standard solutions and partly developed a dedicated annotation interface. The fact that the annotation does not concern exclusively the determiners but involves also their linguistic and textual context makes ELICO distinct from other databases containing diachronic data, such as FRANTEXT (http://www.frantext.fr/). The annotation allows one to classify occurrences with the help of features, giving them the status of linguistic sets of observations. Moreover, it is possible to link these observations to textual types. For instance queries sent to ELICO can help the

---

[12] We wish to thank all the members of ELICO who contributed to various aspects of the activity of the project. We are particularly grateful to Margot Colinet, Audrey Fontaine, Julie Glickman, Rozenn Guérois, Vanessa Obry, Sandrine Pescarini, Dana Sleiman and Prescillia Vigneron for annotating the database, and to Asma Ben Abacha and Clément Plancq for developing the interfaces and providing reliable technical support.

user determine whether a given type of text contains significantly more/less occurrences of *tout,* but also whether it contains significantly more/less occurrences of *tout* in certain environments, for instance interrogative or negative sentences, etc. In this respect, it is possible to study the evolution of determiners through their specific uses in specific types of text, thus extending the traditional approach in terms of frequency in texts and offering research facilities that even powerful script-based treatments using regular expressions on tagged corpora do not make easily available.

Admittedly, the ELICO database has some of the usual imperfections characteristic of prototypes, for instance in terms of limited coverage. However, its realisation is in itself a novel fact, which opens the way to designing other similar tools over different empirical domains (other grammatical units, other languages, etc.) and creates a first methodological standpoint, which illustrates the merits and the limits of the approach. The knowhow acquired in constructing the basis enhanced our awareness of the theoretical and practical issues of diachronic annotation and can be exploited to create more refined products.

References

Adam, Jean-Michel (1992). *Les textes, types et prototypes: récit, description, argumentation, explication et dialogue.* Paris: Fernand Nathan.

Adam, Jean-Michel (1999). *Linguistique textuelle. Des genres de discours aux textes.* Paris: Nathan.

Aijmer, Karin and Altenberg, Bengt (eds.) (2004). *Advances in Corpus Linguistics.* Amsterdam: Rodopi.

Bach, Emmon, Jelinek, Eloise, Kratzer Angelika and Partee, Barbara H. (eds.) (1995). *Quantification in Natural Languages.* Dordrecht: Kluwer.

Bosveld, Leonie, Marleen, van Peteghem, Daniele, Van de Velde (2000). *De l'indétermination à la qualification. Les indéfinis.* Arras: Artois Presses Université.

Coene, Martine, D'hulst, Yves (2003). *From NP to DP.* Amsterdam: John Benjamins.

Carlier, Anne and Goyens, Michèle (1998). De l'ancien français au français moderne: régression du degré zéro de détermination et restructuration du système des articles. *Cahiers de l'Institut de Linguistique de Louvain* (Louvain-la-Neuve; internationaal tijdschrift) 24, 77-112.

Chesterman, Andrew (2005). *On Definiteness.* Cambridge: Cambridge University Press.

Combettes, Bernard (2004). *Quelque* : aspects diachroniques. *Scolia 18,* 9-40.

Corblin, Francis (2004). Quelque. Dans Francis Corblin and Henriëtte de Swart (eds.), *Handbook of French Semantics,* Stanford: CSLI Publications, 99-109.

Diessel, Holger (1999a). *Demonstratives. Form, Function, and Grammaticalization.* Amsterdam : John Benjamins.

Diessel, Holger (1999b). The morphosyntax of demonstratives in synchrony and diachrony. *Linguistic Typology 3,* 1-49.

Dobrovie-Sorin, Carmen and Beyssade, Claire (2004). *Définir les indéfinis.* Paris: CNRS Éditions.

Fries, Charles Carpenter (1952). *The Structure of English*. New York: Harcour, Brace and Company.

Gomeshi, Jila, Paul Ileana and Wiltschko Martina (eds.) (2009). *Determiners*. Amsterdam: John Benjamins.

Guillot, Céline, Heiden, Serge and Lavrentev, Alexis (2007). Typologie des textes et des phénomènes linguistiques pour l'analyse du changement linguistique avec la Base de Français Médiéval. Dans Malrieu, D. (dir.), *Corpora et Questionnements du littéraire, Actes des Journées d'étude internationales, LINX,* numéro spécial, p. 125-139.

Haspelmath, Martin (1997). *Indefinite Pronouns.* Oxford: Clarendon Press.

Himmelmann, Nikolaus (2001). Articles. Dans Haspelmath, Martin, König, Ekkehard, Oesterreicher, Wulf and Raible, Wolfgang (eds.), *Language Typology and Language Universals*, vol. 1, Berlin and New York: de Gruyter,

Jayez, Jacques and Tovena, Lucia M. (2006). Epistemic determiners, *Journal of Semantics 23*, 217-250.

Jayez, Jacques and Tovena, Lucia M. (2008). Evidentiality and Determination, in *Proceedings of Sinn und Bedeutung 12*, 271-286.

Kepser, Stephan and Reis Marga (eds.) (2005). *Linguistic Evidence. Empirical, Theoretical and Computational Perspectives*. Berlin: Mouton–de Gruyter.

Landman, Fred (2004). *Indefinites and the Type of Sets*. Oxford: Blackwell Publishing.

Lee, David (2001). Genres, registers, text types, domains and styles : clarifying the concepts and navigating a path through the BNC jungle. Language Learning & Technology 5, 37-72.

Lee, David (2006). *Modelling Variation in Spoken and Written English The Multi-Dimensional Approach Revisited*. Londres: Taylor and Francis.

Lehrberger, J., « Automatic translation and the concept of sublanguage », dans R. Kittredge et J. Lehrberger (éds.), *Sublanguage: Studies of Language in Restricted Semantic Domains*, de Gruyter, 1982.

Leistyna, Pepi and Meyer, Charles, F. (eds.) (2003). *Corpus Analysis. Language Structure and Language Use*. Amsterdam: Rodopi.

Lyons, Christopher (1999). *Definiteness*. Cambridge: Cambridge University Press.

Mortelmans, Jesse (2006). *Ledit* vs *le* démonstratif en moyen français : quels contextes d'emploi? *Langue Française 152*, 70-81.

Müller, Henrik H. and Klinge Alex (eds.) (2008). *Essays on nominal determination*. Amsterdam: John Benjamins.

Peters, Stanley and Westerståhl, Dag (2006). *Quantifiers in Language and Logic*. Oxford: Oxford University Press.

Renouf, Antoinette and Kehoe, Andrew (eds.) (2005). *The Changing Face of Corpus Linguistics*. Amsterdam : Rodopi.

Reppen, Randi, Fitzmaurice, Susan M. and Biber, Douglas (eds.) (2002). *Using Corpora to Explore Linguistic Variation*. Amsterdam: John Benjamins.

Stark, Elisabeth, Leiss Elisabeth and Abraham Werner (eds.) (2007). *Nominal determination*. Amsterdam: John Benjamins.

Steen, Gerard (1999). Genres of discourse and the definition of literature. *Discourse Processes* 28, 109-120.

Swales, John (1990). *Genre Analysis: English in Academic and Research Settings.* Cambridge: Cambridge University Press.

Wilson, Andrew, Archer, Dawn and Rayson, Paul (eds.) (2006). *Corpus Linguistics Around the World.* Amsterdam: Rodopi.

de Wolf, Anouk (2003). Un nouveau déterminant: Le déterminant anaphorique *-dit* en français médiéval. *Verbum 25*, 335-351.

CE N-CI AND *CE N-LÀ* IN MIDDLE FRENCH

W. De Mulder (University of Antwerp)

C. Guillot (ENS Lyon)

J. Mortelmans (University of Antwerp)

Abstract

This text aims to describe the evolution of the semantics of the French "complex" demonstratives *ce N-ci* 'this' and *ce N-là* 'that' from their first occurrences onwards. We will look in particular into the semantics of the elements *–ci* and *–là*, hypothesizing that the semantics of the simple demonstrative (*ce*), which has been extensively described in the literature, has remained unchanged in the complex forms. After an analysis of the uses of *ce N-ci* and *ce N-là* in a corpus of Middle French texts, we will verify whether these complex forms have taken over the distribution of the semantics of the Old French paradigms *cist* and *cil*.

1   Introduction

According to Marchello-Nizia (1995, 170-171), the French complex demonstratives CE N-CI and CE N-LA[1] have replaced in the 15th century the so-called "long" or "very long" versions of the demonstrative determiner, which had a prefix *i-* (ICIST / ICIL, etc.). These Old French forms carried a tonic accent and were used as marked determiners, to thematize or focalize. When the tonic accent was lost, the doubly accentuated phrases such as *icestui chevalier* 'this knight' or *icele table* 'that table' disappeared and were replaced by phrases that only carried an accent on the final particle: *ce-chevalier-ci* 'this knight', *cette table-là* 'that table', etc.[2] Whereas the essentials of the phonetic and morphological evolution of the complex demonstrative *ce N-ci* 'this' / *ce N-là* 'that' thus seem to be clear, their semantic

---

[1] Demonstrative determiners in small capitals refer to the entire paradigm and not only to the forms quoted in the text. N stands for "noun", NP for "noun phrase".

[2] This substitution has not been instantaneous, though: Dees (1971, 72) shows that the combinations *ce + ci* / *ce + là* were already sporadically used before the 15th century. Moreover, as pointed out by Dees (1971) and Marchello-Nizia (1995, 124), the postponed adverbs and suffixes *ci* and *là* were already used in the pronominal forms *ceus-ci* and *ceus-la* since the 13th century.

evolution still remains to be described. This article aims to offer at least some elements to fill up that lacuna.

The demonstrative discontinuous determiner was initially composed of forms of the paradigms CIST, CIL or CE on the one hand (henceforth DEM) and the adverbial particles –CI and –LA on the other. The determiners CIST or CIL seem to have lost their respectively proximal and distal deictic meaning, as is suggested by the existence of forms such as CIL N-CI 'that N-here' and CIST N-LA 'this N-there' that can be found since at least 1350 (Dees 1971, 71). This might explain why *ce*, the singular masculine determiner that has always been neuter with respect to the deictic differences, has ousted the other forms. Thus the subject case *cist* 'this' disappeared from the middle of the 13th century on, and *cil* 'that' disappeared nearly two centuries later.[3] The second component of the discontinuous determiner corresponded to the adverbs *(i)ci* 'here' and *la* 'there' of Old French, as is confirmed by the fact that one still finds the form DEM N *ici* around the same time.[4] These observations also suggest that in Middle French, the discontinuous determiner was not as unified as in Modern French and that the components –CI and –LA were grammaticalized in the following centuries. This process of grammaticalization consisted in a "paradigmaticalization" (Lehmann 2002, 120-121) of the paradigm of demonstratives, the number of forms being reduced to *ce / cet / cette / ces* on the one hand, and to –CI and –LA on the other. In this evolution, the adverbial particles also lost their autonomy and progressively turned into suffixes, which can be seen as an increase in bondedness (Lehmann 2002).

In our analysis of the semantics of these forms, we will adopt as a starting point the hypothesis that the demonstrative determiner (CIST / CIL / CE) has kept its token-reflexive meaning and thus conveys the instruction to identify the referent of the NP by using elements present in the context of use of the demonstrative token.[5] The adverbial particles –CI and –LA can then be said to add the following supplementary information:

(i) –CI signals that the referent of the NP has to be identified on the basis of particular elements of its context of utterance, to wit, the location of the demonstrative token or other, non spatial, elements associated with it, such as the speaker and the time;

(ii) –LA signals that the referent is to be identified starting from elements of a situation other than its context of use in the strict sense, a situation that can contain the addressee,

---

[3] This evolution is also directly related to morpho-syntactic factors and to the specialization of the forms that is characteristic for French. It can be observed moreover that before its disappearance from the system, *cil* 'this' was used more frequently as a pronoun than as an adverb. Other forms of the CIST and CIL paradigms have continued to be used. For a more detailed presentation of the evolution of the French demonstratives, cf. Marchello-Nizia (1995, 157-172).

[4] In Middle French the morpheme *icy* was not linked to the noun by a hyphen. In the critical editions we used the segmentation in words, and also of written forms, are chosen by the editor and only partially reflect the data in the medieval manuscripts.

[5] Cf. Kleiber (1986) and De Mulder (1997) for more details.

but also other elements.[6] In its spatial use, –LA thus signals that the place where the referent of the NP is to be found is not part of the context of use – an indication that may imply that the use of –LA signals a disjunction with respect to the context:

(1)   De quele pays esties vous ? Ou fuistes vous nee ? Mon sire, je su de Henoude. Que dea, vous esties un Englois donques ! Nonil dea, mais nous aymons bien <u>les Engloys</u> a cause que les plus vaillantz seignours de **ceste pais la** sont de nostre linage. (*Manières de langage* 1396, p. 23)

De quel pays êtes-vous ? Ou êtes-vous né ? Mon seigneur, je suis de Henoude. Que diable, vous êtes donc un Anglais ! Certes non, mais nous aimons bien les Anglais parce que les plus vaillants seigneurs de ce pays-là sont de notre lignage

Which country do you come from? Where were you born? My lord, I'm from Henoude. Goodness, you're an Englishman then! Not at all, but we like the English well because the worthiest lords of that country are our kinsmen.

In the following, we will show that the most frequent uses, in which –CI and –LA do not express purely spatial relations, can be explained on the basis of these definitions of their semantics.

Our definitions can be seen as a continuation of those advanced by Perret (1988, 41) for the adverbs CI and LA in Middle French: "*ci* désigne le lieu de sa propre occurrence, *la*, tout autre lieu, du moment que ce n'est pas celui de la présente occurrence du mot *la*" ('*ci* designates the place of its own occurrence, *la* every other place, as long as it is not that of the present occurrence of *la*'). This continuity is justified by the fact that in the first stage of the evolution leading to the formation of the complex demonstratives, phrases of the type CIST / CIL / CE N were "completed" by adding the adverbs CI and LA, which were not attached formally to the nouns involved:

(2)   Nous appellons, en **ce païs icy**, sainctz tous ceulx qui nous font du bien. (Commynes, vol. III, p. 57)

Nous appelons saints, en ce pays où nous sommes, tous ceux qui nous font du bien

In this country, we call all those who do good for us saints.

---

[6] This definition is based, amongst other things, on a proposition by Maes (1991, 179-188), who formulates comparable hypotheses with respect to *deze* and *die*, the Dutch equivalents of (respectively) CE ...-CI 'this' and CE ...-LA 'that'.

We will begin our contribution by studying the occurrences of –CI and –LA in a corpus consisting of 15 texts written between 1305 and 1546, mostly narrative (novels, romances, historical texts, brief stories) and generally in prose. In order to introduce the necessary diversification in the data, we have also decided to include in the corpus two short didactic works on French (the *Manières de Langage* of 1396 and 1399), as well as a drama text (the *Farce de maître Pathelin*, written between 1456 and 1469). Since this part of our study is also concerned with Middle French, we further included some data from the first part of the 16th century, more in particular from the *Tiers Livre* of Rabelais (1546). In the table below, these texts are subdivided in four periods of time; the share of the 14th century is smaller than that of the 15th, as the attested uses of complex demonstratives are rare in the 14th century and mainly become more frequent in the 15th.[7]

14th century	1st half of the 15th century (until 1456)	2nd half of the 15th century	16th century
Mémoires of Joinville (between 1305 and 1309)	*Quinze joies de mariage* (around 1400)	*Roman du comte d'Artois* (around 1453-1467)	*Tiers Livre* of Rabelais (1546)
Manières de langage de 1396	*Chronique* of Monstrelet, book I (around 1425-1440)	*Cent nouvelles nouvelles* anonymus (1456-1467)	
Griseldis (1395)	*Cligès en prose* (1454)	*Farce de maître Pierre Pathelin* (1456-1469)	
Manières de langage of 1399	*Jean de Saintré* by Antoine de la Sale (1456)	*Roman de Jehan de Paris* (1494)	

After the analysis of the uses of CE N-CI and CE N-LA, we will examine whether the discontinuous determiners CE...- CI and CE...-LA have taken over the semantics of Old French CIST 'this' and CIL 'that', adopting as a starting point the hypotheses advanced by Kleiber (1985, 1987, 1991) and Marchello-Nizia (1992, 1995, 2003, 2004) on the meaning of these demonstratives in Old and very Old French.

---

[7] Table 2 (cf. the annex at the end of the text) indicates the number of occurrences of CE N CI and CE N LA in each text of the corpus.

2 CI and LA in Middle French

2.1 The uses of CI[8]

In our corpus, CI is used

(i) with nouns designating parts of space, to signal that they contain the location of the token of CI:

(3)   Et puis qu'il vous convient tout dire, meschant et lasche bonhomme que vous estes, et aultre ne fustes oncques, pensez vous qu'en **ce monde cy** soit medicine qui plus puisse aider et susciter la maladie [...] (*Cent nouvelles nouvelles*, p. 516)
Et puisqu'il faut tout vous dire, méchant et lâche bonhomme que vous êtes, vous qui n'avez jamais été autre, pensez-vous qu'en ce monde-ci il y ait une médecine qui puisse favoriser et susciter la maladie...
And since I've got to spell it out for you, wicked and cowardly little man that you are and always have been, do you think that in this world there is any medicine which could help and inflame the illness any more [...]

(ii) with nouns designating a temporal entity, to signal that it contains the moment of utterance of the demonstrative or that it must be identified through the moment of utterance:

(4)   Il fault bien necessairement que **ceste annee icy** advienne quelque grand cas (*Pronostication nouvelle pour l'an 1560*, f.A3r)
Il faut bien nécessairement que cette année-ci arrive quelque grand événement
It is very necessary that during this year a great event should occur

(iii) with nouns designating persons or objects, in order to signal that these have to be identified through the context of utterance of the token of CI ; in that case, the demonstrative can be accompanied by a pointing gesture:

(5)   [...] a part lui dist : « Beaus hostes, en ceste ville a il nul gentil homme ou bourgois de la forme de **cest grant escuier cy** ? » et lui monstra un de ses gens. (*Jehan de Saintré*, p. 290)
il lui dit en privé : « Cher hôte, y a –t-il dans cette ville un homme noble ou bourgeois de la stature de ce grand écuyer-ci ? », et il lui montra un de ses serviteurs

---

[8] In this article, we will use the notations (-)CI and (-)LA to designate the different forms of the deictic adverbs *ci* and *la*, but also to refer to the particles that have undergone a process of grammaticalization originating in these adverbs.

33

Aside, he said to him: 'Good host, is there any nobleman or other citizen in this town the size of this squire here?' and pointed one of his servants out to him.

(6)   Il vint a l'heure accoustumée veoir cest oeil malade, et quand il l'eut descouvert fist bien de l'esbahy : « Comment ! dit il, je ne vis oncques tel mal ; **cest oeil cy** est plus mal qu'il y a XV jours. » (*Cent nouvelles nouvelles*, p. 504)
Il vint à l'heure habituelle voir cet œil malade et quand il l'eut découvert, il fit mine de s'ébahir : « Comment ! dit-il, je n'ai jamais vu une telle maladie ; cet œil-ci va plus mal qu'il y a quinze jours. »
He came at the usual time to see the sick eye, and when he had looked at it he appeared very shocked: 'Goodness,' he said, 'I've never seen a sickness like it: this eye is worse now than it was a fortnight ago.'

These examples confirm the definition proposed in the introduction, according to which CI signals that the referent of the NP must be identified starting from elements of the context of its utterance.[9] This definition does not seem to explain the use of CE N CI in the following passage, though:

(7)   Et, pour parler d'Allemaigne en general, il y a tant de fortes places et tant de gens enclins à mal faire et à piller et robber et qui usent de force et violence les ungs contre les autres pour petite occasion, que c'est chose merveilleuse ; car ung homme qui n'aura que luy et son varlet desfiera ung grosse cité et ung duc, pour myeulx povoir robber avec le port de quelque petit chasteau rochier, où il se sera retiré, ouquel il y aura vingt ou trente hommes à cheval. **Ces gens icy** ne sont guaires de foiz pugniz des princes d'Alemaigne [...] (Commynes, vol. II, p. 210)
Et, pour parler d'Allemagne en général, il y a tant de places fortes et tant de gens enclins à faire le mal, piller et voler, et qui usent de force et de violence les uns contre les autres à la moindre occasion, que c'en est chose étonnante ; car un homme qui [...]. Ces gens dont il est question ici sont rarement punis par les princes d'Allemagne
And, speaking of Germany in general, there are so many strongholds and so many people inclined to do evil things and to pillage and steal and who use force and violence against each other on the slightest of pretexts that one can only wonder at it; for a man who [...]. These people are rarely punished by the German princes.

---

[9] Maes (1991, 172) has advanced a comparable hypothesis to describe the semantics of the Dutch proximal demonstrative *deze* 'this': "A dezeNP expresses the association of the underlying referent with one or more coordination point(s) of the deictic reference domain (DRD) of the discourse involved".

In this case, the function of *icy* seems to be to attract attention to the part of the text where the adverb can be found (or to the moment where it is actualized by the reading of the text) and to signal that *ces gens* refers to an entity that is present in the mind of the speaker (and in that of the addressee / the reader). Although the presence of this referent in the mind of the speaker (and of the addressee) can be justified on the basis of information that was given in the context immediately preceding the demonstrative NP, it is presented as "the one that is present or given "here", independently of what may have been said about it before". As a consequence, it is isolated from the context; for this reason, CE N CI can be used to refer to an entity that is situated outside of the main line of the narrative, as in example (8):

(8)   [...] ordonnèrent plusieurs mandemens pour rompre une très excessive taille et cruelle, que nouvellement il avoit mise sus par le conseil de monsr des Cordes, son lieutenant en Picardye, pour entretenir vingt mil hommes de pied tousjours paiéz et deux mil cinq cens pyonniers (et s'appelloyent **ces gens icy** les gens du camp) et ordonna avec eulx quinze cens hommes [...] (Commynes vol. II, 284)

ils ordonnèrent plusieurs dispositions pour rompre une taille très excessive et cruelle, qu'il avait récemment imposée sur le conseil de monseigneur des Cordes, son lieutenant en Picardie, pour entretenir vingt mille hommes de pied toujours payés et deux mille cinq cent terrassiers (et les gens dont il est question ici s'appelaient les gens du camp) et ordonna [...].

They ordered several measures to be taken to abolish a cruel and very excessive tallage [land tax], which he had newly levied on the advice of my lord des Cordes, his lieutenant in Picardy, to support twenty thousand paid infantry and two thousand five hundred labourers (and these men were called gens de camp) and he ordered fifteen hundred men with them [...].

The function of *icy* is still the same in (9): it attracts attention to the place where its token is located and in this way, it prompts the reader to find a referent for *cette année* that is associated with that place. But this time, this referent cannot be found through information given before (since nothing can be classified as being "a year") and the reader consequently identifies the referent with what follows:

(9)   [...] Et puis leur sembloit qu'on ne leur pourroit charger d'avoir fait venir le roy en Ytalie, veü qu'ilz ne luy en avoient donné conseil ne aide, comme apparoissoit par la responce qu'ilz avoient faict audit Peron de Bache. En **ceste année icy** M CCCC IIIIxx XIII, tira le roy vers Lion, pour entendre [...] (Commynes, vol. III, p. 29)

Et puis il leur semblait qu'on ne pourrait les accuser d'avoir fait venir le roi en Italie, vu qu'ils ne le lui avaient pas conseillé et ne l'avaient pas aidé à le faire, comme cela apparaissait au travers de la réponse qu'ils avaient faite audit Peron de Bache. En cette année-ci 1493 le roi alla jusqu'à Lyon...

> And then it seemed to them that they could not be accused of making the king come to Italy, since they had given him neither advice nor assistance, as was apparent from the reply that they gave to the said Peron de Bache. In this year 1493, the king went to Lyon, to hear...

Briefly put, these examples show that CI is used to signal that the referent must be identified through elements of the context of the token of CI and, consequently, that the referent is not to be found in continuity with the preceding discursive context.

2.2 The uses of LA

As we have proposed in the introduction, LA signals that the referent of the NP must not be identified through elements associated with its utterance.[10] Consequently, the referent will frequently be identified through information associated with a situation different from the context of utterance; this explains why LA frequently has an anaphoric value. It can be used

(i) with nouns designating a part of space:

> (10)　　[...] car a la paroy du cloistre ou le roy mangoit, qui estoit environné de chevaliers et de serjans qui tenoient grant espace, mangoient a une table .XX. que evesques que arcevesques ; et encore aprés les evesques et les arcevesques mangoit encoste cele table la royne Blanche, sa mere, au chief du cloistre, de **celle part la** ou le roy ne mangoit pas. (Jean de Joinville, p. 48)
> Car vers le mur du cloître où mangeait le roi, qui était environné de chevaliers et de serviteurs qui prenaient beaucoup de place, 20 évêques et archevêques mangeaient à une table. Et encore après les évêques et les archevêques, la reine Blanche, sa mère, mangeait à côté de cette table au bout du cloître, du côté où le roi ne mangeait pas
> For near the wall of the cloister where that king was eating, surrounded by knights and servants who took up a lot of space, 20 bishops and archbishops were eating at a table. And beyond the bishops and archbishops, Queen Blanche, his mother, was eating next to this table, at the end of the cloister, on the side where the king was not eating.

In this example, the referent is identified through the information given by the relative clause, whose content is integrated in the whole of the narrative. It thus is the narrative, and not the context of use, that furnishes the situation allowing the identification of the referent.

---

[10] This might be more evident in Middle French than in Modern French, since a sentence such as *je suis là* (to say 'I am here') was not acceptable in Middle French (cf. Perret 1988, 59). It should be clear that the definition we propose implies that LA is always a token-reflexive expression, since in order to find the referent, it is necessary to start from the particular token of *la*.

The referent of *cel pays la* in the following example is also identified by using information given by the narrative:

(11)   [...] Jadys i avoit en Burgoyne une dame bone, gentele et sage que passoit toutz lez autres dames de **cel pays la** auxi bien de bealté com de bontee. (*Manières de langage* 1396, p. 13)

Il y avait jadis en Bourgogne une dame bonne, noble et sage qui surpassait toutes les autres dames de ce pays-là aussi bien en beauté qu'en bonté.

There was once in Burgundy a good lady, kind and wise, who surpassed all the other ladies of that land both in beauty and in goodness.

By substituting *cel pays la* by *ce pays-ci* it can be shown that the referent of the phrase accompanied by LA is identified relative to a situation that is not identical to its context of utterance.

(ii) with nouns designating temporal entities, in order to signal that the referent is a moment in time implied by the narrative:

(12)   Li contes monta a ceval et se departi de la Sale a petite gens, mais casquns se mist a voie apriés li. Qant il vint ou marchiet de Valenchiennes, il i avoit gardes qui gettoient au berrefroi ; si dist tout hault : « Sonnés, sonnés les cloces ! Esmouvés la ville ! » On fist son conmandement, les cloces furent sonnees a esfort ; toutes gens sallirent sus sans ordenance, car on avoit mervelles quel cose ce voloit estre a **celle heure la**, et alerent as armes, et se traist casquns ou marchiet. (Froissart, p. 353)

Le comte monta à cheval et quitta [l'hôtel de] la Sale avec quelques personnes, mais chacun se mit en chemin après lui. Quand il arriva au marché de Valenciennes, il y avait des gardes qui faisaient le guet sur le beffroi ; il dit d'une voix forte : « Sonnez, sonnez les cloches ! Remuez la ville ! On obéit à son ordre, les cloches furent sonnées à toute force ; tout le monde se leva dans le désordre car on se demandait avec étonnement quelle chose ce pouvait être à cette heure-là, et ...

The count mounted his horse and left [the hotel of] la Sale with a small group, but the others set out after him. When he reached the marketplace in Valenciennes, there were sentries looking out from the watch-tower; he said out loud: "Ring the bells ! Get the town's people moving!" His order was carried out; the bells were rung loudly; everyone scrambled to their feet in confusion, for they wondered what could be happening at that time of night.

(iii) with nouns designating persons or other entities; thus the army designated by *ceste armée là* in (13), is the one that was described before in this passage; it must not be identified relative to the context of use of LA:

(13)   [...] Entre les autres y estoit le conte de Dunoys, fort estimé en toutes choses, le mareschal de Lohehac, le conte de Dampmartin, le seigneur de Bueil et maintz autres, et estoient partyz de l'ordonnance du roy et bien cinq cens hommes d'armes qui tous s'estoient retyréz vers le duc de Bretaigne, dont tous estoient subjectz, et néz de son pays, qui estoyent la fleur de **ceste armée là**. (Commynes, vol. I, p. 20)

Parmi les autres il y avait le conte de Dunoys, très estimé en toute chose, le maréchal de Lohehac, le conte de Dampmartin, le seigneur de Bueil et beaucoup d'autres, qui avaient quitté la maison du roi, et bien cinq cent hommes d'armes, qui tous s'étaient retirés du côté du duc de Bretagne, dont tous étaient les sujets – ils étaient issus de son pays – qui étaient la fleur de cette armée-là.

Among others, there was the count of Dunoys, well respected in all things, the marshall of Lohehac, the count of Dampmartin, the lord of Bueil and many others, all of whom had left the service of the king, and five hundred men-at-arms who had all joined the duke of Brittany, as they were all his subjects and born in his land, and they were the flower of that army.

(iv) with abstract nouns, as in the following passage, where LA again demands that the referent be linked to elements that are not part of its context of utterance:

(14)   Et disoient aussi que ledit duc de Calabre avoit envoyé homme exprès à Venise pour empoisonner les citernes, au moins celles où il pourroit joindre, car plusieurs sont fermées à clef ; mais audit lieu ne usent de nulle aultre eaue, car ilz sont de touts poincts assis en la mer, et est l'eaue très bonne, et en ay beü huyt moys, pour ung voyage seul, et esté une autre foiz depuis, en la saison dont je parle. Mais leur principalle raison ne venoit point de **ces raisons là**, mais pour ce que les dessusdits les gardoient d'acroistre à leur povoir, tant en Ytalie que en Grèce (Commynes, vol. III, p. 29)

Ils disaient aussi que ledit duc de Calabre avait envoyé un homme exprès à Venise pour empoisonner les citernes, au moins celles qu'il pourrait atteindre, car plusieurs sont fermées à clé ; mais dans ledit lieu ils n'utilisent aucune autre eau, car ils sont totalement environnés par la mer, et l'eau est très bonne, j'en ai bu pendant huit mois au cours d'un seul voyage, et j'y ai séjourné une autre fois depuis, pendant la saison dont je parle. Mais leur motif principal ne tenait pas à ces raisons-là, mais à ce que les dessus dits les empêchaient d'étendre leur pouvoir...

And they were also saying that the duke of Calabria had sent a man to Venice to poison the cisterns; at least those he could reach, as several are locked. But in the said place, they use no other water, for they are surrounded by the sea on all sides and the water is very good, and I have drunk it for eight months during a single voyage, and I have been there once since, in the season of which I was speaking. But their main motive was not to do with those reasons, but was because the aforementioned men prevented them from increasing their power, in Italy as well as in Greece.

LA gets a quasi anaphoric interpretation in a lot of these uses, in conformity with what can be expected from its basic value. This idea is again confirmed by the following example:

(15)   [...] portes de Paris, où estoient dedans monsr de Nantouillet, grant maistre, qui bien y servit, comme j'ay dit ailleurs, et le mareschal Joachin. Le peuple se veit espoventé et d'aucuns autres estatz eussent voulu les seigneurs dedans, jugeans à leur advis ceste entreprinse bonne et profitable pour le royaulme. Autres en y avoit de leurs seigneuries et se meslans de leurs affaires, esperans que par leurs moyens pourroient parvenir à quelques offices ou estatz, qui sont plus desiréz en **ceste cité là** que en nulle autre du monde. Car ceulx qui les ont les [...] (Commynes, vol. I, p. 51)
Portes de Paris, où étaient monseigneur de Nantouillet [...] il y en avait d'autres appartenant à leurs seigneuries et se mêlant de leurs affaires, espérant que grâce à eux ils pourraient parvenir à quelques offices ou états qui sont plus désirés en cette cité-là qu'en aucune autre au monde.
[...] gates of Paris, and within them was my lord of Nantouillet [...] Others were there from their estates or involved with their affairs, hoping that through them they could obtain office or land, which are more desirable in that city than in any other anywhere else in the world.

The referent of *ceste cite là* is indeed identified by using information that was given before in the text (the mention of *Paris*), but the relative ("qui sont plus desiréz en ceste cite là que en nulle autre du monde") is justified by knowledge that is presumed to be shared by the speaker and the interlocutor, and not by elements related to the context of utterance, as would be signalled by CI, which would also present the referent from the point of view of the speaker.

2.3 Provisional conclusion

In Middle French, an NP of the type DEM N CI / LA identifies its referent by combining information coming from its three composing parts:

-   The demonstrative determiner of CE / CIST / CIL (where the last two forms no longer imply the semantic opposition that is traditionally defined in terms of distance (but see section § 3.2.3.)) has its habitual token-reflexive semantics: it signals that the referent is to be identified starting from the context of use of the demonstrative;
-   The postponed adverbs, and later suffixes, CI and LA are also token-reflexive, as they give the instruction that the referent is to be identified starting from their occurrence, but whereas CI signals that the referent is to be linked to an element of its context of utterance, such as the speaker, the moment and the location of

utterance, etc., LA signals that the referent is to be identified by using elements that are not directly associated with its utterance.[11]

- The noun provides a classification of the referent, which makes it possible, amongst other things, to decide whether the final interpretation of the demonstrative determiner is spatial, temporal or other.

3 The semantics of CIST and CIL in Old French

It has been pointed out above that phrases of the type DEM N CI / LA have been used since the 15th century to take over the functions of the phrases of ICIL / ICIST N. This raises the question whether the Old French demonstrative determiners ICIL N / ICIST N[12] had the same value as those defined above for DEM N CI/LA. In order to answer this query, we will look into Kleiber's (1985, 1987, 1991) analysis of the functioning of the Old French demonstratives CIST and CIL. We will show (i) that Kleiber's approach can be completed by the definitions advanced above, and (ii) that it can be combined with the functioning of CIST and CIL in very Old French presented in Marchello-Nizia (2003, 2005, 2006a/b).

3.1 A question of contiguously saturated referential matching or not

After a critical presentation of earlier analyses of the functioning of CIST and CIL, Kleiber (1985, 1987, 1991) defines the difference in meaning between the two forms on the basis of the role of the immediate context of the demonstrative token. This context is double: (i) since the use of an expression is a spatio-temporal event, each token has a spatio-temporal context; (ii) as a linguistic expression, it also has a discursive environment. According to Kleiber, CIST indicates that the referent that must be matched with the NP is entirely identified by information present in this double environment (Kleiber 1987, 19-20; this will be called "contiguous saturation"); CIL, on the contrary, signals that the referent cannot be entirely identified by using information contained in the double environment of its token (Kleiber 1987, 22). Kleiber proposes, moreover, to combine this semantic distinction with a difference in markedness, considering CIL to be the unmarked term with respect to CIST, and thus implying that in certain contexts, CIL does not imply the absence of "contiguous saturation", whereas in others, it gets the same interpretation as CIST. These definitions can be illustrated by example (16):

---

[11] In the spatial domain, this means that the referent is "distant" with respect to the occurrence of the demonstrative determiner; in the non spatial domains, this means that the referent is "rejected" out of the context of utterance of the demonstrative.

[12] As we already pointed out, ICIST and ICIL are long versions of CIST and CIL ; the studies on the opposition between the different paradigms of the demonstratives mainly concern the short forms, but can of course be extended to cover the long forms too.

(16)   Tuit dient : « Ja ne passera
        Cist jorz, se vos feites que sage,
        Qu'ainz n'aiez fet le mariage
        Que molt est fos qui se demore
        De son prue feire une seule ore.
        (*Le chevalier au lion* 2134-2138)

        Ce sera donc **aujourd'hui même**, lui répondent-ils,
        si vous voulez agir sagement,
        que vous conclurez le mariage ;
        car celui qui tarde, une heure ou un instant,
        à faire son profit commet une grande sottise.
        (translation Hult, 1994)

        All said: "Before this day is through, if you're wise, you'll have concluded the marriage, for anyone who delays even a single hour in acting for his own benefit is a fool."

Cist indicates here that the referent of the NP has to be identified on the basis of information contained in the double environment of the demonstrative. The discursive context does not contain any indication that might lead to the identification of the referent, but the spatio-temporal environment of the utterance does, since the referent can be matched with the day on which the token of *cist jorz* is pronounced (Kleiber 1987, 21).[13] This basic value also makes it possible to explain the spatial uses of these demonstratives, as exemplified by (17):

(17)   Or tien, fet il, **cest mantel gris**
        (*Guillaume de Dole* 723)
        Tiens donc, dit-il, ce manteau gris
        "Now," he said, "take this grey cloak."

In this case, the immediate spatio-temporal environment can contain an ostensive gesture that contributes to finding the referent. The idea that CIST expresses spatio-temporal proximity can thus be seen as a contextual effect of the basic meaning as defined above. Consequently, this basic meaning makes it possible to explain uses which a theory formulated in terms of proximity or distance cannot explain, such as those implying non spatial (and non temporal) entities, as exemplified by (18):

(18)   Asez savum de la lance parler,
        Dunt Nostre Sire fut en la cruiz nasfret ;

---

[13] Note that the noun also contributes to the identification of the referent, as it signals that it is a temporal entity.

> Carles en ad la mure, mercit Dieu ;
> En l'oret punt l'ad faite manuvrer.
> Pur **ceste honur** e pur **ceste bontet**,
> Li nums Joiuse l'espee fut dunet.
> (*La chanson de Roland* 2503-08)

> Nous savons très bien parler de la lance
> dont Notre Seigneur fut blessé sur la croix ;
> Charles en a la pointe, grâce à Dieu ;
> il l'a fait enchâsser dans le pommeau d'or.
> C'est à cause de **cet honneur** et de **cette grâce**,
> que le nom de Joyeuse fut donné à l'épée.
> (translation Moignet, 1969)

> We know well the story of the lance with which Our Lord was wounded on
> the cross; Charles has its tip, thanks be to God; he has had it fitted in a gilded
> handle. Because of this honour and grace, Joyous was the name given to the
> sword.

In order to explain these uses, some have proposed to replace the notion of spatial proximity by that of proximity of interest. Kleiber (1987, 11-12) has shown, however, that this notion is too vague and has proposed an analysis of the use of CIST based on the idea that the demonstrative indicates that the information necessary to identify the referent is "close' to its occurrence' (Kleiber 1987, 22). It is clear, indeed, that these SN resume the events narrated before by qualifying them as "honur" and "bontet".[14]

As the demonstrative CIL has been analyzed as the unmarked term of the pair CIST / CIL, it can get in context (i) an interpretation opposed to that of CIST, to wit, (- contiguous saturation), but also (ii) a neuter interpretation (ø contiguous saturation) and even (iii) an interpretation that is identical to that of CIST (+ contiguous saturation). The first possibility can be illustrated by (19):

(19)   Por **cel apostre qu'en quiert en Noiron pré** (*Le Charroi de Nîmes* 279, Kleiber 1987, 23)
        Au nom de l'apôtre qu'on vénère dans les jardins de Néron
        In the name of that apostle who is revered in Nero's gardens.

Of course, in this example, the information necessary for finding the referent is present in the immediate environment of the demonstrative token; nevertheless, CIST is not used in these contexts because the addressee (or the reader) is invited to relate the referent to

---

[14] This is in fact the only example given by Kleiber where the use of *cist* must be justified with respect to the discursive environment and thus seems to be "anaphoric" (also see Debruyn 1992, 11).

previous knowledge (which is based on the shared knowledge that the apostle in question is Peter).[15]

However, as a pronoun, CIL can also appear in contexts where the notion of (- contiguous saturation) does not apply, such as (20):

(20)   Tant li fu la chose celee
        qu'il avint une matinee,
        la ou il jurent an un lit,
        qu'il orent eü maint delit ;
        boche a boche antre braz gisoient,
        come cil qui molt s'antre amoient.
        Cil dormi et **cele** veilla.
        (*Erec et Enide* 2469-2475, Kleiber 1987, 27),

        Le secret fut gardé
        jusqu'au jour où, un matin,
        ils étaient couchés dans leur lit
        après y avoir connu maints plaisirs ;
        ils étaient étendus, bouche à bouche,
        dans les bras l'un de l'autre, en amoureux passionés.
        Il dormait, **elle** était éveillée.
        (translation Fritz, 1994)

        The secret was kept until one morning they lay down in the bed where they had known many pleasures; they were lying in each other's arms, mouths together, as do those who love each other very much. He slept and she was awake.

CIL can also be used in contexts where it refers to entities that are entirely identified by the spatio-temporal environment of their occurrence:

(21)   car set homes molt forz et granz
        i covandroit au descovrir,
        qui la tonbe voldroit ovrir,
        qu'ele est d'une lame coverte.
        Et sachiez que c'est chose certe
        qu'au lever covandroit set homes

---

[15] This is also the case in the Old French uses of the demonstrative known as "demonstrative of notoriety", which also demand that the reader use extra-discursive knowledge and is only used to refer to stereotypical scenes describing battles, springtime, etc. See Kleiber (1991) and Guillot (2010) for more details.

plus forz que moi et vos ne somes.
Et letres escrites i a
Qui dïent : « Cil qui levera
cele lanme seus par son cors [...]
(*Le chevalier de la Charrette* 1892-901, Kleiber 1987, 29)

Il faudrait sept hommes très grands
et très forts pour qu'on le découvre,
si on voulait ouvrir la tombe,
car elle est recouverte d'une dalle,
qui, sachez-le comme une chose sûre,
pour être levée exigerait sept hommes
plus forts que vous et moi ne le sommes.
Sur elle sont inscrites des lettres
disant : Celui qui levera
cette dalle par lui seul [...]
(translation Méla, 1994)

for seven very large and strong men would be needed to find it by anyone wanting to open the tomb, as it is covered by a flat stone. And know this for certain: seven men would be needed to lift it, stronger than me or any of you. On it letters were inscribed, which read: "He who lifts this stone by his own might..."

In these uses, CIL has the same interpretation as CIST, which explains that it can be combined with *ci*, as can be seen in the following example:

(22)   [...], il est bon que nous dions après en **cel chapitre ci** des essoines et des contremans [...] (Philippe de Beaumanoir, p. 62)
         Il est bon que nous parlions ci-après en ce chapitre des excuses et empêchements de comparaître...
         It is right that we speak later in this chapter about pleas for delay and essoin...

Although Kleiber's analysis clearly presents some advantages as compared to the earlier ones, it also raises further questions, concerning (i) the notion of contiguity, (ii) the role of markedness and (iii) the "scope" of the proposed definitions: can they be applied as such to all attestations of CIL and CIST in Old French? We will now look into these three questions in the order as indicated.

3.2 Questions

3.2.1 The notion of contiguity[16]

Kleiber's definitions of CIST and CIL are formulated in terms of contiguity with the spatio-temporal or the discursive environment of the demonstrative. But whereas the idea of contiguity seems clear with respect to the spatio-temporal environment of the demonstrative token, is it also clear with respect to the discursive environment? In view of the considerable number of verses that sometimes separates demonstrative tokens from their antecedent, it is clear that the notion of contiguity cannot be defined in exclusively spatial terms and that it will probably be necessary to appeal to other factors as well. These may be cognitive factors that determine the accessibility of the referent and that take into account, for instance, the thematic status of the demonstrative NP. The relevance of the thematic status for the use of CIST seems to be confirmed by Moignet (1976, 112), who notes that in the *Queste del Saint Graal*, "la "Quête" est généralement évoquée par *ceste Queste*, tout au long du roman" ('the "quest" is generally evoked by *ceste Queste* ('this quest') all through the novel). It is thus probably necessary to define the notion of "contiguity" more precisely, but the preceding observations confirm, in our view, that CIST N signals that the referent should be identified through the spatio-temporal context in which the demonstrative token has been used or with one of its elements, such as, in this case, the speaker and the on-going discourse.[17]

Besides the reservations already formulated with respect to the exact definition and the limits of the notion of contiguity, Kleiber's definition also encounters problems to explain the use of *cil* in (23), which exemplifies a kind of use that was relatively frequent throughout the Middle Ages and has been well noted by the grammarians:

(23)   Dont commande li rois que li esquiers viengne devant lui, et **cil** i vient tout maintenant. (*Tristan en prose*, I, 175, 10)
         Alors le roi ordonne que l'écuyer se présente devant lui, et **l'autre** se présente aussitôt.
         Then the king commanded that the squire come before him, and the latter came right away.

In this kind of uses, the pronoun (singular or plural) in the subject case indicates a change of syntactic subject, but also a change of role in an interaction between two characters, most frequently a scene of verbal exchange. *Cil* then refers in general to the addressee of the preceding words, and above all to the utterer of the following words. As can be seen in this

---

[16] Cf. Debruyn (1992, 15) for comparable critical remarks.

[17] This last element shows that our formulation of the meaning of CIST is situated in continuity with that of Kleiber. CIST would from that point of view be comparable to the Dutch demonstratives *deze / dit*, which correspond to *ce…ci* (cf. Maes 1991, 172).

example, there can be complete discursive contiguity between the source (*li esquiers*) and the anaphorically used demonstrative. Moreover, both referents are co-present in the same situation of utterance. If it does not come as a surprise that *cil*, the unmarked term of the system, can be used in this context, why is that *cist* is never used?[18]

3.2.2 Marked / unmarked

As we already explained above, Kleiber holds that CIL is the unmarked form of the pair CIST/CIL.[19] As a consequence, if CIL signals in (19) that the referent has to be linked to knowledge that is supposed to be shared by the addressee (or reader), the demonstrative gets this interpretation in context. However, if CIL is indeed only unmarked with respect to contiguous saturation (cf. 3.2.1.), it is not clear what prevents it from signalling in (19) that the information necessary to identify the referent is available in its immediate environment. As noted by Kleiber (1987, 22), the use of CIL brings about a difference in meaning, that becomes clear when one compares *cil apostre qui N* with *cist apostre qui N* et *l'apostre qui N* : only the NP introduced by CIL requires that the referent be linked to knowledge outside of the situation of utterance. We propose, then, that this is exactly what CIL expresses: that the identification of the referent requires that it be linked to a situation other than the context in which its token appears.

This idea is not incompatible with the use of CIL in contexts such as (20) and (21): it is clear that in (20), the referent is not linked to the context of utterance, but to the reference points of the narrative, whereas (21) shows that it is not spatial proximity as such that is relevant, but the way the referent is given. Even if *cele lanme* refers to a blade that is present in the scene, the use of CIL has the effect of presenting the blade as mythical, of signalling that it is known from elsewhere, that it has already been the object of other tales, etc. Briefly put, the use of CIL signals that the blade is linked to knowledge that does not have to be related to the context of utterance of the demonstrative, which comprises the speaker, the moment and the place of utterance and the immediate environment of the demonstrative NP. It seems to us, moreover, that if CIL can be used in a context such as (21), where the intended referent is present, this might explain the confusion between CIST and CIL that appears according to Dees from 1350 onwards. Starting from that moment, one finds not only occurrences of CIL + CI, but also of CIST + LA.

3.2.3 Very Old French: a "personal" system

Marchello-Nizia (2003, 2005, 2006a and b) proposes to explain the use of demonstratives in very Old French without using the notions of markedness or contiguity. She advances the hypothesis that in the first French texts, CIST signals that the referent of the NP must be situated in the personal sphere of the speaker, which includes everything that is close to the

---

[18] Also see Guillot (to appear) for a more extensive discussion of this kind of uses.

[19] He refers to McCool (1981) for that idea.

speaker, but also everything that in some sense "belongs" to him (including the words he just spoke) (Marchello-Nizia 2006b, 107). CIL, on the other hand, signals that the referent of the NP is to be situated outside of this sphere. Thus in the following examples, *ceste meschinne* refers to the wife of the speaker when he talks about their common happiness, whereas he uses *celle* later on in his story to refer to his wife after she has left him:

(24)   « Li roi meïzmez qui France a a baillier / M'i ot donné Lubias a moillier, / **Ceste meschinne** au gent cors afaitié » (*Ami et Amile*, 2200, cité par Marchello-Nizia 2006b, 109)
« Le roi lui-même, qui gouverne la France, m'a donné Lubias comme épouse, cette belle jeune fille au corps élégant »
"The king himself, who rules all France, had given me Lubias to be my wife, this beautiful young maiden with her elegant, fine body. "

(25)   « **Celle** me faut qui me deüst amer. » (*Ami et Amile*, 2444, cité par Marchello-Nizia 2006b, 109)[20]
« Celle qui aurait dû m'aimer me trahit. »
"She who ought to love me failed me."

3.2.4 A second provisional conclusion

We thus propose that the meaning of demonstrative has undergone in Old French an evolution in which three stages can be distinguished:

1)   In very Old French, CIST locates the referent in the personal sphere of the speaker whereas CIL excludes it from this sphere.
2)   Subsequently, CIST signals that the referent must be found through an element of the context of utterance, comprising the speaker, but also the moment or place of utterance, or the text or discourse being produced; CIL signals that the referent is to be located outside of this context.[21]
3)   Finally, the form *cist* falls progressively into disuse from the middle of the 13th century onwards and *cil* approximatively two centuries later, in favour of the undifferenciated forms *ce* and *ces*, whereas other forms of the demonstrative paradigms, such as *cet*, *cette*, *celle* and *celui* continue to be used.

---

[20] This hypothesis also suggests that by using CIL in (21), the speaker excludes the referent from his personal sphere. Does it follow that there are still "traces" of the older opposition in the French language of the 12th and 13th centuries? More extensive research is needed to confirm that conclusion.

[21] This does not mean that the idea of token-reflexivity is no longer valid: the referent still has to be identified starting from the occurrence, or the token, of CE N CI/LA, but, on top of that, CI and LA say whether or not the element leading to the referent is part of the context of utterance of the demonstrative token.

These are not neatly separated stages, however, and it is not always clear which "rules" one needs in order to explain the use of certain forms. Moreover, there is continuity between the "rules". When ICIST N and ICIL N are replaced by CE / CIST / CIL N-CI/LA, their use can be explained by the definition under 2). In the following section, we will verify whether this "rule" is still the one that explains their use in Modern French.

4 -CI and -LA in Modern French

The great majority of uses of CE N-CI and CE N-LA in Modern French seems to respect the definition proposed above: -CI signals that the referent must be identified through the context of utterance and its elements, to wit, the speaker, the place and the moment of utterance, and the text / discourse produced; -LA on the other hand signals that the referent has to be identified through reference points that are not contained in the context of utterance. This definition is best illustrated by NPs containing temporal nouns: when CE N-CI contains a temporal noun, the NP cannot be used anaphorically (Debruyn 1992):

(26)　　J'ai reçu votre lettre le mardi 19 janvier. C'est d'ailleurs justement [*ce jour-ci/ OK ce jour-là] que Jean-Paul est rentré d'Amérique. (Debruyn 1992, 32)
I received your letter on Tuesday, January 19. It was [on this day / on that day] exactly that Jean-Paul came back from America.

The referent of the NP must obligatorily be identified through the context of utterance:

(27)　　– [...] On ferme.
– Comment, on ferme ? A **cette heure-ci** ? (Queneau 1942, 26, cité dans Debruyn 1992, 32)
"We're closing."
"What do you mean, 'you're closing?' At this time?"

Even if the referent is situated outside of the context of utterance, this is initially identified through the context:

(28)　　En 1988, pendant **ce mois-ci**, il y avait de la neige. (Debruyn 1992, 34)
There was snow in this month in 1988.

As formulated by Debruyn (1992, 34), -CI has the preceding noun in its scope.

It can be seen in (26) that anaphoric uses are easier with -LA than with -CI. This is not surprising, if -LA indeed signals that the referent must be identified with respect to a situation which is not the context of utterance and can thus be given by the narrative. We believe that this analysis also makes it possible to explain the use of CE N-LA when the noun refers to a concrete entity (29), an abstract entity (30), or a localizing entity (31):

(29)   [...] de l'ombre du couloir, deux hommes avaient surgi. Tarrou eut à peine le temps d'entendre son compagnon demander ce que pouvaient bien vouloir **ces deux oiseaux-là** (Camus, 1962, 1447, cité dans Debruyn 1992, 20)
[...] from the shadow of the corridor, two men had burst forward. Tarrou barely had time to hear his companion ask what those two nutters could possibly want.

(30)   – Vous avez pensé tuer votre femme et à vous tuer ensuite ?
– C'est romantique, n'est-ce pas ? Cependant, l'homme le plus intelligent a eu **cette tentation-là** au moins une fois dans sa vie. (Simenon, 1948, 184, cité dans Debruyn 1992, 29)
"You thought about killing your wife and then yourself?"
"Romantic, isn't it? But even the cleverest man has had that urge at least once in his life."

(31)   Des noyaux de curieux se tenaient çà et là ; de temps à autre, la police les faisait rouler, et ils s'arrêtaient un peu plus loin. Au coin de l'avenue de la porte d'Argenteuil, ça n'avait pas brûlé. On discutait ferme de **ce côté-là**. Mais on ne savait pas grand-chose. (Queneau 1942, 138, cité dans Debruyn 1992, 42)
Small groups of curious onlookers were hanging around here and there; from time to time the police moved them on, and they stopped again a bit further away. At the corner of avenue de la porte d'Argenteuil, nothing had burned. A lively argument was going on over there. But nobody knew much.

If CE N-LA is used deictically, the referent is situated at a place other than the context of utterance in a strict sense:

(32)   Pierre, tu veux bien me passer **ce livre-là** ? (Debruyn 1992, 21)
Pierre, can you give me that book?

(33)   (en voyant deux personnes s'embrasser dans la rue)
– **Cet amour-là** me va droit au cœur. (Debruyn 1992, 29)
That kind of love really touches me.

(34)   (en montrant du doigt un endroit particulier)
– C'est à **cet endroit-là** qu'il y avait autrefois la sculpture de la Sainte Vierge. (Debruyn 1992, 43)
It's over there that there used to be the statue of the Virgin.

The most problematic uses are then those that contain an anaphorically used -CI, such as (35), (36) and (37):

(35)   – « C'est bien », dit-elle. Il monta l'escalier. Ça le démangeait de se remettre à écrire. Et il se félicitait à l'idée que **ce roman-ci** ne serait pas édifiant pour un sou : il n'avait encore aucune idée précise de ce qu'il allait faire ; sa seule consigne, c'était de s'amuser gratuitement à être sincère. (Simone de Beauvoir 1954, 119, cité dans Debruyn 1992, 20)
         "It's fine," she said. He went upstairs. He was itching to get back to writing. And he was pleased by the idea that this book wouldn't be the slightest bit enlightening: he still had no clear idea of what he was going to do. The only requirement was to enjoy being gratuitously frank.

(36)   Michael Smith avait dû encaisser beaucoup de refus dans sa vie, mais **ce refus-ci** lui alla droit au cœur. (Debruyn 1992, 28)
         Michael Smith must have had to deal with many refusals in his life, but this one really affected him.

(37)   Hier, le comte et la comtesse ont fait la visite de Bruxelles et c'est **cette ville-ci** qu'ils ont trouvé la plus belle, bien qu'ils aient aussi visité Bruges et Anvers. (Debruyn 1992, 41)
         Yesterday, the count and countess visited Brussels, and this was the city they found the most attractive, even though they had also been to Bruges and Anvers.

Indeed, it is not evident that -CI is used anaphorically, if it signals that the referent must be identified through an element of the context of utterance. Nevertheless, our definition seems capable of explaining the use of *ce roman-ci* in (35): this expression refers to an element in the mind of the character designated by *il*, who thus functions as an instance having a point of view.

The demonstrative NP suggests moreover that the referent is contrasted with other referents of the same category, especially in (36) and (37). This effect should not to be wholly attributed to the particle -CI, however: Corblin (1987) and Kleiber (1986) have already shown that this is a characteristic effect of using a demonstrative determiner. Indeed, if this determiner signals that the referent must be identified starting from elements of the context of utterance, its use also implies that the preceding context is at least back-grounded. Since the particle -CI signals in this context that the referent must be identified using the context surrounding the token of the demonstrative NP, it reinforces this effect. This can be shown by replacing *ce refus-ci* in (36) by *ce refus-là*: -LA requires that the referent be associated with knowledge situated outside of the context of utterance (in this case knowledge supposed to be known), whereas the use of -CI has the effect of blocking this appeal to a larger context and to incite the addressee (or the reader) to identify the referent starting from the immediate context. But since in this context, the only information that makes it possible to find the referent are the noun, which expresses a classification, and the demonstrative determiner, which requires that the NP be matched with a particular referent and conveys the idea of an opposition that is internal to the category designated by the noun, the result is a contrastive interpretation. This is confirmed by the context, as this makes it possible to oppose the refusal referred to by *ce refus-ci* to other refusals.

5 Conclusion

The particles -CI and -LA have the meanings that we have assigned them above since their creation:

(i)   -CI signals that the referent must be identified through an element of the context of utterance, which contains the speaker, the moment and the place of utterance, and the discourse that accompanies the demonstrative token;

(ii) -LA signals that the referent must be identified through elements that are not part of the context of utterance.

Our study also confirms that (i) CE N-CI and CE N-LA progressively replace the Old French long forms of the demonstratives ICIST and ICIL, and (ii) that in doing so, they take over the semantics of Old French CIST and CIL. The grammaticalization involved in this evolution consists on the one hand in a paradigmatization by reducing the number of forms and on the other in a transformation of the adverbs *ci* and *là* into suffixes, thus creating more unified or "bonded" forms.

References

Corpus

Antoine de la Sale. *Jehan de Saintré*, edited by J. Misrahi and C. A. Knudson. (1965). Droz, Geneva.

de Beauvoir, S. (1954). *Les Mandarins*, Gallimard, Paris.

Camus, A. (1962). *La peste*, in *Théatre, récits, nouvelles*, ed. R. Quillot, Gallimard, Paris.

Cent nouvelles nouvelles, edited by Sweetser, F. P. (1966). Droz, Genava.

Enguerrand de Monstrelet, *Chronique* (livre 1), edited by Douët d'Arcq, L. (1857-1860). Société de l'Histoire de France (SHF), Paris.

Estoire de Griseldis en rimes et par personnages (1395), edited by Roques, M. (1957). Droz/Minard, Geneva/Paris.

Farce de maître Pierre Pathelin, edited by Dufournet, J. (1986). Garnier-Flammarion, Paris.

François Rabelais, *Tiers Livre*, edited by Jourda, P. (1962). Garnier-Flammation (Classiques Garnier), Paris.

Jean de Joinville, *Mémoires ou vie de saint Louis*, edited by Monfrin, J. (1995). Garnier-Flammarion (Classiques Garnier), Paris.

Jean Froissart, *Chroniques* (livre 1), edited by Diller, G. T. (edition of the manuscript of Rome Reg. lat. 869) (1972). Droz, Geneva.

Livre de Alixandre empereur de Constentinoble et de Cligés son filz. Roman en prose du XVᵉ siècle, edited by Colombo Timelli, M. (2004). Droz, Geneva.

Manières de Langage (1396, 1399), edited by Kristol, A. M. (1995). Anglo Norman Text Society, London.

Philippe de Beaumanoir, *Coutumes de Beauvaisis*, édité par Salmon, A. (1970). Picard, Paris.

Philippe de Commynes, *Mémoires*, edited by Calmette, J. (1964-1965). Belles Lettres (Classiques de l'Histoire de France au Moyen-Age), Paris.

Pronostication nouvelle pour l'an 1560, Lyon, Jean Brotot & Antoine Volant

Queneau, R. (1942), *Pierrot mon ami*, Gallimard, Paris.

Quinze joies de mariage, edited by Rychner, J. (1963), Droz, Geneva.

Roman de Johan de Paris, edited by Wickersheimer, E. (1923), Champion, Paris.

Roman du comte d'Artois, edited by Seigneuret, J.-Ch. (1966), Droz, Geneva.

Simenon, G. (1948), *Les vacances de Maigret*, Presses de la cité, Paris.

Tristan en prose, édité par Ménard, P. (1987), Droz, Geneva.

Other works

Corblin, F. (1987). *Indéfini, défini, démonstratif*. Genève, Droz.

Corblin, F. (1998). « Celui-ci » anaphorique : un mentionnel, *Langue française 120*, 33-44.

Debruyn, J. (1992). *L'opposition de Ce+N-ci/Ce+N-là : un double fonctionnement*, UIA, Antwerp (*Antwerp papers in linguistics* 68).

Dees, A. (1971). *Etude sur l'évolution des démonstratifs en ancien et en moyen français*, Wolters-Noordhoff, Groningen.

De Mulder, W. (1997). Les démonstratifs: des indices de changement de contexte. In : N. Flaux, D. Van De Velde & W. De Mulder (eds) *Entre général et particulier: les déterminants*, Artois Presses Université, Artois, 137-200.

Guillot, C. (2010). Le démonstratif de notoriété de l'ancien français : approche textuelle. In B. Combettes, C. Guillot, E. Oppermann-Marsaux, S. Prévost & A. Rodriguez Somolinos (eds) *Le changement en français*, Peter Lang, Bern, 217-233.

Guillot, C. (to appear). Le pronom anaphorique *cil* de l'ancien français : continuité ou discontinuité topicale ? In : Actes du colloque international *Anaphore et anaphoriques : diversité des grammèmes, diversité des langues* (May 2009, Rouen).

Kleiber, G. (1985). Sur la spécialisation grammaticale des démonstratifs du français ancien, *De la plume d'oie à l'ordinateur. Etudes de linguistique offertes à Hélène Naïs, Verbum special issue*, 99-113.

Kleiber, G. (1986). Adjectif démonstratif et article défini en anaphore fidèle. In J. David & G. Kleiber (eds) *Déterminants: Syntaxe et sémantique*, Recherches Linguistiques Université de Metz, Metz, 169-185.

Kleiber, G. (1987). L'opposition cist / cil en ancien français ou comment analyser les démonstratifs ?, *Revue de linguistique romane 51*, 5-35.

Kleiber, G. (1991). Sur le démonstratif de notoriété en ancien français, *Revue québecoise de linguistique 19/1*, 11-32.

Lehmann, C. (1985/2002²). *Thoughts on Grammaticalization. Second, revised edition*, Universität Erfurt, Seminar für Sprachwissenschaft, ASSidUE 9

Maes, A. (1991). *Nominal Anaphors and the Coherence of Discourse*. Ph.D.. Catholic University of Brabant, Tilburg.

Marchello-Nizia, C. (1992). L'évolution du système des démonstratifs en moyen français. In: R. Van Deyck (ed.) *Le moyen français en langue et en discours, Travaux de linguistique 25*, 77-91.

Marchello-Nizia, C. (1995). *L'évolution du français. Ordre des mots, démonstratifs, accent tonique*, Armand Colin, Paris.

Marchello-Nizia, C. (2003). « Se voz de ceste ne voz poez oster, je voz ferai celle teste coper » (*Ami et Amile* 753) : La sphère du locuteur et la deixis en ancien français ». In : P. De Wilde, S. Kindt, A. Vanneste & J. Vlemings (eds) *Mémoire en temps advenir. Hommage à Theo Venckeleer*, Peeters, Leuven, 413-427.

Marchello-Nizia, C. (2004). La sémantique des démonstratifs en ancien français : une neutralisation en progrès ?, *Langue française 141*, 69-84.

Marchello-Nizia, C. (2005). Deixis and subjectivity : the semantics of demonstratives in Old French (9th-12th century), *Journal of Pragmatics 37*, 43-68.

Marchello-Nizia, C. (2006a). Du subjectif au spatial : l'évolution des formes et du sens des démonstratifs en français, *Langue française 152*, 114 -126.

Marchello-Nizia, C. (2006b). From personal deixis to spatial deixis : The semantic evolution of demonstratives from Latin to French. In: M. Hickmann & S. Robert (eds). *Space in Languages. Linguistic Systems and Cognitive Categories*, John Benjamins, Amsterdam/Philadelphia, 103-120.

McCool, G. (1981). *A Semantic Analysis of the Old French Demonstrative System*, Ph.D., Cornell University.

Mathews, C. E. (1907). *CIST and CIL : a syntactical Study*, J.H. Furst, Baltimore.

Moignet, G. (1976). *Grammaire de l'ancien français*, Klincksieck, Paris.

Perret, M. (1988). *Le signe et la mention. Adverbes embrayeurs ci, ça, la, iluec en moyen français (XIVᵉ – XVᵉ siècles)*, Droz, Geneva.

Annexe

The following table contains the number of occurrences of CE N CI and CE N LA in each text of the corpus.

Textes	Nombre total d'occurrences-mots	Nombre d'occurrences de CE N CI	Nombre d'occurrences de CE N LA
Mémoires de Joinville	75629	0	6
Griseldis	16243	0	1
Manières de langage de 1396	15494	5	2
Manières de langage de 1399	4788	0	0
Chroniques de Froissart	216518	5	9
Quinze joies de mariage (vers 1400)	34680	0	0
Chronique de Monstrelet	29165	0	0
Cligès en prose	31759	0	0
Roman du comte d'Artois	45806	0	1
Jean de Saintré d'Antoine de la Sale	89892	2	0
Cent nouvelles nouvelles anonymes	151925	3	0
Farce de maître Pierre Pathelin	10674	4	2
Roman de Jehan de Paris	25094	0	0
Mémoires de Commynes	204 646	12	32
Tiers Livre de Rabelais	54472	2	1

FROM *MULTUM* TO *BEAUCOUP* :
BETWEEN ADVERB AND NOMINAL DETERMINER[1]

Anne Carlier
University of Lille / North of France, Lille 3
CNRS UMR 8094 – STL

Anne.Carlier@univ-lille3.fr

Abstract

The morphosyntactic status of the French quantifying expression *beaucoup* 'a lot / much, many' has been extensively discussed in the literature. Three hypotheses have been put forward: *beaucoup* has been categorized as an adverb, as having a double categorial status, both a determiner and an adverb, or as an expression which is underspecified as to its categorial status. This paper reconsiders the question from a diachronic viewpoint. It highlights two parallelisms between *multum* in Classical Latin and *beaucoup* when it becomes a quantifying expression in Middle French: (i) both quantifying expressions can combine with a noun or a verb, but never with an adjective or an adverb; (ii) they occur in direct object position (expressed in Latin by an accusative NP not headed by a preposition) or in subject position in combination with unaccusative verbal predicates, but they are unattested in other syntactic positions. These similarities can be explained on the basis of the nominal origin of *multum* and *beau-coup* 'beautiful knock'. Being nominal expressions, *multum* and *beaucoup* are used for quantification of the direct internal argument of the verb and may occur with a genitive complement or a prepositional complement introduced by *de*. Since they quantify the direct internal argument of the verb, they also quantify the verbal process as such and become in this way full adverbs without saturating an argument position. It is only in a later stage that they can quantify an NP external to the VP and that they become full-fledged

---

[1] This research on quantification has been initially conducted in collaboration with L. Melis (*cf.* Carlier & Melis 2005, Carlier & Melis 2006). Earlier versions of this paper have been presented in Paris, Lyon, Strasbourg, Valenciennes and Antwerp. Thanks to my audience at these different occasions for their suggestions and critical comments. The paper has also benefited from the insightful comments of Lucia Tovena, Christiane Marchello-Nizia and of two anonymous referees.

nominal determiners. They keep however their hybrid status, between adverb and nominal determiner, when they quantify the direct internal argument of the verb.

The diachronic perspective of this study offers a better understanding of the use of *beaucoup* in Modern French: (i) from a distributional viewpoint, it explains why *beaucoup* used as an adverb can modify a verb but not an adjective or an adverb; (ii) it offers a fine-grained account of the morphosyntactic categorization of *beaucoup* in its different uses in Modern French and clarifies its syntactic differences with respect to quantifying determiners like *plusieurs* 'several'; (iii) from a semantic viewpoint, it explains in which contexts *beaucoup* behaves as an ordinary quantifier, having normal scope relations.

Although substantial research effort has been devoted to the question, the morphosyntactic status of *beaucoup* in its uses exemplified by (1a) and (1b) is still under debate.

(1)	a.	Il	mange	***beaucoup***	*de* pain.
		He	eat-PRST.3SG	a lot	of bread.
	b.	Il	lit	***beaucoup***	*de* livres.
		He	read-PRST.3SG	a lot	of books

The present study intends to shed new light on this topic by introducing the diachronic perspective.

Beaucoup belongs, together with *peu* 'little, few', *assez* 'enough', *trop* 'too much/many, tant / tellement* 'so much/many', *plus* 'more', *moins* 'less', ... to the paradigm of expressions quantifying both extension (1) and degree or 'intension' (2) (Doetjes 1997, Abeillé & Godard 2003, Abeillé *et al.* 2004).

(2)	a.	Il aime	***beaucoup***	cet auteur.
		He like-PRST.3SG	a lot	this author.
	b.	Il	éprouve	***beaucoup***	de respect pour son père.
		He	feel-PRST.3SG	a lot	of respect for his father.

Recent studies insist upon the categorial flexibility of these quantifying expressions. As illustrated by (3), *beaucoup* can be used as an adverb (3a), for nominal determination (3b/3c) and even as a pronoun (3d). Finally, it can reinforce another quantifier (3e-f).

(3)	a.	Marie	a	***beaucoup***	dansé.
		Mary	has	a lot	danced.
		'Mary danced a lot'			

    b. Marie a lu   ***beaucoup***   *de*   livres.
        Mary   has read   a lot   of   books.
        'Mary has read a lot of books'
    c. ***Beaucoup***   *de*   filles   ont dansé.
        A lot   of   girls   have danced.
        'A lot of girls danced'
    d. ***Beaucoup***   ont assisté   à la réunion.
        A lot   have assisted to the meeting.
        'Many attended the meeting'
    e. Marie a lu   ***beaucoup***   (plus / moins / trop / trop peu)   de livres.
        Mary   has read   a lot   (more / less / too many / too less) of books.
        'Mary has read much more/less/... books'
    f. Marie a   ***beaucoup***   (plus / moins / trop / trop peu / mieux)   dansé.
        Mary   has a lot   (more / less / too much / too less)   danced.
        'Mary danced much more / less /...'

How can we conceptualize this flexibility of the grammatical categorisation of *beaucoup* and of the other members of its paradigm? Section 1 provides a critical survey of the previous accounts (§ 1). The following sections offer a diachronic perspective on the problem of the morphosyntactic categorization and specifically focus on *beaucoup (de)* and its predecessors *multus / mult / moult* in Latin (§ 2), in very Old French (§ 3), in Old French (§ 4) and in Modern French (§ 5). The final section (§ 6) will highlight the parallelism between *multum* in Latin and *beaucoup* in Middle French and suggest some directions for further research.

1   The morphosyntactic categorization of *beaucoup* in Modern French : three hypotheses

In order to account for the categorial flexibility of *beaucoup, peu, trop, assez, tant, ...*, several hypotheses have been explored. Firstly, these quantifying expressions have been described as underspecified with respect to their morphosyntactic categorization (§ 1.1). Secondly, they have been analyzed as adverbs in all their uses (§ 1.2). According to the third hypothesis, these quantifying expressions are ambivalent as to their morphosyntactic status: they can be either adverb or nominal determiner (§ 1.3).

1.1   Hypothesis 1: *Beaucoup* is categorially underspecified

The hypothesis of the categorial underspecification has been defended by Doetjes (1997: 1-2), on the basis of the following observation: contrary to *souvent* 'often' (4) and *plusieurs* 'several' (5), *beaucoup* does not impose categorial restrictions and can be used with both NPs and VPs.

(4)   a. Les linguistes ont   ***beaucoup***   dansé   la salsa.
           The linguists have   a-lot   danced the salsa.
       b. ***Beaucoup***   de linguistes   ont dansé   la salsa.
           A lot   of linguists   have danced   the salsa

(5)   a. Les linguistes   ont   souvent   dansé   la salsa.
           The linguists   have   often   danced   the salsa.
       b. *** *Souvent***   (de) linguistes ont   dansé   la salsa.
           Often   of linguists   have   danced   the salsa.

(6)   a. *Les linguistes   ont   ***plusieurs*** dansé la salsa.
           The linguists   have   several   danced the salsa.
       b. ***Plusieurs*** linguistes   ont dansé   la salsa.
           Several   linguists   have danced   the salsa   (Doetjes 1997: 1-2)

Therefore, *beaucoup* is analyzed by Doetjes as having the syntactic status of an adjunct. The only distributional constraint characteristic of *beaucoup*, as well as of the other similar quantifiers like *peu* 'little, not much/many', *assez* 'enough', *trop* 'too much/many', *(au)tant* 'as much' etc., is of a semantic nature: they are only compatible with open-scale predicates, and do not accept non gradable (7) or closed-scale (8) predicates (Doetjes 1997[2] ; Kennedy & McNally 2005) :

(7)   a. *Elle   est ***peu***   enceinte / morte.
          She   is   not-much   pregnant / dead.
       b. *Une carte   ***trop / assez***   géologique.
          A map   too/enough   geological.

(8)   a. La bouteille est ***à moitié / complètement / *peu*** vide.
          The bottle   is   half- / completely /not-much   empty
       b. Cette image est ***partiellement / complètement / *peu*** invisible.
          This picture is   partially / completely / not-much   invisible

The hypothesis of categorial underspecification accounts for the flexible distribution of *beaucoup* and the similar quantifying expressions, *i.e.* their ability to combine with different categories. But it fails to explain the limits of this flexibility. For instance, if it is true that all quantifiers belonging to the paradigm of *beaucoup* lack in the same way categorial selection, why is the adnominal position more natural for *beaucoup* than for *assez* in example (9)?

---

[2] A more fine-grained analysis of the specific distributional constraints of the different quantifiers or degree-markers is offered by Doetjes (2008): on the basis of their compatibility with different morphosyntactic categories, she establishes a typology of the English, Dutch and French quantifiers or degree markers.

(9)   a. **Beaucoup** de filles   ont dansé.
            A-lot   of girls   have danced.
      b. ??**Assez** de filles   ont dansé[3].
           Enough of girls   have danced.

A second problem relates to the presence of *de* when the quantifier is in an adnominal position. The explanation offered by Doetjes (1997: 157) is based on a comparison with the English quantifying expression *a lot of* :

(10)   a. Jean   a lu   **beaucoup / peu**   <u>de</u> *livres.*
       b. John has read *a-lot / few*   <u>of</u> *books.*

Doetjes argues that *a lot of* is a classifier construction. In the framework of generative grammar, where every NP has to receive case, it is assumed that case is assigned to the nominal classifier, leaving the NP *books* without case. The insertion of the genitive case marker *of* allows complying with the requirement to assign case to the NP *books* (Chomsky 1981). According to Doetjes (1997: 158) and Battye (1991: 32), the presence of *de* when *beaucoup, peu, trop, assez, ...* are used in adnominal position has to be explained along the same lines: given that the quantifier absorbs the case assigned by the verb, the use of *de* is necessary in order to assign case to the NP *livres*.

It should however be noted that this analysis of *beaucoup, peu, ...* as nominal classifiers absorbing the case assigned by the verb is incompatible with their syntactic status of adjuncts, since adjuncts do never receive case from the verb. Hence, the hypothesis of the categorical underspecification leaves unexplained the presence of *de* when the quantifier *beaucoup* is adnominal.

1.2   Hypothesis 2: *Beaucoup* is an adverb

The morphosyntactic category of the adverb is heterogeneous, in part because it served as ragbag throughout the history of grammar. In this perspective, it is not sure that the addition of the quantifying expressions like *beaucoup* to the category is judicious, because their adverbial status is far from unquestionable in all their uses.

Let's focus on two particular cases.

-   Quantifying expressions like *beaucoup* can hold on their own the position of preverbal subject, which is a typically nominal position :

(11)   **Beaucoup** ont   participé   à la manifestation.
        A-lot   have-PRST.3PL participated in the demonstration.

---

[3] This acceptability judgment was empirically assessed by a small corpus study on the basis of *Frantext*: in comparison with the number of preverbal subjects introduced by *beaucoup*, the frequency of *assez* in this same syntactic context amounts to only 1 %.

- They can serve as an NP governed by a preposition :

(12) <u>Pour *beaucoup*</u>, le vocabulaire et   la syntaxe qu' ils   utilisent   en famille
For a-lot,   the vocabulary and the syntax that they use-PRST.3PL in family

n'   ont   rien à   voir   avec le vocabulaire en usage à l'école.
not have-PRST.3PL   anything to do with the vocabulary in usage   at the school.

'For a lot of people, the vocabulary and the syntax they use in their family have nothing to do with the vocabulary used at school.' (F. Dolto, *La cause des enfants*)

These pronominal uses are difficult to explain if we accept that *beaucoup* is an adverb, but they naturally follow from its categorization as a nominal determiner, since it is not exceptional that a nominal determiner has a parallel use as a pronoun.

1.3 Hypothesis 3: *Beaucoup* is both an adverb and a nominal determiner

The hypothesis of a double morphosyntactic categorization, as an adverb and as a nominal determiner, has been defended, among others, by Gross (1977), by Milner (1978a) and by several descriptive grammars. The distinction between the adverbial use and the determiner use is however complicated by the existence of an intermediate structure, illustrated by (13b), which has been labelled 'remote quantification' ('quantification à distance).

(13) a. Il   a lu   *beaucoup*   de livres.
          He has read a-lot   of books.
      b. Il   a   *beaucoup*   lu   de livres.
          He has a-lot   read of books

This structure has been identified by Milner (1978a-b) and has been analyzed as the result of a derivation :

(14)   V $[_{SN} Q \ de \ N']$ → Q_i V $[_{SN} \varnothing_i \ de \ N']$

According to this analysis, remote quantification would be the result of an extraction of the quantifier from its adnominal position and a movement towards the typically adverbial position between the auxiliary and the participle. In support of this analysis, Milner (1978b) observes that the only adverbs compatible with remote quantification are those that can be used in adnominal position, as is illustrated by (15).

(15) a. J'ai   *énormément / abondamment*   lu.
          I have enormously / abundantly   read.

b. J'ai **énormément /*abondamment** lu *de livres.*
    I have   enormously / abundantly   read   of books.

c. J' ai   lu **énormément /*abondamment** *de livres* (Milner 1978b)
    I   have   read   enormously / abundantly   of books.

In this perspective, remote quantification is basically a nominal quantification bearing on the NP « *de* N' ».

Milner's hypothesis has been re-examined by Obenauer (1983) and by Doetjes (1997). Both convincingly show that the scope of quantifier in adverbial position in (13b) is not restricted to the NP « *de* N' », but includes the verb. They argue that the so-called remote nominal quantification is in fact a quantification of the VP, including the nominal direct object. Since this quantifying structure is related both to the verb and to the nominal object, it could be the missing link between the adverbial use of *beaucoup, trop, assez, ...* and its use as a nominal determiner, allowing us to understand why these expressions can express nominal and verbal quantification.

The quantifying structure « Q V *de* N' » is rather uncommon in Modern French, but had a high vitality in older stages of the French language (Buridant 2000, Marchello-Nizia 2000, 2006, Carlier & Melis 2005)[4]. This suggests that the determiner use and the adverbial use of expressions like *moult / beaucoup, peu, assez, trop, ...* separated progressively throughout history. Hence, the diachronic viewpoint can shed a new light on the problem of the morphosyntactic categorization of these quantifying expressions. It is in this perspective that we will examine *beaucoup* and its antecedents *multus / multum* in Latin and *m(o)ult* in medieval French.

2   *Multus / multum* in Classical Latin

In Classical Latin, the quantifier *multus* is an inflected form and agrees in gender and number with the noun. Latin does not have a clear distinction between determiner and adjective. As is illustrated by the following examples, quoted from Menge (2000: § 263), *multus* can be coordinated to an adjective (16) or can occur without coordinating conjunction, in the way of a determiner (17).

(16) **Multi**   *ac*   *summi*   *viri* (Cicero, *Catil.* 1: 10)
      'numerous   and   important   men'

(17) **Multi**   *docti*   *homines* (Cicero, *Fam.* 9,6,5)
      'numerous   learned   men'

Moreover, *multus* is used in a very flexible way as pronoun.

---

[4] The positional constraints and interpretation of the structure « Q V *de* N' » in Modern French will be detailed in § 5.

(18) *Occident   nonnullos,   vulnerant   **multos***
kill-PRST.3PL   several-ACC.M.PL   wound-PRST.3PL many-ACC.M.PL
'They kill some of them, they injure many of them' (Cicero, *Pro Sextio* 75, 8)

One of these pronominal uses is precisely the nominative or accusative singular neutral form *multum*, also labelled adverbial. This form can be complemented by a genitive (19-20-21) or by a prepositional phrase introduced by *ex* 'out of' or *de* 'from, of', taking the ablative case (22). This last case is the ancestor of Modern French pattern *beaucoup de N'*.

(19) ***Multum***   *operae*   *dabam*   *Quinto*   *Scaeuolae*
a-lot-ACC.SG.N work-GEN.SG give-IMPF.1sg Quintus-DAT.SG Scaevola-DAT.SG
'I worked a lot with Quintus Scaevola, son of Publius' (Cicero, *Brutus*, 89, LXXXIX, 304)

(20) *ne*   ***multum***   *operae*   *impendas*
in-order-to-NEG   a-lot ACC.SG.N   work-GEN.SG   devote-CONJ.PRS1.2SG
'in order to avoid that you devote much work to …' (Seneca, *Letters to Lucilius*, V, 1:6)

(21) *Tum   uero   **multum**   sanguinis   fusum   est.*
Then   however a-lot-NOM.SG.N blood-GEN.SG shed.PST.PTCP be.PRST.3SG
'Then a lot of blood has been shed' (Quintus Curtius Rufus, *History of Alexander the Great*, I, 3,11)

(22) *Proximo bello si aliquid de summa grauitate Pompeius,*
multum   *de cupiditate*   *Caesar*   *remisisset,*
a-lot-ACC.SG.N of cupidity-ABL.SG Caesar-NOM give up-CONJ.PQPF.3SG
et pacem stabilem et aliquam rem publicam nobis habere licuisset.
'During the last war, if Pompeius had given up a little bit of his noble gravity and Cesar a lot of his cupidity, we could have kept a stable peace and a shadow of the Republic'. (Cicero, *Philippics*, 13 (2).

This adverbial use of *multum* obeys to strict syntactic constraints: it can occur in syntactic positions that correspond to the nominative case (21) and to the accusative case not governed by a preposition (19/20/22). In the other syntactic functions, it is replaced by the inflected form. The examples (23a-b) illustrate this same distribution of the inflected form and the uninflected form for *tantus*: *tantum* combined to a complement in the genitive case can be used as the object of *dare*, but the inflected form is required for an accusative governed by a preposition.

(23) a. ***Tantum***   *operae*   *mihi*   *ad*   *audiendum*
datis
So-much.ACC.SG.N work-GEN.SG me-DAT to listen-GERUND.ACC

give.PRST.2PL
You give me so much work to listen' (Cicero, *De oratore*, 2: 122)

b. *Propter*   **_tantam_**   *operam.*
because-of   so-much.ACC.SG.F   work-ACC.SG
'because of so much work'

It has been argued that the distributional constraints imposed upon *multum* are due to the fact that *multum*, although analyzed as an adverb, is originally a nominalised neuter adjective in the nominative or accusative case and has to respect the constraints of its case marking (Maurel 1985: 126). However, this hypothesis does not explain why *multum* can be used for direct objects but not if the accusative case is governed by a preposition.

The hypothesis that will be put forward in this paper in order to account for these distributional constraints of *multum* relies on a structured representation of the arguments of the verb. I will adopt the distinction, established by Williams (1981), between the external argument, outside the VP and which takes the syntactic function of subject, and the internal arguments, included in the VP. I will further distinguish between the direct internal argument and the indirect internal arguments (Marantz 1984): the direct internal argument is directly governed by the verb, whereas the indirect internal arguments are governed by a preposition or, in case inflected languages, have a case marker which is not the nominative or the accusative. This structured representation of the verbal arguments allows us to establish a typology of the major verbal predicates: the direct transitive verbs have both an external argument and a direct internal argument, the intransitive verbs split into the inergative verbs, having only an external argument, and the unaccusative verbs, whose unique argument is a direct internal argument. (Perlmutter 1978, Levin & Rappaport 1995)[5].

---

[5] Argument structure is also put into service by Kratzer (1995) in order to distinguish between two types of verbal predicates: **stage-level predicates** such as *standing on a chair, available* would have an extra argument position for an event argument or for spatio-temporal location, whereas **individual-level predicates** such as *altruistic, having long arms* lack this argument position. This locative argument is conceived of as an external argument in the sense of Williams (1981).
The hypothesis of an argument of spatio-temporal location occupying the external argument position contributes to define the correlation between aspect, information structure and the referential interpretation of indefinite NPs. However, as has been observed by Grimshaw (1994: 64) and by Fernald (2000: 44 ff), it is unclear how to articulate this hypothesis with the theory of argument structure. Williams assumes that only one argument can be external to the VP. According to Kratzer, all stage-level predicate have an argument for spatio-temporal location and this argument will be necessarily the external argument. From this hypothesis, it follows that all 'stage-level' predicates are unaccusative insofar as their subject is an internal argument (Fernald 2000: 44-45). In this perspective are considered as unaccusative not only the verbs that have been identified as such (*come, leave, ...*), but also those that are commonly recognized as unergative (*cry, dance, work...*) and even agentive transitive verbs (*hit, kill,...*). In order to accommodate the hypothesis of the locative argument to the theory of argument structure, it would be necessary to clarify the exact status of the locative argument, a debate which is beyond the scope of this study.

The argument structure has been correlated to the aspectual properties of the verbal predicate (Dowty 1979, 1991, Tenny 1994, Grimshaw 1994, Van Valin 1990). Relevant for this study is the fact that only the direct internal argument, whether it is the direct object of the transitive verb (24a) or the subject of the unaccusative verb (24b), plays a crucial role in aspectual structure: only the direct internal argument can 'measure out the event' to which the verb refers (Tenny 1994: 10). The delineation of the external argument, be it the subject of a transitive verb (24c) or the subject of an intransitive verb of the unergative type (24d), does not have this effect. This can be shown by the test of compatibility with telic and atelic aspectual complements introduced respectively by the prepositions *en* 'in' and *pendant* 'during'.

(24) a. Marie   a bu   *trois verres*   en une heure /   *pendant une heure.
          Mary   drink-PST.3SG   three glasses   in one hour /   during one hour.
          'Mary drank three glasses in one hour / during one hour'
     b. *Trois hommes*   sont arrivés   en une heure   /* pendant une heure.
          Three men   arrive-PST.3PL   in one hour   / during one hour.
          'Three men arrived in one hour / during one hour'.
     c. *Trois hommes* ont apporté   des caisses   *en une heure /   pendant une heure.
          Three men   bring-PST.3PL of-the boxes   in one hour/   during one hour.
          'Three men brought boxes in one hour / during one hour'.
     d. *Trois hommes*   ont travaillé   *en une heure /   pendant une heure.
          Three men   work-PST.3PL   in one hour/   during one hour.
          'Three men were working in one hour / during one hour'.

This 'measuring-out' of the verbal process by means of a quantified internal argument is not characteristic of all verb classes. As has been noted by Verkuyl (1972), for static verbs, the boundedness of its direct object does not have any incidence on aspect (25a). Moreover, even in combination with certain dynamic verbs, the boundedness of the direct object does not yield telicity (25b).

(25) a. Pierre   connaît /   apprécie   *les voisins.*
          Peter   know-PRST.3SG   like-PRST.3SG   the neighbours.
     b. Pierre   caresse   *le lapin*
          Peter   stroke-PRST.3SG   the rabbit.

The quantification of the direct internal argument is relevant for the aspect calculus only if there is a homomorphism between the spatial properties of the internal argument and the temporal structure of the verbal process, in such a way that the referential properties of the internal argument carry over to the temporal constitution of the verbal process. This homomorphism has been analyzed in detail by Krifka (1992) and by Jackendoff (1993) for verbs that describe the coming into being and disappearing of their internal argument (26), a change of the properties of the internal argument (27), or that conceive the internal argument as a path (28).

(26) a. Pierre construit   *une maison.*
         Peter   build-PRST.3SG a   house
      b. Pierre mange   *une pomme.*
         Peter   eat-PRST.3SG   an   apple.
(27) a. Le cuisinier caramélise   *le sucre.*
         The cook   caramelize-PRST.3SG   *the sugar.*
      b. *Le sucre*   caramélise.
         The sugar   caramelize-PRST.3SG
(28) a. Pierre joue   *un   concerto*
         Peter   play-PRST.3SG   a   concerto
      b. Pierre monte   *l'   échelle.*
         Peter   climb-PRST.3SG the   ladder

I argue that the argument structure is the relevant factor to explain the distribution of *multum* in Latin. An expression like *multum*, having the form of a singular neutral nominative or accusative can quantify the direct internal argument, be it the direct object of a transitive verb (19/20/22), the subject of an intransitive verb of the unaccusative type or the subject of a passive predicate (21). On the contrary, it is not used for indirect internal arguments, neither for adjuncts (23b). Upon this quantification can be grafted a genitive complement (19-21) or a prepositional complement (22).

This syntactic constraint is crucial for understanding how the nominal form *multum* could evolve into an adverb. According to the hypothesis of a correlation between argument structure and aspect, the quantification of direct internal argument can amount to a quantification of the verbal process as such. Hence the quantification by *multum* in structures like **multum** *operae* dabam (19) or **multum** *sanguinis fusum est* (21) offers evidence for the double nature of the quantification. On the one hand, this quantification is nominal, because *multum* fills an argument position whose nature is specified by the genitive or the prepositional complement. On the other hand, this quantification is also verbal, insofar as the quantification of the internal argument yields a quantification of the verbal process[6].

In this way, *multum* tightens its relationship with the verb. It becomes a full-fledged adverb when it occupies no longer a syntactic position corresponding to a NP (28). Witness the fact that it can be coordinated in this use with forms endowed with the adverbial suffix (29).

(29) **Multum**   *te*   *amamus* (Cicero, *Epistulae ad Atticum*, 1,1,5)
      Much   you-ACC   love-PRST-1PL
      'We love you very much'

---

[6] Le Goffic (1993: § 17), observes « an important contact area [...] between the adverb and the preposition-less NP in the domain of the quantificational expressions » (my translation). The hypothesis defended in this paper ties up with this observation.

(30) **longe   multumque**   *superamur*   *a bestiis* (Cicero, *Fin.* 2,11)
     long-ADV   much-and   surpass-PASS.PRST.1PL   by animal-ABL.PL
     'Animals are by far and in many respects ahead of us'

However, it is not attested in all the contexts of use of the adverb. It only sporadically occurs with an adjective (31/32) (Menge 2000: § 360). Moreover, the consulted corpora did not contain any occurrence in combination with an adverb.

(31) *Hac*   *in re*   *scilicet*   *una*   **multum** <u>*dissimiles*</u>
     This-ABL.FEM.SG in thing-ABL.SG of-course one-ABL.FEM.SG much different-
     NOM.PL
     'In this respect only, they are very different.' (Horatius, *Epist.*, 1,10)

(32) *medicus*   **multum**   <u>*celer*</u>   *atque*   *fidelis*
     doctor-NOM.SG much   swift-NOM.SG and   faithful-NOM.SG
     'a very swift and faithful doctor.' (Horatius, *Satira*, II: 3, 145)

As a matter of fact, in Latin, high degree quantification in relationship with an adjective or an adverb is expressed by a synthetic superlative (e.g. the adjective *celer, celerrimus* 'swift' / 'very swift' or 'the swiftest'; the adverb *celeriter / celerrimē* 'swiftly / very swiftly' or 'the most swiftly'). The form *multo,* analyzed as an ablative of measure, is however used to reinforce the comparative or the superlative of adjectives and adverbs (**multo** <u>*crudelior*</u> 'much more barbaric', Cicero, *Pro Roscio Amerino*, 53 (153); **multo/longe** <u>*optimus*</u> 'the very best / by far the best' *cf.* Ernout & Thomas 1951: §§ 117 & 190).

These data show how *multum*, the (pro)nominal use of the adjective-determiner *multus*, enters into the verbal sphere and acquires the status of an adverb. As we will see in sections §§3-4, in the shift from Latin to Old French, the categorial status of the adverb *mult* strengthens; on the contrary, the inflected form of *mult* moves towards its decay.

3   *Mult* in very Old French

Mult in very Old French retains some morphological and syntactic features of *multus* in Latin even if there is evolution on some points.
Firstly, in the oldest French texts, predominantly Anglo-Norman[7], *mult* is still inflected according to case, gender, and number: the examples (33) and (34/35) contain respectively a masculine and feminine plural.

(33) **Mulz**   *malades*   guari   de sun relief demaine.
     Many-REG.M.PL sick-REG.PL   cure-PST.3SG

---

[7] This study is based on the corpus *Corptef* (http://w7.ens-lsh.fr/corptef/). All the inflected forms of *mult* have been taken into account. Outside the Anglo-Norman area, the inflected form of *mult* also occurs in the *Passion de Clermont* (end 10th C. or beginning 11th C.). The much debated question of the language of this poem will not be dwelt upon in this paper.

La fille a un riche humme en devint tute saine,
Qui out esté fievrose mainte lunge semaine
'He cured a lot of sick persons of his domain obtained by relief. The daughter of rich man, who had been feverish during several long weeks, fully recovered' (Guernes de Pont-Saint Maxence, *Life of Saint Thomas Becket* [1173], v. 3671)

(34) Pantere est de **multes** *culurs* : neire, ruge, verte, pale, purpre, ...
Panther is of many-FEM.PL colors
'The panther has a-lot of colours : black, red, green, pale, purple.' (*Lapidary in prose,* middle 12th C.)

(35) Par **multes** *terres* fait querre sun amfant
throughout many-FEM.PL country-PL make-PRST.3SG search-INF his child.
'he made look for his child throughout many countries' (*Life of Saint Alexis* [1050], v. 112)

The singular form, however, has lost its gender agreement: the feminine form is not attested[8]. As will be shown below, this at first sight enigmatic asymmetry between singular and plural, inexistent in Latin, can be explained by the specific conditions of use of the inflected form at this language stage.

Contrary to its Latin homologue, the inflected quantifier cannot be coordinated with an adjective and behaves in this respect as a determiner:

(36) *Tanz* *riches* *reis*
So-many-REG.M.PL rich-REG.M.PL king-REG.PL.M
'so many rich kings' (*Song of Roland* [1100], v. 527)

Like *multus* in Latin, the inflected form *mult* is used not only as a determiner, but also as a pronoun.

(37) A **molz** l' ai veü avenir
to many-REG.M.PL this have-PRST.1SG seen happen -INF
'I have seen happen this to many' (Thomas [end 12th C.], *Tristan & Iseult*, v. 397)

Alongside this use as a pronoun or a determiner, *mult* in its uninflected form fulfils also the role of an adverb and, unlike *multum* in Latin, it occurs in the whole range of contexts characteristic of the adverb: it can modify not only a verb (38), but also an adjective (39) or

---

[8] It has however to be noted that the feminine singular form *multe* is attested in one single text, namely the *Psalter of Oxford*, with no less than seven occurrences. On the basis of the other linguistic features of the text, it can be reasonably assumed that the use of this form is due to an interference with the translated Latin source.

an adverb (40). Finally, it is used to reinforce the analytical comparative or superlative, in a similar way as *multo* in Latin (41).

(38) Jo vos   *aim*   **mult**
      I   you-2PL love-PRST1SG   much
      'I love you a lot' (*Song of Roland* [1100], v. 634)

(39) Si fut   Ionas **mult** *correcious*
          be-PST.3SG   Jonas much   angry
      'Jonas was very angry' (*Sermon on Jonas* [940], cf. Marchello-Nizia 2006)

(40) **Mult** *dulcement* a   regreter   le   prist
      Much   slowly   to regret-INF   him-ACC.SG take-PST.3SG
      'very slowly, he began to regret it' (*Song of Roland* [1100], v. 2036)

(41) Car   **mult** *plus* *grief*   martyre suffri
      because much   more   serious   martyr   suffer-PST.3SG
      'because he suffered a much more serious martyr.' (Guernes de Pont-Saint
      Maxence, *Life of Saint Thomas Becket* [1173], v. 5811)

Though more properly adverbial than its Latin predecessor, the uninflected form *mult* can also serve as a quantifier in the nominal domain. *Mult* can be contiguous to the noun it quantifies (42/43/44), but it is often separated from this noun (45/46).

(42) E   **mult** *ennois*   ad   a   traire
      And much   difficulties   has to   endure
      'and he has to endure a lot of troubles' (Benedeit, *saint Brendan* [1120], 614)

(43) **Mult** *gemmes*   et   mult or esméré   i   posa
      Much gems-PL   and much gold   there put-PST.3SG
      'he put there a lot of gems and pure gold' (Guernes de Pont-Saint Maxence, *Life of Saint Thomas Becket* [1173])

(44) Par   la   mer   **mult** *de* *morz* en gist
      Throughout   the sea   much of   dead   lay-PST.3SG
      'in the sea were laying a lot of corpses' (Wace, *Brut* [1155], v. 13093)

(45) **Mult** unt   oüd *e*   *peines*   *e* *ahans*.
      Much   have-PST.3PL had and sorrows   and torments.
      'They had a lot of sorrows and torments' (*Song of Roland* [1100], v. 267)

(46) **Mult** sunt   *de* *malvais*   *estres*
      Much   be-PRST.3PL   of bad   creatures
      'There are a lot of bad creatures' (Philippe de Thaon, *Bestiary* [around 1130])

This existence of an uninflected form for nominal determination raises two questions.
- Which is its categorial status in the examples (42) to (46)?
- How to account for the respective distribution of the inflected and the uninflected forms of *mult*?

A first principle which determines the distribution of the inflected and the uninflected forms is of a syntactic nature: in the oldest French texts, only the inflected form is used in the case of a NP headed by a preposition.

(47)   Escuz   unt   genz,   *de mult-e-s*   *cunoisances*
        Shields have-PRST.3PL   nice,   of many-FEM.PL   armorials
        'They have nice shields, adorned with many armorial bearings' (*Song of Roland* [1100], 3090)

(48)   *De   multes*   *choses*   unt   entr'els dous   desputé -PST.PTCP
        Of   many-FEM.PL   things   have-PRST.3PL between them two   discussed.
        'Ils ont discutés entre eux de beaucoup de choses' (Guernes de Pont-Saint Maxence, *Life of Saint Thomas Becket* [1173], v. 4391)

(49)   li   pains   est fait   *de mulz greins*
        the   bread-SG.NOM   is   made   of many-REG.M.PL grains-REG.M.PL
        'Bread is made of a lot of grains' (*Elucidaire*, 3th translation [ca. 1200])

In the very same way as *multum* in Latin, the uninflected form *mult* does not occur in this context: be it in adverbal position (45/46) or in adnominal position (42/43/44), the uninflected form *mult* can quantify a nominal constituent when this NP is the direct object of a transitive verb (42/43/45), or the subject of an unaccusative verbal predicate (44). This constraint shows that even in adnominal position, *mult* is not a full-fledged nominal determiner, but still behaves as an adverb: the uninflected quantifier applies to the VP and can in this way quantify the internal argument of the verb. Hence, the syntactic structure of the examples (42) à (46) corresponds to (50a) rather than (50b).

(50)   a. Q [V N']
        b. Q$_i$ [V] [N']$_i$

A second principle accounting for the distribution of the inflected and uninflected quantifiers is of a semantic nature: the use of the inflected form tends to evoke a distributive plural, whereas the uninflected form expresses a collective plural[9]. For

---

[9] This semantic opposition between inflected and uninflected forms meaning 'a lot' also exists in other languages. In Dutch, the inflected form expresses an individuated plural, whereas the uninflected form allows a collective apprehension of the quantified set.

(i)   Ik heb vele$_{[+inflected]}$ mensen gegroet op de receptie. 'I greeted a lot of people at the reception' (one by one)

instance, (33), containing an inflected form, suggests that the sick are cured one by one, whereas in the examples (42) and (43), containing the uninflected form, the verbal process affects the troubles and the gems as a collection without individuating them.

(33) **Mulz**   *malades*   guari   de sun relief demaine.
Many-REG.M.PL   sick-REG.PL   cure-PST.3SG
La fille a un riche humme en devint tute saine,
Qui out esté fievrose mainte lunge semaine
'He cured a lot of sick persons of his domain obtained by relief. The daughter of rich man, who had been feverish during several long weeks, fully recovered '
(Guernes de Pont-Saint Maxence, *Life of Saint Thomas Becket* [1173], v. 3671)

(42) E   **mult** *ennois*   ad   a traire (Benedeit, *Saint Brendan* [1120], 614)
And   much difficulties has   to endure
'and he has to endure a lot of troubles'

(43) **Mult** *gemmes*   et   mult or   esméré   i   posa
Much gems-PL   and much gold pure   there put-PST.3SG
'he put there a lot of gems and pure gold' (Guernes de Pont-Saint Maxence, *Life of Saint Thomas Becket* [1173])

This correlation between the inflection of the quantifier and the concept of distributive plural in very Old French accounts for the fact that the inflected forms exist only for the plural and are not attested for the singular, since inflection does have no 'raison d'être' in the singular.

The following table shows the frequency of *mult* in the different uses listed above in a corpus composed of the six following texts: *The Passion of Clermont* [980], *The Life of Saint Léger* [975], *The Life of Saint Alexis* [1050], *The Song of Roland* [1100], *The Comput*, written by Philippe de Thaon [1113], *The alphabetic Lapidary* [1st third of the 12th C.]. It should be mentioned that the frequency of the inflected form is uneven in the different texts. For instance, there are few occurrences in the *Song of Roland*.

(ii)   Ik heb veel[-inflected] mensen gezien op de receptie. 'I saw a lot of people at the reception'

TABLE 1:
Absolute frequency of *mult* as a determiner / pronoun and as an adverb in a very Old French corpus (980-1130)

TOTAL NUMBER OF OCCURRENCES OF *MULT*	**292**
DETERMINER / PRONOUN	22
Inflected form in a PP	8
Uninflected form in a PP	0
Inflected form in a NP, which is a direct object or a subject of an unaccusative predicate	3 (+3)[10]
Uninflected form in a NP, which is a direct object or a subject of an unaccusative predicate	8
ADVERB	270
Adverb modifying a verb	38
Adverb modifying an adjective	174
Adverb modifying a PP (often a genitive of quality)	7
Adverb modifying an adverb	51

4 *Moult* in Old French

From the 13th century on, the inflected form of *moult*, already infrequent in very Old French, disappears. The example (52) corresponds to the last occurrence in the corpus.

(52) Sire, fet li rois, de vostre venue avions nos mout grant mestier por ***moltes***
                                                                      for   many-FEM.PL

choses
thing-PL
'Lord, said the King, we needed very urgently your arrival for many things. (*Quest for the Holy Grail* [1220])

---

[10] These three occurrences are undecidable, since the inflected form appropriate in the context corresponds to *mult*, which is also the uninflected form.

Only subsists the invariable form *moult*, which extends its use to NPs headed by a preposition.

(53) Vraiement   a Moysi   fut   offert   ke   ilh
     Really   to Moses be-PST.3SG offer-PST.PTPC   COMP he
     seroit   sires de   ***mult***   de   genz
     be-COND.3SG lord-NOM.SG_of a-lot   of   people
     'really, Moses has been proposed to be lord of a lot of people' (Saint Bernard,
     Sermones in Cantica, last quarter of the 12th C.)

This evolution shows that within the category of quantifying determiners, a new categorial borderline emerges: only nominal determiners like *maints* 'many', *plusieurs* 'several' that exclusively apply to count nouns endowed with a plural form remain inflected, whereas determiners that are not specified according to this feature become invariable.

In parallel to the disappearance of the inflected form, there is a rise of the pattern *mult de N'*. It has been argued that this rise of *de* before the quantified noun phrase is a sign of reanalysis: the quantifier which primitively applies to the entire VP (54a) would have its scope limited to the object NP (54b) and would become in this way a remote nominal quantifier:

(54)   a. Q [V N']
       b. Q$_i$ [V] [*de* N']$_i$

In Carlier & Melis (2005), this hypothesis was rejected on the basis of the following arguments.

- Firstly, the empirical data offer no evidence for the fact that the presence or absence of *de* corresponds to a difference in scope. For instance, it seems unlikely that in the two following examples, quoted from the same text, the quantifier has a different scope according to the presence or absence of *de*.

(55)   Cil   Ewruins   ***molt*** li   vol   *miel*
       That Ebroïn   much him-DAT want-PRST.3SG   harm
       'That Ebroïn intends to harm him a lot.' (*Life of Saint Léger* [975], v. 101)

(56)   Por quant   il pot,   ***tan***   fai   **de** *miel*
       For as-much he can-PRST.3SG, as-much do-PRST.3Sg of   harm.
       'He does as much harm as he can' (*Life of Saint Léger* [975], v. 135)

- Secondly, in Old French, the presence of *de* is more systematic when the quantifier is in adnominal position than when it is separated from the nominal object by the verb. Yet, in adnominal position, the marking of the scope of the quantifier is superfluous because there is no risk of ambiguity.

(57) mostreir **mult** <u>de</u> *signes* (*Li Dialoge Gregoire lo Pape*, end 12th C.)
      show-INF a-lot of signs

- Finally, if *de* has the role of a scope marker, why does it never appear when the quantifier modifies an element which does not have the morphosyntactic status of noun, such as an adjective, for instance?

(58) Entre les dous oilz **mult**   out *large* le front
      Between the two eyes much/very had large the brow'
      'His brow between his two eyes was very large' (*Roland*, [1100], v. 1217)

Since the presence of *de* is conditioned by the morphosyntactic category to which *moult* applies, the reason for its emergence seems to be a gradual shift of the categorial status in the evolution from *multus* in Latin to *moult* in Old French.

As pointed out before, *multus* in Latin is endowed with a great categorial flexibility. It appears not only in its inflected form, but has also developed the pronominal form *multum*. *Multum* as a pronoun quantifies the verbal process by quantifying its internal argument (e.g. **multum** <u>operae</u> *dabam* (ex. 19) or **multum** <u>sanguinis</u> *fusum est* (ex. 21)). It has however shifted towards the category of the adverb when it quantifies the verbal process as such, without saturating an argument position (cf. **multum** <u>te</u> *amamus* (ex. 29)). In the evolution from Latin to Old French, the inflected form is lost and the uninflected form has strengthened its adverbial status: it extends its distribution to adjectives and adverbs. Given that *moult* is an adverb, it looses its capacity to appear freely in combination with a noun, in the way of a nominal determiner, unless *de* is inserted. Hence, *de* fulfils a syntactic role: it enables an adverbial quantifier to combine with a noun, whether it is contiguous to the noun or separated from it by a verb. This explains why *de* does not occur when the quantifier applies to an adjective (cf. example (58)). The syntactic role of *de* also accounts for the fact that *de*, in the stage where it is still optional, occurs more readily when the quantifier is in adnominal position (59) than when it is in adverbal position and quantifies the nominal object at a distance (60).

(59) Avec **assez** <u>de</u> *pain*
      with enough of bread (Gaston Phébus, *Le livre de chasse*[=The book of hunting] [1387])
(60) Car **assez** ont   *pain et pictence*
      Since enough have-PRST.3PL bread and food
      'Since they have enough bread and food' (F. Villon, *The Testament* [1461], p. 38)

Eventually, the use of *de* will become obligatory, at the time when the partitive article is no longer optional. It thus appears that *de* has a double role: it is not only a relator but it also partakes in determination (Carlier & Melis 2006).

In conclusion, *moult* in Old French has two distinct uses. On the one hand, it quantifies the VP and can take into its scope the NP corresponding to the direct internal argument of the verb. On the other hand, after the disappearance of the inflected form, the invariable form *moult* acquires a role in nominal determination: it becomes part of a complex nominal determiner and can also quantify an NP external to the VP.

5 *Moult / beaucoup* in Middle French and in Modern French

Besides the 'obligatorification' of *de*, two major evolutions occur in the period of Middle French.

- The form *moult* is gradually replaced by *très* 'very' and *beaucoup* 'a lot'. The rise of *beaucoup* is dramatic : although its frequency becomes significant only from the 15th century on, it has, along with *très*, already spread by the end of the 16th century to all contexts of use of *moult,* which in turn becomes obsolete (Marchello-Nizia 2000; 2006: 140-141) (§ **5.1**).
- The pattern Q V N' becomes rare and is replaced by V Q N' (§ **5.2**).

5.1.   From *moult* to *beaucoup*

The disappearance of *moult* and its replacement by *beaucoup* and *très* have been investigated in detail by Marchello-Nizia (2000; 2006, chapter 4). In the context of this paper, only some elements of this evolution, relevant for the analysis, will be mentioned. Marchello-Nizia's analysis offers evidence for the fact that the loss of *moult* is due to the tendency towards higher morphosyntactic specialization. *Très* (< Latin *trans* 'through') is primitively a prefix or preposition with the spatial meaning 'through', but it can also express high degree (*tres-tot* 'absolutely everything', *tres-fremir* 'tremble entirely'). Furthermore, as a degree marker, it can also be used as an adverb modifying adjectives or adverbs. In this use, it enters in competition with *moult* from the 12th century on. *Beaucoup* develops in complementary distribution with respect to *très*: whereas *très* is restricted to adjectives and adverbs, *beaucoup* combines with nouns and verbs. According to Marchello-Nizia (2006:250), the replacement of *moult* by *très* and *beaucoup* introduces in this way a new marking of a grammatical distinction: nouns and verbs are first level units, since they are head of an immediate constituent of the sentence, whereas adjectives and adverbs are units of an inferior level.

On the basis of the empirical data of Marchello-Nizia's study (2006: 147) and in accordance with the observation of Le Goffic (1993: § 166), I will argue that the nominal origin of *beau-coup* (< 'beautiful knock') can contribute to account for its specific distribution in Middle French. In the same way as for *multum* in Latin, the (pro)nominal form of the adjective-determiner *multus*, the first uses of *beaucoup* are those where it fills the direct argument position of the verbal predicate, *i.e.* the direct object of a transitive verb[11] (61) or the subject of an inaccusative verbal predicate, most often in inverted position, behind the verb (62/63). It may occur with a complement of the form « *de* N' ».[12]

---

[11] Marchello-Nizia (2006: 186) spots one early occurrence of *beaucoup* in an indirect or prepositional object :

    Et   parlerent   ensamble de   **biaucop** *de choses* (Froissart, *Chronique* [1400])

(61) Et leur pel est moult bonne pour <u>fere</u> ***biau coup*** *de choses* quant elle est bien conreiee et prise en bonne sayson.
'Their skin is very good to do ***plenty*** *of things* when it is well finished and taken in the good season.' (Gaston Phébus, *Le livre de chasse* ['the Book of Hunting'][1387])

(62) Et cest livre j'ay comencié a ceste fin que je vueil que chascuns saichent qui cest livre verront ou orront que de chasce je ose bien dire qu'il peut <u>venir</u> ***biau coup*** *de bien*.
'I wrote this book because I want that everyone who sees or hears this book knows that from the hunting – I dare say it – there can <u>come</u> ***a lot*** *of good things*.' (Gaston Phébus, *Le livre de chasse* ['the Book of Hunting'] [1387])

(63) En la ville de Malignes   <u>vinrent</u>   ***biaucop***   *de signeurs*
In the town of Malines   come-PST.3PL   a-lot   of lords
'In the town of Malines, there <u>came</u> ***a lot*** *of lords*' (Froissart, *Chronicle* [1400])

Next, *beaucoup* develops its use as a degree marker of the VP without saturating an argument position.

(64) Et pour ce, chieres amies, veu que ce ne vous puet riens valoir et ***beaucoup*** <u>nuire</u>, ne vous vueilliez en tieulx fanfelues moult delicter. (Chr. De Pisan [1405])
'and therefore, dear friends, given that this can offer you nothing and <u>harm</u> you ***a lot***, please do not delight in such banalities.'

(65) Vous m'*avez* ***beaucop*** celé les amours d'une telle et de vous.
'you <u>have</u> ***much*** <u>hidden</u> the amorous adventures of Mrs so-and-so and of yourself'
(*Cent nouvelles nouvelles*, p. 229, quoted from Marchello-Nizia, 2006: 147)

Beaucoup appears only later on as a quantifier of an NP headed by a preposition.

(66) et en ***beaucoup*** *de lieux* en France, et mesmement en la viconté de Paris, femmes en ligne collateral ne succedent point en fiefs nobles (Jean Juvénal des Ursins, *Audite celi* [1435])
'<u>in</u> **many** *regions* of France and even in the viscount of Paris, women in collateral lineage do not inherit noble fiefs.'

And speak-PST.3PL together of   a-lot   of things
'And they spoke together about a lot of things'

[12] On the basis of the similarity with *beaucoup* [...] *de* N', Muller (1995: 266-267) offers an analysis along this lines of the negation *pas ... de N'*.

Hence, the same evolutionary stages are observed as in the case of *multum* > *m(o)ult* : nominal form > adverb > nominal determiner. Moreover, *beaucoup* as a nominal determiner gives rise to a pronominal use:

(67) ***Beaucoup*** furent esbahiz de ceste fantaisie
'Many were surprised by this fantasy'. (Ph. De Commynes, *Mémoires* [1489], quoted by Marchello-Nizia 2006)

Besides, like *multo* in Latin and *moult* in Old French, *beaucoup* appears early to strengthen the degree morphemes 'more'/ 'less'. (Marchello-Nizia 2000: 5).

(68) ***biaucop*** _plus_ de signeurs de France
much more (of) lords of France (Froissart, *Chroniques* [1400])

(69) L'autre chemin, a dextre, par ou je montay, est assez plus longs,
mais il est ***beaucop*** _plus_ aysié
but it is much more easy
'the other path, on the right, by which I went up, is longer, but it is much easier.'
(A. de la Sale [1442])

5.2. The positional shift of the quantifier: a sign of reanalysis?

A second evolution occurs in Middle French : the pattern Q V *de* N' (70a) declines and is replaced by the pattern V Q *de* N' (70b)[13].

(70) a. En celle assemblee ***moult*** en y ot
in that melee, a-lot of-them there have-PST.3SG
de mors et de navrez de chascune partie
of dead and of wounded at each side'
'In that melee, there were a lot of dead and wounded at each side.' (*Bérinus* [1350], p. 128)

---

[13] According to Hopper's principle of layering, the emergence of a new grammatical pattern does not yield the elimination of the older one (Hopper 1991). In the case of the shift from Q V *de* N' to V Q *de* N', the old pattern continues to occur sporadically during a very long period, especially with the quantifier *tant*. Witness the following example from the 19th century, where the quantifier *tant* applies to the whole VP, composed by an inaccusative verb and its inverted subject in the internal argument position.

On eût dit sous le chêne un essaim de frelons,
tant arrivaient *d'esprits, d'ombres et d'âmes folles* pour recueillir le miel des savantes paroles.
so-much arrive-IMPF.3PL *of spirits, of shadows, and of foolish souls* ...
'There arrived so much spirits, shadows, foolish souls to gather the honey of the wise words, you would have said a swarm of hornets under the oak' (A. Brizeux, *Marie* (1840))

b. en   y   ot   **moult**   *de*   *mors*   de chascune partie
of-them there have-PST.3SG a-lot of dead at each side.
'There were a lot of dead at each side' (*Bérinus* [1350], p. 123)

In the new pattern, the quantifier is next to the NP *de N'*. This positional shift has been analyzed as a sign of reanalysis: the quantifier would no longer apply to the entire VP, but would be restricted to the NP *de N'*. In this way, *moult* would have reached the status of a nominal determiner.

(71)   a   Q [V [*de* N']]
       b. V [Q *de* N']

(72)   a. **moult**   a   *de dolour*
          a-lot   has of sorrow
          'He suffers a lot' (Eustache Deschamps, *Miroir de mariage* ['Mirror of marriage'] [1385])
       b. il eut **beaucoup**   *de chagrin*
          he had a-lot   of sorrow
          'he felt very upset' (Antoine Galland, *Les mille et une nuits* ['Thousand and one nights'][1715])

It is important to note that this positional shift of the quantifier is linked to a more general change of word order. On the basis of the description offered by Marchello-Nizia (1999; 2006: chapter 3), this evolution can be summarized as follows. From Latin to French, the order of the constituents radically changes. In Latin, word order was relatively free, even though there is a tendency towards SOV (subject – object – verb) (Adams 1976, Bauer 1995, Pinkster 1991). Old French is dominantly V2: the verb is in second position and the theme is before the verb, i.e. TVX (T=theme). From the 13th century on, the nominal object is fixed in the postverbal position (Combettes 1988), which results in the order TVO. The preverbal position is nevertheless not only available to the subject, but is also open to other thematic constituents, often anaphoric elements (Marchello-Nizia 2006: 48).

(73) **Lors** appella   un chevalier   chipprien   qui bien savoit toute la contree, et
       lui dist :
       Then call-PST.3SG   a knight   Cyprian   who well know-IMPF.3Sg whole
       the region and him.DAT say-PST.3SG
       'Then he called a Cyprian knight who knew well the whole region and he said to him : ...'
       (Jean d'Arras, *Mélusine* [1392])

It is in this position that we can also find an adverbial quantifier linked to the nominal object behind the verb.

(72a) **moult** a   <u>de dolour</u>
      A-lot   have-PRST.3SG   of pain
      'He suffers a lot' (Eustache Deschamps, *Miroir de mariage* ['Mirror of marriage']
      [1385])

During the period of Middle French, word order shifts from TVO to SVO. The subject tends to be systematically expressed and to occupy the preverbal position. As a result, whereas Middle French still allows Q V (*de*) N', with Q in front position, this pattern is gradually replaced by V Q (*de*) N', with the subject in front of the verb.

(72b) il   eut   **beaucoup**   de chagrin
      he   have-PST.3SG   a-lot   of sorrow
      'he felt very upset' (Antoine Galland, *Les mille et une nuits* ['Thousand and one nights'][1715])

If it is true that the positional shift of the quantifier has to be understood in the light of a more general change of word order, the tightening of the link with the NP *de N'* can not be invoked as the determining factor. Moreover, this shift does not necessarily place the quantifier immediately before the nominal object. In the case of complex verbal predicates where the finite verb form, inflected for person and for tense, is followed by a non finite verb form, *i.e.* an infinitive or a participle, this non finite verb form can be inserted between the quantifier and the nominal object *de N'*.

(74)   se vous   me   voulez   **tant**   <u>fere</u>   *de courtoisie*
      if you-PL me   want-PRST-2PL   so-much   do-INF   of courtesy
      'si vous voulez me faire tant de courtoisie' (*Bérinus* [1350])

(75)   depuis   monpartement, ilz   auront   **beaucoup**   <u>aprins</u> *de nouvelles*
      since   my-departure,   they have-FUT.3PL   a-lot learn-PST.PRTC of news-PL
      'since I left, they will have got a lot of news. (Jean de Bueil, *Le Jouvencel* [1461])

(76)   Et   vous   en   avez   **beaucoup**   <u>ouÿ</u>   <u>dire</u>   *d'exemples*
      and   you-PL of-it have-PRST.2PL a-lot   hear-PST.PRTC say-INF   of examples
      'and you heard mention a lot of examples' (Jehan Bagnyon, *L'Histoire de Charlemagne* [1465])

This pattern is still possible in Modern French (*cf.* § **1.3**), although it is less frequent.

(77)   On   doit   **beaucoup**   <u>gagner</u>   *d'argent*   ici.
      One must-prst.3sg   a-lot   earn-INF   of money   here.
      'You probably earn a lot of money here' (M. Barrès, *Mes Cahiers* [1902])

(78)   On   a   **beaucoup**   <u>écrit</u>   *de poèmes* en prose depuis trente ou quarante ans
      One has   a-lot   written   of poems in prose since thirty or forty years.
      (M. Jacob, *Le cornet à dés* [1923])

It appears even possible to insert another constituent between the quantifier in postverbal position and the nominal object *de N'*.

(79) Ils   ont   ***assez*** pour lui *de respect* dans le cœur
      They have-PRST.3PL enough for him of respect in the heart. (Georges de
      Brébeuf [1655])

These data lead to the conclusion that the positional shift of the quantifier – although it decreases the number of occurrences where the quantifier is separated from the nominal object *de N'* in the linear surface order – is not necessarily correlated to a categorial change of this quantifier: if the quantifier is analyzed as an adverb applying to the entire VP in (72a), it lends itself to the same analysis in (72b).

(72) a. ***moult*** a   *de dolour* (Eustache Deschamps, *Miroir de mariage* [1385])
          a-lot   has of sorrow
      b. il   eut ***beaucoup*** *de chagrin*
          he had a-lot   of sorrow (Antoine Galland, *Les mille et une nuits*
          [1715])

It seems at least necessary to consider two possible analyses

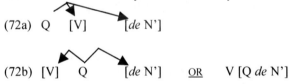

(72a) Q   [V]   [*de* N']

(72b) [V]   Q   [*de* N']   OR   V [Q *de* N']

and to explore if there are independent arguments in favour of one or the other analysis.

Several studies, conducted on the basis of Modern French data, have been devoted to the relationship between the so-called remote quantification, where the quantifier is separated from the object NP *de N'* by a non-finite verb form (cf. 80a) and the adnominal quantification illustrated by (80b).

(80) a. Pierre a   lu   ***beaucoup*** *de journaux.*
          Peter has read a-lot   of newspapers
      b. Pierre a   ***beaucoup*** lu   *de journaux.*
          Peter has a-lot   read of newspapers

As shown in § 1.2, Milner (1978) argues that (80b) is derived from (80a), without any semantic difference. Disputing the validity of this hypothesis, the studies of Obenauer (1983), Haïk (1982), Doetjes (1997), and Carlier & Melis (2005) offer evidence for the fact that the position of the quantifier in surface structure is significant[14]: the so-called remote quantification and the adnominal quantification are different with respect to the syntactic constraints and from a semantic point of view. The quantification is nominal in (80a), whereas it applies to the VP and in this way on the direct object NP of the verb in (80b). The following arguments corroborate this opposition:

- In order to account for the fact that the quantifier in adverbal position can take scope over a nominal object of a coordinated VP, we have to postulate the analysis Q [$_{SV}$V (*de* N') & V *de* N'] (Carlier & Melis 2005: 373).

(81) Nous   avions   **énormément**   mangé   ou pris   *d'alcool.*
     We   have-IMPF.1PL enormously   eaten   or taken of alcohol.
     'We have eaten enormously and we have drunk an enormous quantity of alcohol
     (oral example quoted by Damourette & Pichon, § 2761)

(82) Ils   ont   **trop**   lu   *de BD*   et   regardé *de feuilletons.*
     They   have-PRST.3PL too-much   read   of cartoons   and   watched of serials
     'They have read too many cartoons and watched too many serials'

- As has been observed by Haïk (1982: 79), contrary to the adnominal quantifier (83-84a), the quantifier *beaucoup* in adverbal position (83-84b) does not allow that the referent is conceived as a set of individuals.

(83) a. Pierre   a fumé   **beaucoup**   *de cigarettes*   l'une après l'autre.
        Peter   has smoked   a-lot   of cigarettes   one after another
     b. *Pierre   a   **beaucoup**   fumé   *de cigarettes*   l'une après l'autre.
        Peter   has a-lot   smoked   of cigarettes   one after another

(84) a. Amélie   avait raconté   **beaucoup**   *d'histoires*   dont la première était
        incompréhensible.
        Amelia   had told   a-lot   of stories   of which the first was
        incomprehensible
     b. *Amélie   avait **beaucoup**   raconté   *d'histoires* dont la première était
        incompréhensible
        Amelia   had   a-lot   told   of stories of which the first was
        incomprehensible

Therefore, *beaucoup* in adverbal position cannot have wide scope. (85a), where the quantifier is in adnominal position, has a double interpretation: either *beaucoup* does not take scope over the plural subject, with the meaning 'Peter and Mary have found

---

[14] For the quantifiers *tout* 'every' and *chaque* 'each', the necessity of an interpretation *in situ* has also been invoked. A first version of this hypothesis has been formulated by Haïk (1982) for the analysis of *tout*. It has been further developed by Junker (1995) for *chaque* and *tout* and by Zimmermann (2002) for *each* in English and *jeweils* in German.

together a lot of proofs', either *beaucoup* takes in its scope the plural subject, which results in the meaning 'Peter has found a lot of proofs and Mary has found a lot of proofs without these proofs being identical'. This second interpretation is not available in (85b), where *beaucoup* is in adverbal position (Azoulay-Vicente 1989: 93; Carlier & Melis 2005).

(85)   a. Pierre et Marie   ont trouvé   ***beaucoup***   *de preuves.*
              Peter and Mary   have found   a-lot   of proofs.
        b. Pierre et Marie   ont   ***beaucoup***   trouvé   *de preuves.*
              Peter and Mary   have   a-lot   found   of proofs.

(85')   [Peter & Mary]$_x$ [[a lot of proofs]$_y$ [x has found y]] - (86a/b)
        [a lot of proofs]$_y$ [[Peter & Mary]$_x$ [x has found y]] - (86a)

- In comparison with *beaucoup* in adnominal position, *beaucoup* in adverbal position brings about aspectual restrictions, which have been analyzed by Obenauer (1983) and Doetjes (1997). Obenauer (1983: 78) observes that, in the example (86), *beaucoup* in adverbal position is only acceptable in the interpretation *beaucoup de fois* 'a lot of times/often'. Witness the example (86b), where the gerund construction *en soulevant le couvercle* blocks this multiple event-reading and makes the sentence is unacceptable. This requirement of a multiple event-reading shows that the quantifier applies to the entire VP.

(86)   a. En   soulevant   le couvercle, il   a trouvé   ***beaucoup***
          de pièces   *d'or.*
          When   lifting   the lid,   he   has found   a-lot
          of coins   of gold.
        b. *En   soulevant   le couvercle, il   a   ***beaucoup***
          trouvé   *de pièces d'or.*
          When   lifting   the lid,   he   has   a-lot
          found   of coins   of gold.
        c. En   cherchant   partout,   il   a   ***beaucoup***
          trouvé   *de pièces*   *d'or.*
          While   looking   everywhere,   he   has   a-lot
          found   of coins   of gold

In line with this observation, we can understand why the existential predicate does not accept the quantifier *beaucoup* in adverbal position[15].

(87)   *Il   y   a   ***beaucoup***   eu   *de personnes*
       3SG.PRON   LOC   have-PRST.3SG   a-lot   have-PST.PTC   of persons

---

[15] I owe this observation as well as the examples (89) and (90) to one of my anonymous reviewers.

> chez nous   hier.
> with us   yesterday

These constraints did not exist in the older stages of French.   Witness the following example from the 16th century:

(88)   ***Beaucoup***   y   a   *de païs*   en nostre   Europe.
       A-lot   LOC   have-PRST.3SG   of countries in our   Europe
       (Charles Estienne, *L'agriculture et maison rustique* [1564]

Taking up the investigation initiated by Obenauer (1983), Doetjes (1997: 261 ff) notes that an example like (89) does not necessarily express the meaning of different events of oil-streaming through the pipeline, this is the *beaucoup de fois* 'a lot of times' reading.

(89)   Cet   oléoduc   a   ***beaucoup***   transporté   *de pétrole*.
       This   pipeline has   a-lot   transported   of oil

So she adjusts the constraint formulated by Obenauer (1983).   In accordance with Obenauer, she argues that the quantification applies to the VP, but she pertinently shows that the interpretation of the quantifier depends upon the referential properties of the nominal object or the internal argument *de N'*.   When the nominal object contains a count noun, a 'multiple event'- interpretation is obtained (86b-c).   In the case of a mass noun, the quantified verbal predicate can be interpreted as one continuous event (89).   There is however a constraint specific to adverbial quantification and ineffective in the case of adnominal quantification: adverbial quantification is only possible if there is a homomorphism between the spatial properties of the internal argument and the temporal structure of the verbal process, in such a way that the referential properties of the internal argument carry over to the temporal constitution of the verbal process.   This is the case in example (90a-b), but not in (90c).

(90)   a.   Il a ***beaucoup*** regardé *de films*. / Il a regardé ***beaucoup*** *de films.*
               He has a-lot watched of movies. / He has watched a-lot of movies
          b.   Il a ***beaucoup*** perdu *de sang*. / Il a perdu ***beaucoup*** *de sang.*
               He   has a-lot lost of blood. / He has lost a-lot of blood
          c.   ??Il a ***beaucoup*** montré *de patience*. / Il a montré ***beaucoup*** *de patience.*
               He has a-lot shown of patience. / He has shown a-lot of patience

If it is true that in (80b) *beaucoup* applies to the entire VP and only indirectly to the object NP *de N'*, whereas in (80a) it expresses a properly nominal quantification, this means the situation of contiguity of the quantifier with respect to the object NP *de N'* resulted in a weakening of its relationship with the verb or the VP.   Hence, there has been reanalysis in the sense of a 'rebracketting' (Langacker 1975, Haspelmath 1998):

(72b) [V]   Q   [*de* N']   →   V [Q *de* N']

Why does this reanalysis take place? This reanalysis has to be situated in the context of a general typological shift affecting the NP during the evolution from Latin to Modern French (Lehmann 1990, Combettes 2001, Carlier 2004, 2006, 2007).

The hierarchical structure of the nominal phrase in Latin is rather loose, the categorial distinction between adjective and noun (cf. also Ernout & Thomas 1951: § 190), between pronoun and determiner, between adjective and determiner (*cf.* examples (16)-(17)) is unclear, and the internal cohesion within the NP is low (Lehmann 1990).

From Latin to French, the NP undergoes a gradual evolution towards the tripartite structure: D–N–XP (with XP being a complement or an adjunct). This evolution towards a tripartite structure of the NP goes along with the emergence of a distinct category of nominal determination. Nominal determiners acquire a specific distribution and develop specific forms (hence, the formal differentiation between demonstrative and possessive pronouns and determiners cf. Marchello-Nizia and Combettes 2001). Moreover, the presence of a determiner becomes obligatory. The obligatory presence of a determiner contributes to the dramatic rise of the partitive article in the 15th century, which renders exceptional zero determination in combination with common nouns (Carlier 2007).

I put forward the hypothesis that, in this context of the emergence of independent category of nominal determination, the presence of an adverbial quantifier contiguous to the nominal object *de* N' has led to a reanalysis of the pattern V Q *de* N' and to a recategorization of the quantifier as a nominal determiner.

And yet, as shown in Carlier & Melis (2005), this reanalysis is not entirely accomplished. This can be shown by the restrictions on the cleft structure. Whereas a nominal object determined by an inflected quantifier (e.g. *plusieurs*) can occur in the focus position of a cleft structure, the cleftage of *beaucoup de* N' is not natural.

(91) a. Pierre a écrit *ce roman*.   C'est *ce roman* que Pierre a écrit.
         Peter has written this novel.   It is this novel that Peter has written.
      b. Pierre a écrit *plusieurs romans*. C'est *plusieurs romans* que Pierre a écrits.
         Peter has written several novels   It is several novels that Peter has written.
      c. Pierre a écrit *beaucoup de romans*. ??C'est *beaucoup de romans* que Pierre a
                                              écrits.
         Peter has written a lot of novels   It is a lot of novels that Peter has written.

The cleftage of the quantified NP of the type *beaucoup de* N' is blocked only when it is a direct object. In the examples (92) and (93), where the quantified NP in focus is not a direct object, the cleft structure is acceptable.

(92) Pierre est venu *peu de fois*.   C'est *peu de fois* que Pierre est venu.
      Peter   came   few of times   It is   few of times that Peter came

(93) Cet appareil coûte ***beaucoup*** *d'argent.*   C'est ***beaucoup*** *d'argent* que cet
                                                        appareil coûte.

      This machine costs   a-lot   of money.   It is   a-lot   of money   that
                                                        this machine costs.

This means that the adverbial quantifier, when it quantifies the direct object, even if it is
contiguous to this object NP, has still not completely broken its bonds with the verb.

6   Conclusion and perspectives for further research

6.1. This study showed that the diachronic evolution of *beaucoup* from Middle French to
Modern French exhibits salient similarities with the pathway from *multum* in Latin to *moult*
in Middle French. The following stages can be distinguished:

Stage I: *Multum* and *beaucoup* are originally nominal forms.
Stage II: This nominal form becomes an adverb: used for quantification of the direct
internal argument of the verb, it can quantify the verbal process as such and it acquires in
this way the ability to quantify the process without saturating an argument position.
Stage III: Whereas in stage II the quantifier can only apply to an NP in the direct internal
argument position, it extends subsequently its context of use to NPs outside the VP and to
NPs headed by a preposition. It becomes in this way a full-fledged nominal determiner,
with the same properties as ordinary quantifying determiners, such as scope ambiguities (*cf.*
ex. (85)).

The diachronic approach leads to a more accurate synchronic account of *beaucoup* as it
functions in Modern French. It explains the specific distribution of *beaucoup*, which, like
multum in Latin, is a nominal or verbal quantifier, but does not apply to adjectives or
adverbs. Moreover, it offers a fine-grained account of the morphosyntactic categorization
of *beaucoup* and defines the contexts of use where *beaucoup* is used as an adverb (stage II),
as a nominal determiner (stage III), or has a hybrid status, between adverb and nominal
determiner. Finally, it accounts for the presence of *de* in its determiner use and clarifies the
relationship with respect to quantifying determiners such as *plusieurs*.

6.2. Several issues require further investigation. Firstly, it would be interesting to compare
multum / beaucoup with other quantifying adverbs such as *peu* 'little/few', *trop (peu)* 'too
much (too little)', *assez* 'enough', *tant, tellement* 'so much', *énormément* 'enormously':
these have been included in the same paradigm as *beaucoup* because they share the
property of quantifying not only nouns but also verbs and some of them even adjectives or
adverbs. A comparative analysis of these different quantifiers would reveal that this class
is less homogeneous than generally admitted. For instance, whereas *beaucoup* is well-
established as a nominal quantifier and has a high frequency in its use as a nominal
determiner or even as a pronoun, *assez* remains more anchored in the verbal sphere and is
still used in a more flexible way in the so-called remote quantification pattern.

(94) a. Pierre a **beaucoup** travaillé.   Pierre a **assez**
           travaillé.
           Peter has a-lot worked   Peter has enough
           worked
      b. *Pierre a **beaucoup** montré *de patience*.   Pierre a **assez**
           montré *de patience*.
           Peter has a-lot shown of patience   Peter has enough
           shown of patience
      c. **Beaucoup** de filles ont dansé. ??*Assez* de filles ont dansé. (cf. fn. 1)
           A-lot of girls danced Enough of girls danced.
      d. **Beaucoup** ont dansé.   *Assez* ont dansé.
           A-lot danced   Enough danced

This more adverbial status of *assez* could be assessed by a diachronic study. More generally speaking, the present analysis dealing with *multum / m(o)ult / beaucoup* should be undertaken for the other quantifying expressions entering into the paradigm of verbo-nominal quantification, in order to identify the peculiar categorial features of each expression of this paradigm.

A second research question that deserves further investigation relates to the tendency towards a categorial specialization, which has been invoked at different stages of the evolution from *multum* in Latin to *beaucoup* in Modern French. In the context of Romance, it is clear that this tendency is in a more advanced stage in French than in the other Romance languages. It would be interesting to consider this evolution in the context of the different typological changes that characterize the evolution from Latin to Modern French.

Electronic Corpora

Classical Latin: *Itinera Electronica* (Université catholique de Louvain)
Very Old French: « *Corptef* » (ENS-LSH Lyon, CNRS UMR 5191 ICAR)
Old French: *Base du français médiéval* (ENS-LSH Lyon, CNRS UMR 5191 ICAR)
Middle French: *Dictionnaire du moyen français* (CNRS UMR Atilf, Nancy)
Classical and Modern French: *Frantext* (CNRS UMR Atilf, Nancy)

References

Abeillé A. & Godard D. (2003). The syntactic flexibility of adverbs: French degree adverbs, *in* S. Muller (éd.), *Proceedings of the 10th International Conference on HPSG*, 26-46, CA: CSLI Publications.

Abeillé A., Doetjes J., Molendijk A., de Swart H. (2004). Adverbs and quantification, *in* Corblin F. & de Swart H. Eds, *Handbook of French Semantics*, 185-209, Stanford: CSLI.

Adams J.A. (1976). A typological approach to Latin word order. *Indogermanische Forschungen* 77-90.

Azoulay-Vicente A. (1989). Cas partitif et quantification à distance. *Recherches linguistiques* 18, 81-99.

Battye A. (1991). Partitive and pseudo-partitive revisited: Reflections on the status of *de* in French. *French Language Studies* 1: 21-43.

Bauer B. (1995). *The Emergence and Development of SVO Patterning in Latin and French. Diachronic and Psycholinguistic Perspectives*. Oxford: Oxford University Press.

Buridant C. (2000). *Grammaire nouvelle de l'ancien français*. Paris: SEDES.

Carlier A. & Melis L. (2005). De la quantification adnominale à la quantification adverbale ?: perspectives diachroniques. *Verbum* 27, 361-382.

Carlier A. & Melis L. (2006). L'article partitif et les expressions quantifiantes contiennent-ils le même *de* ? , *in:* G. Kleiber, C. Schnedecker, A. Theissen Eds. *La relation partie – tout* 449-464. Peeters: Louvain.

Carlier A. (2004). Sur les premiers stades de développement de l'article partitif. *Scolia* 18, 115-146.

Carlier A. (2006). *Grammaire, grammaticalization et référence*. Mémoire HDR.

Carlier A. (2007). From Preposition to Article: the Development of the French Partitive Article. *Studies in Language* 31: 1, 1-49.

Chomsky N. (1981). *Lectures on government and binding*. Cambridge Ms.: MIT Press

Combettes B. (1988). *Recherches sur l'ordre des éléments de la phrase en moyen français*. Doctoral Thesis, Univ. of Nancy.

Combettes B. (2001). L'émergence d'une catégorie morphosyntaxique: les déterminants du nom en français. *Linx* 45: 117-126.

Damourette J. & Pichon E. (1911-1940). *Des mots à la pensée: essai de grammaire de la langue française*, tome 6. Paris: d'Artrey.

Doetjes J. (1997). *Quantifiers and Selection: On the Distribution of Quantifying Expressions in French, Dutch and English*. The Hague: Holland Academic Graphics.

Doetjes J. (2008). Adjectives and degree modification, *in* McNally L. & Kennedy Ch. Eds. *Adjectives and adverbs*. Oxford: Oxford UP, 123-155.

Dowty D. (1979). *Word meaning and Montague grammar*. Dordrecht: Reidel.

Dryer M. S. (1997). On the six-way word order typology. *Studies in Language* 21: 69-103.

Ernout A. & Thomas F. (1951). *Syntaxe latine*. Paris: Klincksieck.

Fernald Th. (2000), *Predicates and Temporal Arguments*. Oxford: Oxford U.P.

Foulet L. (1965[3] [1919[1]]). *Petite syntaxe de l'ancien français*. Paris: Champion.

Greenberg J. (1963). Some Universals of Grammar with Particular Reference to the Order of Meaningful Elements, *in* J. Greenberg Ed. *Universals of Language*, 73-113. Cambridge/Ms.: MIT Press.

Grimshaw J. (1992). *Argument structure*. Cambridge Mass.: MIT Press.

Gross M. (1977). *Grammaire transformationnelle du français: syntaxe du nom*. Paris: Larousse.

Haïk I. (1982). On clitic *en* in French. *Journal of Linguistic Research* 2, 63-87.

Haspelmath M. (1998). Does grammaticalization need reanalysis?. *Studies in Language* 22: 315-251.

Hopper P. J. (1991). On some principles of grammaticization », *in* Traugott, E.C. & Heine, B. Eds, *Approaches to Grammaticalization* I, 17-35. Amsterdam: Benjamins.

Jackendoff R. (1993). The Role of Conceptual Structure in Argument Selection. *Natural Language and Linguistic Theory* 11, 279-312.

Junker M.-O. (1995). *Syntaxe et sémantique des quantifieurs flottants* tous *et* chacun. Genève: Droz.

Kayne R.S. (1977). *Syntaxe du français*. Paris: Seuil.

Kayne R.S. (1984). *Connectedness and Binary Branching*. Dordrecht: Foris.

Kennedy Ch. & McNally L. (2005). Scale Structure and the Semantic Typology of Gradable Predicates. *Language* 81.2: 345-381.

Krifka M. (1989). Nominal Reference, Temporal Constitution and Quantification in Event Semantics. In R. Bartsch, J. van Benthem, P. von Emde Boas Eds. *Semantics and Contextual Expression*. Dordrecht: Foris Publication.

Krifka M. (1992). Thematic Relations as Links between Nominal Reference and Temporal Constitution. *In* I. Sag & A. Szabolcsi Eds. *Lexical Matters*, 29-53. CSLI Publications, Chicago University Press.

Kupferman L. (2001). Quantification et détermination dans les groupes nominaux, *in* X. Blanco *et al.* (éds), *Détermination et formalisation*. Amsterdam: Benjamins.

Langacker R. (1977). Syntactic reanalysis, *in* Charles N. Li (éd.). *Mechanisms of Syntactic Change,* 59-137. Austin: University of Texas Press.

Le Goffic P. (1993). *Grammaire de la phrase française*. Paris: Hachette.

Lehmann C. (1990). The Latin nominal group in typological perspective, *in*: Coleman, R. Ed. *New Studies in Latin Linguistics*. 203, Amsterdam: Benjamins.

Lehmann W.P. (1973). A structural principle of language and its implications. *Language* 49, 47-66.

Levin B. & Rappaport Hova M. (1995). *Unaccusativity: At the Syntax-Semantics Interface*. Cambridge. MA: MIT Press.

Marantz A. (1984). *On the Nature of Grammatical Relations*. Cambridge: MIT Press.

Marchello-Nizia Ch. (1992). *Histoire de la langue française aux XIVe et XVe siècles*. Paris: Dunod.

Marchello-Nizia Ch. (1999). *Le français en diachronie: douze siècles d'évolution*. Paris: Ophrys.

Marchello-Nizia Ch. (2000). Les grammaticalisations ont-elles une cause ? *L'information grammaticale* 67, 3-9.

Marchello-Nizia Ch. (2006). *Grammaticalisation et changement linguistique*. Bruxelles: De Boeck.

Maurel J.-P. (1985). Génitif et quantification. *in* Touratier Ch. Ed. *Syntaxe et latin,* 121-138. Aix-en-Provence: Presses de l'Université de Provence.

Menge H. (2000). *Lehrbuch der lateinische Syntax und Semantik*. Darmstadt: Wissenschaftliche Buchgesellschaft.

Milner J.-C. (1978a). *De la syntaxe à l'interprétation: quantités, insultes, exclamations*. Paris: Seuil.

Milner J.-C. (1978b). Cyclicité successive, comparative et Cross-over en français (première partie). *Linguistic* Inquiry 9: 4, 673-693 (annexe 2).

Muller C. (1995). *De* partitif et la négation, *in*: Forget D. *et al.* Eds. *Negation and Polarity: Syntax & semantics*, 253-270. Amsterdam: Benjamins.

Obenauer H.-G. (1983). Une quantification non-canonique: la quantification à distance. *Langue française* 58, 66-88.

Perlmutter D. M. (1978). Impersonal passives and the Unaccusative Hypothesis. *Proceedings of the 4ᵗʰ Annual Meeting of the Berkeley Linguistics Society.* 157–189.

Pinkster H. (1991). Evidence for SVO in Latin ?, *in* Wright R. Ed. *Latin and the Romance Languages in the Early Middle Ages*. London: Routledge.

Riegel M. & *al.* (1994). *Grammaire méthodique du français*. Paris: PUF.

Skårup P. (1994). La place de *de* en français contemporain: devant ou dans le syntagme nominal. *Revue romane* 29, 195-211.

Tenny C. (1994). *Aspectual Roles and the Syntax-Semantics Interface*. Dordrecht: Kluwer.

Van Valin R. (1990). Semantic Parameters of Split Intransitivity. *Language* 66, 221-260.

Vennemann Th. (1974). Topics, Subjects, and Word Order: From SXV to SVX via TVX, *in* J. Anderson & Ch. Jones Eds. *Proceedings of the 1ˢᵗ International Congress of Historical Linguistics*. Edinburgh, Sept. '93. Amsterdam: Benjamins, 339-376.

Verkuyl H.J. (1972). On the compositional nature of the aspects. Dordrecht: Kluwer.

Williams E. (1981). Argument structure and morphology. *Linguistic Review* I:1, 81–114.

Zimmermann M. (2002). Binominal each-constructions in German and English. *In*: Zwart J.-W., Abraham W. Eds. *Studies in Comparative Germanic Syntax*, Amsterdam: Benjamins.

SOME *QUELQUE(S)* IN LATIN[1]

B. Bortolussi
UMR ArScAn, équipe THEMAM
Paris Ouest Nanterre-La Défense
bernard.bortolussi@u-paris10.*fr*

Abstract

There are many Latin words corresponding to French *quelque(s)*; they are in a quasi-complementary distribution, their uses depending on syntactic or pragmatic contexts. Three plural forms, *aliquot*, *quidam* and *aliqui*, share the meanings and functions of *quelques* between them. In the same way, three singular forms – *quidam*, *aliquis* and *quis* – match Haspelmath's tripartition – [specific, known], [specific, unknown] and [*irrealis* nonspecific] respectively. *Quis* contrasts with yet another indefinite pronoun, *quisquam*, in negative contexts.

Late Latin diachronic changes reveal a tendency for the earlier indefinite pronouns getting confused with one another, and also a competition with distributive pronouns such as *quisque* and Free Choice indefinites (*qualiscumque/qualisque*).

1   Introduction

There is no Latin ancestor to French *quelque(s)* (Combettes 2004) or Italian *qualche*; however there is a large set of indefinite pronouns matching *quelque(s)* uses[2] : *quis, quisquam/ullus, aliquis, quidam, quispiam*…

(1)   a. *censor aliusue quis magistratus* (CIL 1[2], 593,144)
            "un censeur ou quelque autre magistrat"
            "a censor or some other magistrate"
         b. *Est quidam homo qui* … (Plaut. *Cist.* 735)
            "il y a un homme qui …"
            "there is some/a man who …"

---

[1]   This is a reworked version of a paper read during the Nancy *Journée d'étude* (May 23rd, 2008). It has been revised by taking Bertocchi & *alii* (2010) into account. It has also been improved by the comments and observations from Lucia Tovena and Alessandra Bertocchi, Mirka Maraldi and Anna Orlandini – whom I thank; one should refer to their work in order to read a comprehensive description of the relevant indefinites.
[2]   We shall (nearly) always give French translations with « quelque, quelqu'un », even in cases when other translations may be as good or even better. English translation are borrowed (and partly adapted) from the Loeb Classical Library.

    c. *At quis appellat ? Magistratus aliquis ?* (Cic. *Verr.* 2, 4, 146)
      "Mais qui forme cet appel ? <u>Quelque</u> magistrat?"
      "Who gives of an appeal (to the governor)? <u>One</u> of the magistrates?"
    d. *Hunc si <u>ullus</u> deus amaret* (Plaut. *Bacch.* 818)
      "Si <u>quelque</u> dieu l'aimait"
      "if <u>any</u> god loved him"
    e. *si <u>quispiam</u> det qui manus grauior siet* (Plaut. *Pseud.* 784)
      "si <u>quelqu'un</u> me donnait de quoi alourdir ma main"
      "if <u>someone</u> gives me something adding to my hand"

Most of these indefinites are morphologically related, deriving from a common root *qui-*, which is enhanced in various ways in Latin and which is well documented in the other Indo-European ancient languages. Another morphological characteristic is that adjectives[3] and pronouns are almost always identical ; I'll assume that adjectives and pronouns behave in the same way apart from the morphological differences – unlike French *quelque* and *quelqu'un*.

The wide range of various forms quoted in (1) suggests that whereas French only uses *quelque(s)*, Latin has clearly differentiated indefinites expressing existential quantification[4]. In a simplified presentation, and following Haspelmath's (1997) criteria and Bertocchi & *al.*'s presentation (2010), I shall assume that *quis* is non specific *irrealis*, *aliquis*, specific unknown, and *quidam*, specific known. *Quisquam / ullus* appear with negations or in negatively oriented contexts. Finally *quispiam* seems to compete with all the above-mentioned indefinite pronouns.

Given this contrastive description of Latin indefinites, I shall start from the distribution in French and from the well-known difference between plural form *quelques* and singular *quelque*. First we shall see that several indefinites are used in Latin to express indefinite plurality, whereas French only uses *quelques*. The second part will deal with the singular form *quelque*, and there again we shall find a subset of the previously mentioned indefinites, but within a more complex picture, with indefinites which are sensitive to the presence of negations play a role. In the last part I shall present an overview of the Late Latin diachronic changes, focusing on new forms originating from *qualis*, which is, as everyone knows, ancestor to *quelque(s)* through *quel que*.

2   Some *quelques*

First of all I shall show how indefinite countable quantity (*cf.* French *quelques*) is expressed in Latin. Like French, Latin used existential pronouns in the plural form [5].

---

[3]   In this paper I will not give a firm opinion about the status of the relevant Latin items: they are traditionally described as determiners, although this view may be criticized, since their syntactic behaviour is mostly comparable to that of ordinary (so-called qualifying) adjectives. However two arguments might be adduced: these indefinites are morphologically akin to interrogatives and relatives, all three groups sharing morphological peculiarities; moreover, all those items are both adjectives and pronouns, with no (or very little) morphological difference between adjectival and nominal forms.

[4]   Contrast between "existential" and "quantitative" is just part of a convenient terminology, which alludes to various classifications. A detailed study proves that it is inappropriate. For instance, we shall see that *quis*, which cannot be used in existential sentences, should not be classified in this way.

[5]   The reader is referred to Bertocchi & Maraldi (2009) on quantifiers.

Latin has an invariable indefinite which is exclusively specially dedicated to indefinite plural: *aliquot*. On the other hand, like French *quelques*, two existential indefinite pronouns may be used in the plural form : *aliqui* and *quidam*. Indefiniteness regarding reference is added to indefiniteness regarding quantity: *aliqui* refers to an indefinite set of elements whose existence is presupposed, but whose identity is unknown; *quidam* refers to a set of known elements whose identity is not revealed.

2.1   *Aliquot*

Like *aliquis*, *aliquot* is a compound word combining *ali(us)* « other » with a *qu*-word; it is indeclinable and only used with plural Ns. It indicates an indefinite quantity, situated at an intermediate level; Bertocchi & Maraldi (2009) call this kind of indefinites *mid-scalars quantifiers* ; they behave in turn as cardinal numbers and proportional ones. An argumentative effect may be associated to *aliquot* in (3a et b): the quantity, no matter how low or relatively high, is real and must be held to be not insignificant.

    a- Adjective (with other determiners)

(2)   *M. Volscius Fictor, qui ante <u>aliquot</u> annos tribunus plebis fuerat* (Liu. 3,13,1)
    "M. Volscius Fictor, qui avait été tribun de la plèbe <u>quelques</u> années auparavant"
    "M. Volscius Fictor, who had been a tribune of the plebs <u>a few</u> years before"

(3)   a. *Quis dicere audeat uera omnia esse somnia ? 'aliquot somnia uera' inquit Ennius 'sed <u>omnia</u> non necesse est'* (Cic. *diu.* 2,127)
      "Qui oserait dire que tous les rêves sont vrais ? '<u>quelques/un certain nombre de</u> rêves sont vrais', a dit Ennius, 'mais pas nécessairement <u>tous'</u> »
      "And further, would anybody dare to say that all dreams are true? '<u>Some</u> dreams are true,' says Ennius, ' but not necessarily <u>all</u>.'"
    b. *saltem <u>aliquot dies</u> / profer, dum proficiscar aliquo, ne uideam.* (Ter. *Andr.* 328)
      "Diffère-le au moins de <u>quelques</u> jours, que j'aie le temps de partir quelque part, pour ne pas en être témoin."
      "Put it off for <u>some</u> days at least, while I go elsewhere, that I may not be a witness."

In (2) *ante aliquot annos* indicates an interval not very long, but indefinite, without specific argumentative effect. In (3a) *aliquot* may refer to a rather great number, but not the totality (*omnia*) ; in (3b) the quantity is low, but the speaker considers it as sufficient, as indicated by the argumentative adverb *saltem* "at least".

    b- Pronoun (animate)

The pronominal use is rather rare; *aliquot* refers to an NP previously introduced and it designates a subset of elements whose number is indefinite:

(4)   a. *cum militarent <u>aliquot</u> apud Romanos* (Liu. 23,4,7)
    "alors que <u>quelques uns</u> servaient dans les armées romaines"
    "while <u>several</u> were serving in the Roman armies"
    b. *<u>aliquot</u> primo impetu perculsi caesique sunt* (Liu. 23,44,4)
    "<u>quelques uns</u> furent atteints et tombèrent au premier assaut"
    "<u>several</u> were knocked down and slain in the first charge"

Aliquot refers in both examples to a subset of previously mentioned soldiers.

2.2   *Quidam* : indefinite plurality of specific[6] known elements

Quidam looks like French *certains*, it refers to a subset of identified elements, whose number remains undetermined:

(5)   a   *apud quosdam ueteres auctores non inuenio Lucretium consulem* (Liu. 2,8,5)
"chez quelques/certains historiens anciens je ne trouve pas mention de Lucretius comme consul"
"In some ancient authorities I do not find Lucretius given as consul"

b   *Video enim esse hic in senatu quosdam qui tecum una fuerunt* (Cic. *Catil.* 1,8)
"J'en vois en effet ici au sénat quelques-uns/certains qui étaient avec toi"
"For I see here in the senate some men who were there with you."

In example (5a), Cicero avoids naming Catiline's accomplices, but he knows them very well; is the same with the historical sources mentioned by Livy.

2.3   *Aliqui* : indefinite plurality of specific unknown elements

In the plural form, *aliqui* refers to a subset of elements whose number remains indefinite, but, in contrast to utterances with *quidam*, the speaker doesn't know their identity :

(6)   a   *Cum cotidie aliqui eorum caderent* (Liu. 38,29,9)
"Alors que chaque jour quelques-uns d'entre eux tombaient"
"Since every day some of their small number were killed"

b   *ex illo ipso numero navarchorum aliqui uiuunt* (Cic. *Verr.* 2,5,21)
"dans ce groupe même des navarques quelques-uns sont vivants"
"out of this very body of naval captains some are alive"

In the above examples the original set is expressed by a partitive genitive (*eorum, ex illo ipso numero nauarchorum*).

Paradoxically, *aliqui* is also used with a numeral adjective:

(7)   a.   *quemadmodum dicuntur* aliqui *tres amici aut tres propinqui aut tres uicini* (Aug. *trin.* 7,6)
"comme on parle de trois amis ou de trois parents ou de trois voisins"
"like one speaks of three friends or three members of a family or three neighbours"

b.   *Contineo me ab exemplis. Graecis hoc modicum est : Leonidas, Epaminondas, tres aliqui aut quattuor.* (Cic. *fin.* 2,62)
"J'arrête avec les exemples. Chez les Grecs ils sont peu nombreux: Leonidas, Epaminondas, quelques trois ou quatre autres."
"I refrain from further instances. The Greeks have but a modest list: Leonidas, Epaminondas, some three or four."

---

[6]   In Haspelmath's (1997) terminology, *specific* means that the existence of a particular referent is presupposed ; the identity of the referent may or may not be known, as the case may be.

    c   *Elleborum potabis faxo <u>aliquos</u> uiginti dies* (Plaut. *Men*. 950)
        "je ferai en sorte que tu boives de l'ellébore pendant <u>quelque</u> vingt jours"
        "I'll make you drink hellebore for <u>some</u> twenty days."

Quantity is determined from the beginning, but the identity of the entities is unknown: in example (7a), the Trinity is compared with trios of unidentified individuals. And from non-identification of individuals one drifts to the approximation of the number itself, as in (7b): Cicero leaves slightly indeterminate the number of temperate great men, because he is unable to quote fast enough all the elements of the list. In (7c) the threat bears on an indeterminate future, only the duration of which is known (20 consecutive days) ; but the length of the hellebore treatment itself may be an approximation. To indetermination of identity is added indetermination of quantity ; quantity which was initially definite becomes vaguer, as it happens also with adverbs such as *paene* « almost », *circa* « about » etc. In French *quelque* changed from an adjective into an invariable adverb[7], while in Latin it remains an adjectival form that agrees with the noun (*aliquos dies*: acc. pl).

3   Some *quelque*

When we compare Haspelmath's implicational maps (1997 : 69) of Latin and French, we can observe that *quelque* corresponds to several latin indefinites: *quidam, aliquis, quisquam/ullus,* and we need to add *quis*. The comparison between French and Latin has to be refined. First we note that, unlike the Latin indefinites, singular *quelque* now belongs to formal registers of the language. Furthermore the distribution of Latin indefinites is based on referential, semantic and pragmatic properties, but it is also based on syntactic criteria ; for instance, *quis* and *quisquam* are used instead of others after a negation. These constraints are quite different from those that apply to French *quelque* : ignorance, inference, modal contexts, etc.[8]

First I shall look at indefinites that are gathered in the left part of Haspelmath's implicational map: *quidam (specific known), aliquis (specific)* and *quis (non-specific)* – I introduce them in the same way as Bertocchi, Maraldi, Orlandini (2010). We shall see that their uses are conditioned by more than the kind of existential reference they have.

In traditional grammars, *quis* and *quisquam* are considered to be in complementary distribution according to the kind of negation that is used. Actually both these indefinites can appear in the same structures, but with different values, in conditional clauses, for example; *quisquam*, as shown by Orlandini (2001), supports a pragmatic negative value, while *quis* is neutral in this respect.

3.1   The quidam / aliquis / quis tripartite division

Haspelmath's division between specific known (*quidam*), specific unknown (*aliquis*) and non specific irrealis (*quis*) is widely illustrated by the data. It appears particularly in some contexts, for example in conditional clauses :

(8)   a. *Si <u>qui</u> alibi <u>motus</u> extitisset* (Liu. 6,32,4)
          "**Pour le cas où** se serait produit ailleurs <u>quelque soulèvement</u>"
          "**if** <u>a revolt</u> should break out anywhere"

---

[7] Cf. Grevisse (1998) § 709, p. 189.
[8] Cf. Jayez & Tovena (2005) and (2008).

b. *Quod si uos aliquis casus conducet in unum, / Mente memor tota, quae damus arma, tene.* (Ou. *rem. am.* 673)
   "Si quelque hasard vous réunit l'un et l'autre dans le même lieu, n'oublie pas de faire usage des armes que je te donne"
   "**If** by any chance you two meet, remember the weapons I gave you"

c. *Si honos quidam, senatus concordiae consulam.* (Cic. *prou.* 47)
   "S'il s'agit de quelque distinction honorifique, je veillerai à préserver l'unité du Sénat."
   "**if** any honour to be paid to him is under discussion, I shall consult the unanimous feeling of the senate"

In (8a) the hostile movement is virtual and therefore it can't be specific nor known (and we cannot exclude the possibility of several hostile movements). In (8b) the existence of a chance (*aliquis casus*) is presupposed, but it remains unknown. In (8c), Cicero knows very well what honours have to be awarded to Caesar, but he deliberately refrains from mentioning them in order to minimize their importance.

However, we may not say that a complementary distribution exists, for three reasons:

a) *Quidam, aliquis* and *quis* occur together in the same clause and it is not always easy in this case to discover a difference in their meaning:

(9) a. *si quis referat mihi casus Vlixen / aut aliquem e sociis, in quem mea saeuiat ira* (Ou. *met.* 14,187)
         "si quelque hasard me ramenait Ulysse ou quelqu'un de ses compagnons, contre lequel ma colère pourrait sévir"
         "Oh! that some chance would but bring Ulysses back to me, or some of his friends, against whom my rage might vent itself"

    b. *Si quid est in me ingeni, iudices, ... aut si qua exercitatio dicendi, ... aut si huiusce rei ratio aliqua ...* (Cic. *Arch.* 1)
         "S'il est en moi, juges, quelque talent, ... ou quelque habitude de la parole, ... ou enfin quelque connaissance de cette affaire ..."
         "If there is any natural ability in me, O judges, or if I have any practice as a speaker, or if I have any method in my oratory"

The distinction between specific (*aliquem*) and non specific (*quis*) is relevant in (9a), since *quis casus* refers to an eventual event or to several events whose existence remains uncertain, while *aliquem* refers to one of Ulysses's companions, whose existence is real. In (9b), however it is difficult to perceive a difference between *ratio aliqua* and *quid ingenii / qua exercitatio*[9]. Stylistic factors and rhythm may play a role, especially concerning the difference between weak (*quis*) and strong (*aliquis*) pronominal forms.

b) They are not always existential pronouns in distributive opposition or competing in the same structure (see infra 2.1.2);

---

[9] One may consider that *aliqua ratio* supports a minimal quantity value: "at least some knowledge" cf. (16).

c) They compete with other "existential" indefinites, among them *quispiam*[10], but also with Free Choice indefinites (*quiuis*) and NPI (*quisquam/ullus*). In conditional clauses introduced by *si*, we can find *quiuis* and *quisquam/ullus* :

(10)   a.   *si tu solus aut quiuis unus cum scuto et gladio impetum in me fecisset* (Cic. *Caecin.* 62)
       "**si** toi tout seul ou quelqu'un/qui que ce soit d'autre m'avait attaqué avec un bouclier et une épée"
       "**if** you by yourself, or **if** anyone person had made an onset on me with shield and sword"

       b.   *Si quisquam huius imperii defensor mori potest* (Cic. *Balb.* 49)
       "**Si** quelqu'un peut mourir en défenseur de cet empire"
       "**if** anyone can die as a defender of this empire"

       c.   *Si ullum uerbum faxo* (Plaut. *Men.* 156)
       "**Si** je prononce quelque parole"
       "**if** I say any word"

Contextual factors are different here. For instance, (10b) and (10c) have a negative orientation : the speaker considers the hypothesis as unlikely or undesirable. However, we can see that the original fine oppositions between all these indefinites seems to have weakened and have turned into actual competition, as shown by the changes in Late Latin[11].

Let us now examine *quidam*, *aliquis* and *quis*, according to Haspelmath's maps.

3.1.1   *Quidam*

a)   specific, known by the speaker :

(11)   *Est quidam homo, qui ait illam se scire ubi sit* (Plaut. *Cist.* 735)
       "Il y a un homme qui dit qu'il sait où elle est"
       "There is a man who says that he knows where she is"

Its semantic properties make it particularly apt in presentational or existential sentences[12]. Here the identity of the person is irrelevant.

b) With proper nouns, it indicates that only identity is known, and nothing else; it may be compared to French *un certain*[13] :

(12)   *Erat Pipa quaedam* (Cic. *Verr.* 2,5,81)
       "Il y avait une certaine Pipa…"
       "There was a woman called Pippa"

---

[10]   This indefinite (which is rare already in the archaic period) seems to compete mostly with *quis*. It will not be studied here ; see Bertocchi & *alii* for more details.

[11]   Cf. Bertocchi & *alii* (2010) and Bortolussi (2009).

[12]   Cf. Rosén (1998).

[13]   According to Serbat (1984), then Touratier (1994 : 57), *quidam* may suggest a plurality which weakens the individuality of a well-identified person ; this, they think, would result in a derogatory nuance of meaning.

According to Rosén (1998: 729), *quidam* « un-defines » proper name, whence a stylistic effect – irony and depreciation, when the person is actually well known[14].

c) With abstract nouns, *quidam* constructs a fictional set of elements of the same kind, from which an element is extracted without being clearly identified. *Quidam* supports an evaluative operation : it indicates the limit, the "hedge" of the relevant abstract notion[15] :

(13)   *nascitur ex adsiduitate laborum animorum hebetatio quaedam et languor* (Sen. *dial.* 9,17,5)
         "naît de l'acharnement au travail une sorte de lenteur et de langueur intellectuelle"
         "continuous mental toil breeds in the mind a certain dullness and languor"

d) in combination with a negation

Quidam rarely appears in the scope of a negation :

(14)   *non solum autem moechandum non est, quod facit non quidam, sed omnis, qui dimittit uxorem suam et ducit alteram* (Aug. *adul.* 1,24,30)
         "non seulement il ne faut pas commettre d'adultère, ce que fait non pas un individu, mais quiconque répudie son épouse et en prend une autre"
         "not only must one avoid adultery, a sin which is committed not by an individual, but by anyone who repudiates his wife and takes another, ..."

This is hardly ever found except in implicature denials (Geurts 1998 : 294 *sqq*)

3.1.2   *Aliqui(s)*

Aliquis presupposes the existence.

a) It is used in assertive sentences, and in particular in existential (15a) or presentational (15b) sentences[16] :

(15)   a.   *Fuit aliquis fatalis casus* (Cic. *Phil.* 6,19)
             "Il s'est produit un coup du sort"
             "There has been a sort of fatality"

         b.   *est aliquis, qui se inspici, aestimari fastidiat* (Liu. 6,41,2)
             "voilà quelqu'un qui refuse de se laisser examiner, de se laisser évaluer"
             "There is many a man who resents being investigated and appraised"

Sometimes several elements may validate the proposition, so that, like with French *quelque*, there is a 'widening' (Jayez et Tovena 2008) from a single individual to a potential plurality. Then *aliquis* comes closer to Free Choice indefinites *quiuis* and *quilibet* :

(16)   *misericordia, odio, motu animi aliquo perturbatos (iudices)* (Cic. *Brut.* 200)
         "(des juges) remués par la pitié, par la haine, par quelque autre/n'importe quelle passion"
         "(in the judges) any strong indications of pity, abhorrence, or any other emotion of the mind"

This interpretative effect is especially noticeable whenever *aliquis* is combined with *unus*[17] :

---

[14]   Bertocchi & *alii* speak of "semantic enrichment implicature".
[15]   "The behavior of *quidam* ... is thus similar to that of a "hedge"." (Bertocchi & *alii* 2010).
[16]   Cf. Rosén (1998).

(17)   a. *(argumenta) siue plura sunt, siue <u>aliquod unum</u>* (Cic. *de or.* 2,292)
            "(les arguments), qu'il y en ait plus ou qu'il y en ait <u>un</u>"
            "whether they are several or <u>only one</u>"
         b. *Haec uitia <u>unus aliquis</u> inducit, ... ceteri imitantur* (Sen. *ep.* 114,17)
            "Ces défauts, il y en a <u>un</u> qui les introduit, les autres l'imitent"
            "<u>Some individual</u> makes these vices fashionable ... the rest follow his lead"

Then identity is unimportant, the only thing that matters being the minimal existence of one entity that validates the predication.

b) Besides its existential use *aliquis* has another use, which may be called quantitative; that indicates a degree that is not well-defined, but must be greater than "none" (*nullus*) and smaller than "all" (*omnes*) :

(18)   *pupillo ... qui iam <u>aliquem</u> intellectum habent ; ... huius aetatis pupilli <u>nullum</u> intellectum habent* (Gaius 3,19,9)
         « le petit enfant qui a déjà <u>quelque</u> (= un certain degré de) conscience ; ... les enfants de cet âge n'ont <u>aucune</u> conscience »
         "little child that has <u>some</u> (degree of) judgment ; ... so young children have no judgment at all"

In the same way as French *quelque*, *aliquis* is rarely found in a negative sentence. There are however important differences, which make it impossible to call *aliquis* an *anti-negative item* (Corblin 2004). One may stress the following points:

a) *aliquis* is outside the scope of negation :

(19)   *Quod incredibilius uidetur, id concedis, aliquem in maximis et continuis doloribus non esse miserum, esse etiam beatum ... Atqui si uirtus potest efficere **ne** miser <u>aliquis</u> sit, facilius efficiet ut beatissimus sit* (Sen. *ep.* 92,15)
         « Ce qui paraît plus incroyable, tu l'admets : que <u>quelqu'un</u> dans de très grandes et perpétuelles souffrances **n'**est **pas** malheureux, et est même heureux. Pourtant si la vertu peut faire en sorte que <u>quelqu'un</u> **ne** soit **pas** malheureux, elle fera en sorte plus facilement qu'il soit parfaitement heureux »
         "you grant what seems more incredible : that <u>someone</u> who is in the midst of extreme and unremitting pain is **not** unhappy, is even happy ... And yet, if virtue can ensure that <u>somebody</u> is **not** unhappy, it will be an easier task for it to make him completely happy."

Even though the whole proposition (from the COMP position)[18] apparently falls within the scope of *ne*, *ne* does not affect the interpretation of *aliquis*, whereas elsewhere it does affect that of *quis* in similar combinations (cf. *infra quis*) : *ne <u>quis</u> miser sit* would mean "that nobody is unhappy".

b) Similarly, in denials, *aliquis* remains unaffected by negation, and there is no scalar effect:

         - in proposition denials (= polemic negation *in* Orlandini 2001) :

---

[17]   Cf. Hofmann & Szantyr (1965 : 211) and Bertocchi & *alii* (footnote 32).
[18]   Actually such a structure might be described in relation to an "intermediate-scope" phenomenon.

(20) *Non aliquis socios rursus ad arma uocat* (Ov. *rem*. 281)

« Il n'est pas vrai qu'il y ait quelqu'un qui appelle encore aux armes ses compagnons »

"No, it is not true that there is somebody who still calls his comrades to arms "

Although this is logically equivalent to "yes, it is true that there is nobody who calls ...", the proposition is first and foremost the negation of the existential assertive proposition *aliquis socios rursus ad arma uocat* "there is somebody who still calls his comrades to arms".

- in implicature denials (Geurts 1998 : 294) :

(21) *non enim declamatorem aliquem de ludo, sed doctissimum quaerimus* (Cic. *Or.* 47)

"ce n'est pas quelque déclamateur d'école que nous recherchons, mais un savant accompli"

"I am not seeking a mere school-declaimer, but a well-accomplished scholar"

c) in the scope of a negation, *aliquis* may exhibit a quantitative meaning; Orlandini (2001) considers it as an NPI; it may be compared to French "le moindre" :

(22) *qui neque exercitationis ullam uiam neque aliquod praeceptum artis esse arbitrarentur* (Cic. *de or.* 1,14)

« en hommes qui n'imaginaient pas qu'il y eût dans cet art ni quelque loi, ni le moindre principe »

"since they thought there was no definite course of training or any / nor the least rules of art"

3.1.3 *Qui(s)*, non-specific *irrealis*, enclitic

Quis is very rare in assertive sentences. Normal contexts are either modal or epistemic, with no presupposition of existence:

(23)   a. *Dixerit quis* (Cic. *off*. 3,76)

"quelqu'un dira » / « quelqu'un pourrait dire"

"someone will say » / « someone may say » / « someone might say"

   b. *Filiam quis habet, pecunia opus est ; duas, maiore* (Cic. *parad*. 6,44)

"Quelqu'un a une fille, il lui faut de l'argent ; (en a-t-il) deux, (il lui en faut) davantage "

"someone has a daughter, he needs money ; two, more money"

= *qui filiam habet, pecunia opus est* "qui a une fille a besoin d'argent" "who has a daughter needs money" ; cf. *Qui placebunt aut custodi aut quis ... emerit* (Cat. *agr*. 145,1) "qui plairont ou au surveillant ou à celui qui aura acheté / à l'éventuel acheteur" "to the satisfaction of the owner or his representative in charge of the work"

= *quicumque filiam habet ...* « quiconque a une fille » "whoever has a daughter"

= *si quis filiam habet ...* « si on a une fille » "if one has a daughter"

In an overwhelming majority of its uses *quis* is combined with and adjacent to another constituent: interrogative adverb (*cf. num quis*), negation (*cf. ne quis*), conjunction (mostly conditional, sometimes temporal – *cf. si quis, ut quis*) ...

This syntactic constraint strongly suggests that *quis* is a NPI; it should be compared with *quisquam/ullus* (cf. *infra* 3.2).

Quis behaves as a variable which is attached to that constituent which determines the modality of the sentence.

a) *num quis* (*numquis*) *?* or *an quis ?* (negatively oriented yes/no questions)

(24)   *An quid est homini Salute melius ?* (Plaut. *Asin.* 717)
        "Y a-t-il quelque chose/rien de meilleur pour l'homme que la Sauvegarde?"
        "Why, is there ever anything better for a man than Salvation?"

(25)   a. *numquis testis Postumum appellauit ?* (Cic. *Rab.* 10)
            "Y a-t-il quelque témoin pour accuser Postumus ?"
            "Did anyone witness then mention Postumus?"
        b. *num quis uestrum ad uim, ad facinus, ad caedem accommodatus est ? nemo.*
            (Cic. *leg. agr.* 3,16)
            "Est-ce que quelqu'un/l'un d'entre vous est porté à la violence, au crime, au meurtre? Non, personne."
            "Is anyone of you a man inclined to violence, or atrocity, or murder? Not one."

b) *ne quis* (*nequis*) "ne … personne, ne … aucun" "nobody, none"

- directive acts (*ne* introduces prohibitions):

(26)   *lex erat : ne quis Dianae uitulum immolaret.* (Cic. *inu.* 2,31,95)
        "La loi était : que personne n'immole un veau à Diane"
        "There was a law that prohibited the sacrifice of a bull-calf to Diana"
        (litt. "let no-one sacrifice a bull-calf to Diana")

- subordinate clauses whose complementizer incorporates a negation (*ne* is a negative conjunction):

(27)   a. *edicto uetuit ne quis se praeter Apellen / pingeret* (Hor. *ep.* 2,1,237-238)
        "il interdit par un édit que personne d'autre qu'Apelle le représentât"
        "so he willed by law none but Apelles might model him."
        b. *Neiquis eorum Bacanal habuise uelet* (C.I.L I², 581, ligne 3)
        "Que personne parmi eux n'ait Bacchanal"
        "No man is to be a Bacchantian"

c) *si quis* (*siquis*)

This construction corresponds to two separate meanings:

- possibility, whether it is still open (28a) or is counterfactual (28b) :

(28)   a. *timorem si quem habetis, deponite* (Cic. *Mil.* 4)
            "si (jamais) vous éprouvez quelque crainte, bannissez-la"
            "lay aside your alarm, if indeed you feel any"

b. me … *si qui* accidisset grauior rei publicae *casus*, si bellum, si morbus, si fames, facile possem defendere (Cic. Phil. 1,13)
"s'il était arrivé quelque malheur plus grave à l'Etat, une guerre, une épidémie, une famine, je pourrais facilement vous en protéger"
"if any more serious calamity had happened to the State, war, pestilence, famine, I should enable to justify myself"

The difference between singular and plural forms seems not to be crucial, as evidenced by their alternation in the same text :

(29)   a. *si qui* alibi *motus* extitisset (Liu. 6,32,4)
"pour le cas où se serait produit ailleurs quelque soulèvement"
"if a revolt should break out anywhere"
b. *si qui* ex Etruria *noui motus* nuntiarentur (Liu. 6,22,1)
"pour le cas où seraient annoncés quelques nouveaux soulèvements depuis l'Etrurie"
"if any fresh commotion might be reported from Etruria"

- universal quantification :

Quis is the indefinite that is used in *donkey sentences*[19] :

(30)   Pudor si *quem* non flectit, non frangit timor. (Publ. Syr. P.45)
"si la pudeur n'arrive pas à fléchir quelqu'un, la crainte n'arrive pas à le briser"
"= quiconque ne plie pas sous l'effet de la honte ne se laisse pas briser par la peur"
"If honour sways one not, fear cannot quell"

Since *quis* is non-specific, it is quite appropriate in generic utterances. Actually, even when there is no adverb or conjunction with the ability to induce the notion of possible or constant iteration of an event, the mere presence of *quis* is enough to trigger a generic reading, see (23b) above.

Universal quantification is the preferred reading when *quis* is in the plural:

(31)   a. Quinctius haec rettulit ad socios : … *perfugas* remittere ac *si qui sint capti* (Liu. 32,35,8)
"Quinctius imposa ces conditions aux alliés : remettre les déserteurs et (tous) les éventuels prisonniers"
"the statement which Quinctius made to the allies was to deliver up the refugees and any prisoners there might be"
b. Dimissis Chaonum <Thesprotorum>que et *si qui alii Epirotae erant* praesidiis (Liu. 43,23,6)
« Après avoir renvoyé les garnisons de Chaonie, de Thesprotie et toutes les autres d'Epire »

---

[19]   Cf. Amsili (2006) for a presentation of this phenomenon and Bortolussi (2009) about its realisation in Latin.

"after sending away the forces of Chaonians, Thesprotians and <u>whatever other Epirotes there were</u>"

So *si qui* becomes an indefinite relative, very similar to *quicumque* «tous ceux qui» (all those who); but when it is compared to *quicumque* (which presupposes the existence of the universally quantified set), *si qui* goes no further than letting it to be possible (31a).

The proposition that is introduced by *si qui* is not a conditional clause any longer, it is becoming a substantive relative clause, as shown by its coordination with a referential NP in (31a)[20].

The group *si* or *ne* + *quis* becomes a fixed expression very early and then a coalescent unit. This change in status is shown by (among other clues) the following two phenomena:

- the group cannot be split up : whatever place *ne* may occupy in the syntagmatic structure, *quis* remains inseparable from it:

(32)   *sacerdos <u>nequis</u> uir eset.* (C.I.L I^2, 581, ligne 10)
         "<u>qu'aucun</u> homme ne soit prêtre."
         "No man is to be a priest."

- NP disjunction : surface cohesion of NPs proves to be less strong than the welding together of *si/ne* and *quis* :

(33)   *<u>si qui</u> accidisset grauior rei publicae <u>casus</u>* (Cic. *Phil.* 1,13)
         si quelque   malheur.
         if any   calamity

If one views *si* – following Lewis' approach – as a quantifier on events, clusters *si quis* and *ne quis* strongly call to mind a logical form, like Operator(variable) preceding the proposition itself.

This analysis is supported by yet another argument : variables are gathered at the beginning of the clause, just after the conjunction:

(34)   *si <u>quis</u> <u>quid</u> quaereret* (Cic. *de or.* 1,102)
         « si <u>quelqu'un</u> demandait <u>quelque chose</u> »
         "if <u>any</u> man want to propound <u>any</u> question"

3.2   Contrast between *quis* and *quisquam*

Another indefinite, *quisquam*, a reinforced form of *quis*, shows a distribution constrained in a way that looks like that concerning *quis* : it occurs after the negatively oriented interrogative adverb *num*, after *si*, and after negations[21].

The adjectival form *ullus* exhibits the same properties ; this form is derived from *unus* « one ».

Quisquam/nullus and *quis* are traditionally viewed as being in complementary distribution:

•   unlike *quis*, *quisquam*, is not subject to the adjacency constraint ;

---

[20]   Amacker (1974) uses this criterion (among others) to prove that *si quis* is (a kind of) nominal item.

[21]   *Quisquam* is used after a negation in a majority of cases, with *si* much less often ; but *quis* is equally frequent with both *ne* and *si*.

- negations with which *quisquam* is found are those of assertive sentences, mostly complex forms *neque* ("and ... not"), *nemo* "nobody"), *nihil* ("nothing"), etc.

According to Orlandini's analysis, *quisquam* and *ullus* are used in two ways:

- *quisquam1*, *ullus1* are "forclusifs"[22] of semantic negation ; therefore they are used in syntaxically negative utterances ; *nec quisquam*[23] and *neque ullus* are accurate equivalents of *nemo* and *nullus* respectively:

(35)   *nec quemquam uidi qui timeret...* (Cic. *nat. deor.* 1,86)
         "et je n'ai vu personne qui craignît..."
         "nor have I ever met anybody more afraid than he was"

(36)   *statuam auream nec in urbe nec in ulla parte Italiae quisquam aspexit* (Val. Max. 2,5,1)
         « une statue d'or, personne n'en a vu ni à Rome ni en aucun endroit d'Italie »
         "nobody has seen any gold statue neither in Rome nor in any place Italy"

But this interpretative equivalence is not verified with sentence negation:

(37)   ***Non** esse seruos peior hoc quisquam potest* (Plaut. *Asin.* 118)
         « **Il ne peut pas** y avoir d'esclave pire que celui-ci »
         "**Not** any servant can there be more artful than this fellow"
         ≠ *nullus seruos esse peior hoc potest* « aucun esclave ne peut être pire que celui-ci »
         "no slave can be worse than this one"

- *quisquam2*, *ullus2* function as « pragmatic negations », *i.e.* they are found in syntactically positive but « pragmatically negative » sentences[24]:

(38)   *Num igitur censes ullum animal quod sanguinem habeat, sine corde esse posse ?* (Cic. *diu.* 1,119)
         "Crois-tu donc par hasard que quelque/un/aucun animal qui a du sang puisse exister sans coeur?"
         "Now do you think it possible for any animal that has blood to exist without a heart?"

(39)   *Hunc si ullus deus amaret* (Plaut. *Bacch.* 818)
         « Si quelque dieu l'aimait »
         "This person, if any God had favoured him"

With rhetorical questions introduced by *num*, the answer the speaker is expecting is negative (38). In (39) the hypothesis is presented by the speaker as unlikely in the extreme:

---

[22] According to the terminology of Damourette and Pichon (1911-1940), `forclusifs' are negation `pas' and all (determiners, pronouns and adverbs) N-words that enter in the negative concord system of French.

[23] Neuter *quidquam* used with a negation is equivalent to *nihil* « nothing ».

[24] Cf. Orlandini (2001).

the probability of a god loving him is very low. While *si quis* does not bring about any orientation, *si quisquam* is negatively oriented.

4   Changes and new-beginnings

4.1   Free alternation of existential indefinites[25]

In Late Latin existential indefinites may cooccur with one another in the same clause; the difference between specific and non-specific (*cf.* 8a) may have become less relevant, particularly in generic sentences. For instance, *quis*, *aliquis* and *quisquam* seem to alternate freely:

(40)   a   *Si aliquis alteri aliquid praestiterit de rebus suis* (*Lex Salica* LI,1)
             "Si quelqu'un prête quelque chose qui lui appartient à quelqu'un d'autre"
             "if somebody lends something of his own to another person"
        b   *si aliquis ab igne quicquam eripuit* (Greg. Tur. *Franc.* 5,33)
             "si quelqu'un a arraché quelque chose aux flames"
             "if someone carried anything away from the fire"

Bertocchi & *alii* (2010) also provide instances of "free alternation" of *quis* and *quidam* in Gregory of Tours' works:

(41)   a   *quae a quibus audiui silere nequeo* (Greg. Tur. *glor. mart.* 7)
             "je ne peux passer sous silence ce que j'ai entendu dire par certains"
             "cannot keep silent on the things I heard from some of them"
        b   *proderit tibi si quiddam nobis profuturum narraueris* (Greg. Tur. *Franc.* 5,19)
             "it will be an advantage for you if you tell us something (which will be) advantageous for us"

Generic contexts too tend to bring *quis* and Free Choice indefinites closer to one another:

(42)   *Si quis animal aut caballum uel quemlibet pecus in messe sua inuenerit* (*Lex Salica* IX,1)
        « Si quelqu'un trouve un animal ou un cheval ou n'importe quel bétail sans sa récolte »
        "If someone finds an animal or a horse or any herd in the harvest"

Quis and *quisquam* cannot always be contrasted either, for (during the archaic and classical periods already) they seem to be free variants of each other in two kinds of context:

-    in directive acts, direct (43a) or indirect (43b) :

(43)   a   *sacerdos **nequis** uir eset. Magister **neque** uir neque mulier quisquam eset.* (C.I.L I², 581, line 10)
             "comme prêtre qu'il n'y ait aucun homme. Comme maître, qu'il n'y ait aucun homme ni aucune femme"

---

[25]   Cf. Bertocchi & *alii* (2010.): "The weakening of precise distinctions among the various indefinites is a generalized phenomenon in Late Latin.".

"No man is to be a priest; <u>no-one</u>, either man or woman, is to be an officer"
b **ne** <u>ullus</u> *modus sumptibus, ne luxuriae sit.* (Liv. 34,3,8)
"Qu'il n'y ait <u>aucune</u> limite aux dépenses, au luxe."
"that there may be <u>no</u> limits to our spending and our luxury."

- after interrogative adverb *num*:

(44)   a   **num** <u>quis</u> *uestrum ad uim, ad facinus, ad caedem accommodatus est ? nemo.*
(Cic. *leg. agr.* 3,16)
"Est-ce que <u>l'un</u> d'entre vous est prêt à l'usage de la force, au crime, au meurtre?
Non, personne."
"Is <u>anyone</u> of you a man inclined to violence, or atrocity, or murder? Not one."

   b   **num** *ergo* <u>quisquam</u> *eos misere uixisse dicet, ut non ipse miserrimus ob hoc omnibus uideatur?* (Sen. *dial.* 12,12,4)
"est-ce que donc <u>quelqu'un</u> dira qu'ils ont vécu malheureux, sans se faire regarder lui-même comme le dernier des malheureux ?"
"Will <u>anyone</u> say, therefore, that these men lived poorly without seeming from his very words to be the poorest wretch alive?"

Irrespective of any indefinite, *num* itself is oriented towards a negative answer ; therefore the use of *quisquam* here happens to be somewhat redundant, unless we hypothesise that *quisquam* then receives a scalar value pointing down to the lowest degree ("the least").

Thus it is not surprising that *quis* and *quisquam* prove to be quite close in Late Latin.

4.2   Expansion of *quisque* ("each")

Distributive indefinite *quisque* is used in contexts where a set of elements is built or presupposed. When it is combined with temporal conjunctions, especially *ut* "when", it indicates exhaustive search over the whole set of elements. Then – even though only in a marginal way – *quisque* becomes a rival to *quis* (which is used for universal quantification, as noted above):

(45)   a   *nam* **ut** <u>quis</u> *destrictior accusator, uelut sacrosanctus erat* (Tac. *ann.* 4,36,3)
"en effet <u>quand</u> un accusateur était mordant, il était pour ainsi dire sacro-saint"
= <u>tout</u> accusateur mordant était pour ainsi dire sacro-saint
"Indeed <u>any</u> conspicuously restless informer was, so to say, inviolable"

   b   *Vt* <u>quisque</u> *acciderat, eum necabam illico.* (Plaut. *Poen.* 486)
"**A chaque fois qu**'il en tombait <u>un</u>, je le tuais sur le champ"
= je tuais sur le champ <u>tous ceux qui</u> tombaient
"**As** <u>each one</u> dropped, I straightway killed him"

Conversely *quisque* comes nearer to *quis*, but nearer to Free Choice[26] indefinites as well, inasmuch as it refers to any individual with no extension to any whole set:

---

[26]   Hofmann & Szantyr (1972: 199) do note that *quisque* and *quivis* come closer (to each other), but they also explain the free alternation of *quis* and *quisque* through phonological weakening of final – *que*. Cf. Bertocchi & *al.*'s (2010) recent synthesis.

(46) *cum quisque de eo procul et abditae quicquam locutus fuisset mali* (Greg. Tur.
      Franc. 9,6)
      « lorsqu'on/quelqu'un avait dit quelque mal de lui de loin et par derrière »
      "after that everyone/anyone at a distance and secretly had said something evil
      about him"

4.3   Uses of *qualis* (« quel ») and derived forms

Even though there is no direct Latin ancestor to French *quelque*, one may wonder whether
qualis (a partial ancestor) has not evolved in Latin from a correlative comparative to an
existential indefinite. This question also concerns some forms derived from *qualis*, such as
qualiscumque, which has been taken up in French as *quelconque*, and the surprising
qualisque, which must of course conjure up *quelque*.

3.2.1   *Qualis*

This morphological ancestor of French *quel* has the same qualitative meaning as its
descendant; it is used both in comparative clauses (47a) in correlation with *talis* and in
interrogative clauses[27] (47b) :

(47) a   *Talis per omnem uitam fuit, qualis in funere* (Sen. *dial.* 6,2,4)
          "Elle fut durant toute sa vie telle qu'elle fut lors des funérailles"
          "Such she remained during her whole life as she was at the funeral"
      b   *Verum meam uxorem, Libane, scis qualis siet.* (Plaut. *Asin.* 60)
          "Mais ma femme, tu sais, Libanus, comment/quelle elle est."
          "But this wife of mine, Libanus, don't you know what sort of a person she is?"

Qualis is always used as a subordinator; it does not combine with other conjunctions,
whereas *quel* does when used in a concessive role (*quel que soit*).

3.2.2   *Qualiscumque* :

Adding *cumque* to indefinite adjectives-pronouns and adverbs turns them into Free Choice
indefinites : *quicumque* "qui que ce soit qui", "whoever", *quandocumque* "n'importe
quand", "whenever". *Qualiscumque* is a subordinator at first, then its use evolves towards
that of an indefinite adjective-pronoun.

-     Relative pronoun :

(48)   *homines benevoli, qualescumque sunt* (Cic. *Att.* 14,14,5)
          " les hommes de bonne volonté, quels qu'ils soient"
          "men who have shown me personal goodwill, whatever their character"

When followed by the subjunctive mood, *qualiscumque* may have a concessive meaning:

---

[27]   Cf. Comorovski (2004).

(49) a *qualemcumque speciem quae fuerit in bestiis* (Colum. 7,2)
        "quelle que fût l'apparence qui présentassent les bêtes"
        "whatever outward appearance the wild animal possessed"
     b *qualiscumque is foret, qui modo esset Herculi stirpe generatus* (Cic. *rep.* 2,24)
        «quel qu'il fût, pourvu qu'il fût de la race d'Hercule»
        "whoever he might be, provided that he is heir of the race of Hercules"

- Indefinite Free Choice adjective-pronoun: "quelconque, qui que ce soit / n'importe
   quel, n'importe qui" "any ... whatsoever, anyone, anything" etc.

(50) a *exiguo et qualicumque pabulo contentus* (Colum. 7,1)
        « se contentant d'une maigre ration de n'importe quel fourrage »
        "content with very little fodder of any sort of quality"
     b *contenta qualicumque principe* (Tac. *hist.* 1,11,2)
        "se satisfaisant de n'importe quel prince"
        "disposed to be content with any emperor"

In this use *qualiscumque* comes close to *aliquis* in Late Latin:

(51) a *si tamen est in te qualiscumque castitas* (Augustin *contra Iulian.* 2,43)
        "si cependant il y a en toi quelque/une quelconque chasteté" = *aliqua castitas*
        "if however there is in you any chastity"
     b *illa habebit qualemcumque locum, tu autem nullum locum* (Augustin *serm.*
        354)
        "elle aura quelque lieu et toi aucun"
        "she will have some place and you, none"

In (51) – comp. (17) – the contrast between *qualiscumque* and *nullus* suggests that the main
value of *qualiscumque* is existential.

4.4   Emergence of *qualisqualis, qualisque*

In Latin there have been a number of ways to reinforce indefinites. One of them,
reduplication, seems to have been continuously productive, as witnessed by Priscian:

(52)   *tam nomina infinita quam aduerbia, si generalem habent pronuntiationem*
       colligentem uniuersitatem numerorum, de quibus loquitur, geminantur apud
       Latinos uel assumunt 'cumque', ut 'quisquis' uel 'quicumque', 'qualisqualis' et
       'qualiscumque', 'quantusquantus' et 'quantuscumque'. (Prisc. *GL* 3,135, 11-15)
       "aussi bien les pronoms que les adverbes indéfinis, lorsqu'ils ont une signification
       générale embrassant la totalité de l'ensemble dont on parle, sont redoublés en latin
       ou bien prennent *cumque*, ainsi *quisquis* ou *quicumque, qualisqualis* et
       qualiscumque, quantusquantus et *quantuscumque*."
       "both indefinite pronouns and adverbs, if they have a general meaning which
       encompasses the whole set of items that are spoken of, are reduplicated amongst
       Latins or take '*cumque*': *quisquis* or *quicumque, qualisqualis* and *qualiscumque,*
       quantusquantus and *quantuscumque*."
While *quisquis* is an old word, *qualisqualis* and *quantusquantus* are never attested until
medieval times.

Complex forms with *cumque* are said to have had a shorter variant (with *que* alone):

(53)   *Inuenitur* quisque *pro* quicumque, qualisque *pro* qualiscumque. *Similiter aduerbia* quoque *pro* quocumque, quaque *pro* quacumque, quandoque *pro* quandocumque. (Prisc. *GL* 3,138,15-17)

"On rencontre *quisque* à la place de *quicumque*, *qualisque* à la place de *qualiscumque*. De même pour les adverbes : *quoque* à la place de *quocumque*, *quaque* à la place de *quacumque*, *quandoque* à la place de *quandocumque*."

"*Quisque* may be found instead of *quicumque*, *qualisque* instead of *qualiscumque*. Same thing for adverbs : *quoque* instead of *quocumque*, *quaque* instead of *quacumque*, *quandoque* instead of *quandocumque*"

Indeed *quandocumque* and *quandoque* seem to be interchangeable in classical times, both as indefinite adverbs ("quelque jour", "some/any day") and as conjunctions ("à quelque moment que", "whenever"). But *qualisque* is practically never attested outside grammarians' treatises[28]:

(54)   a *unde si uelimus secundum latinae linguae proprietates ista discernere more loquendi, nostram uel qualemque scientiam fortasse tenebimus* (Aug. *epist.* 149, 2)

"si donc nous voulons distinguer dans la façon de parler suivant les usages du latin, nous arriverons peut-être à notre sens ou à quelque (autre) sens"

b *Facile est qualemque* (corr. *quemque) sibi degere* (Cassiod. *Varia* 4,3)

« il est facile pour quelqu'un/n'importe qui (/chacun) de vivre pour soi »

"It is easy for any one / every man to live for himself"

In any case, *qualisque* cannot be a direct ancestor of *quelque*: phonetics prove it.[29]

Priscian's testimony also bears witness to the above-mentioned 'free alternation' of *quisque* and those indefinites which express universal quantification (such as *quicumque*.[30])

5   Conclusion

The break between Latin indefinites and the indefinites of Roman languages may be less absolute than lexical data suggest it is. The wide range of uses *quelque(s)* has in French can be found for Latin *aliquis* too; *aliquis* gradually extended its range until it included the whole domain of *quis*, *quisquam* or *aliquot*, with (at first) the exception of negative contexts – as though polyvalence overwhelmed the functional distribution exhibited by (literary) Classical Latin.

---

[28]   Such a form, both rare and non-classical, may have been 'corrected' in the course of ms transmission until it all but disappeared. Cf. (51b).

[29]   Preserving such an ending is extremely rare in French : it can only happen through the resurrection of a Latin form, cf. *quelconque*, reconstructed from *qualiscumque*.

[30]   We must not, however, blindly take what Priscian says at its face value. He may have reversed the sequence of causes: morphological kinship between *quisque* and *quicumque* may be artificial, re-motivated at a late date from the *cumque/que* paradigm.

We are not dealing only with an evolution (or resurgence) of so-called Vulgar Latin, since those late writers who were most influenced by classicism (Augustine, for instance) are aware of these changes and grammarians record them.

Aliquis itself has not escaped the tendency to morphological reinforcement of indefinites : its descendants originate from the late coalescence of *aliquis unus*. Adding *unus* to *aliquis* was originally a way to reinforce referential unity:

(55)   a   *in qua re publica est <u>unus aliquis</u> perpetua potestate* (Cic. *Rep.* 2,43)
          "un état dans lequel <u>une seule personne</u> est dotée d'un pouvoir permanent"
          "a State in which one person has permanent power"
    b   *si omnino laborantem in illo opere uirum ab diis adiuuari oportebat, non sufficeret <u>aliquis unus</u> aut <u>aliqua una</u> ?* (Aug. *ciu.* 6,9)
          "s'il fallait absolument que le mari à la peine dans cette entreprise soit secouru par les dieux, n'aurait-il pas suffi d'<u>un seul</u> dieu ou d'<u>une seule</u> déesse"
          "If it was absolutely necessary that a man, laboring at this work, should be helped by the gods, might not <u>some one</u> god or goddess have been sufficient?"

Unus was weakened and evolved towards indefinite status, whence the linked evolution of *aliquis unus*.

References

Amacker, R. (1974). Latin *si quis* et la distinction entre nom et adverbe, *Cahiers Ferdinand de Saussure* 31,15-35.

Amsili, P. (2006). Donkey sentence. In *Sémanticlopédie: dictionnaire de sémantique*, D. Godard, L. Roussarie et F. Corblin (ed.), GDR Sémantique & Modélisation, CNRS, http://www.semantique-gdr.net/dico/.

Bertocchi, A. et Maraldi, M. (2005). Indefinite pronouns in conditional clauses, *Papers on Grammar IX 1*, 453-466.

Bertocchi, A. et Maraldi, M. (2009). Mid-scalar quantifiers in Latin. Talk delivered to ICLL, Innsbruck, March 2009.

Bertocchi, A., Maraldi, M. et Orlandini, A. (2010). Quantification. In P. Baldi & P.L. Cuzzolin (eds) *New perspectives on Historical Latin Syntax*, Berlin-New York, Mouton de Gruyter.

Bortolussi, B. (2001). Sur la distinction entre place et position syntaxique en latin : l'exemple de *quis* (quelque, quelqu'un). Dans J.-M. Marandin (ed.) *Cahiers J.-C. Milner*, Paris, Verdier, 99-115.

Bortolussi, B. (à paraître). *Si quis*. Communication à ICLL, Innsbruck, mars 2009.

Combettes, B. (2004). La grammaticalisation d'un déterminant indéfini : "quelque" en Moyen-Français, *Scolia*, 18, 9-40.

Comorovski, I. (2004). Quel. In F. Corblin & H. de Swart (éds) *Handbook of French Semantics*, Stanford, CSLI, 131-140.

Corblin, F. (2004). Quelque. In F. Corblin & H. de Swart (eds.) *Handbook of French Semantics*, Stanford, CSLI Publications, 99-107.

Damourette J. & Pichon E. (1911-1940). *Des mots à la pensée: essai de grammaire de la langue française*, tome 6. Paris: d'Artrey.

Geurts, B. (1998). The mecanism of denial, *Language*, *74*, 274-307.

Grevisse, M. (1980). *Le bon usage*, Genève, Duculot.

Haspelmath, M. (1997). *Indefinite Pronouns*, Oxford University Press.

Hofmann J. & Szantyr, A. (1965). *Lateinische Syntax und Stilistik*, München, Beck.

Jayez J. & Tovena L. (2005). Free-choiceness and Non Individuation. *Linguistics and Philosophy*, 28, 1-71.

Jayez J. & Tovena L. (2008). Evidentiality and determination. In A. Gronn (ed.), *Proceedings of the 12th Sinn & Bedeutung*, 271--286, Oslo NO.

Orlandini, A. (2001). *Négation et argumentation en latin. Grammaire fondamentale du latin. Tome VIII*, Louvain, Peeters.

Rosén, H. (1998). Latin presentational sentences. In B. García-Hernández (ed.) *Estudio de lingüística latina*, Madrid, Ediciones Clásicas, 723–742.

Serbat, G. (1984). *Erat Pipa quaedam ....* , *Revue des Études Latines* 62, 344–356.

Szabolcsi, A. (2004). Positive Polarity – Negative Polarity, *Natural Language and Linguistic Theory*, *22*, 479-532.

Touratier, Chr. (1994). *Syntaxe latine*, Louvain-Paris, Peeters.

THE MEANING AND (A BIT OF) THE HISTORY OF *quelque**

Jacques Jayez
ENS-LSH and L2C2, Lyon
jjayez@ens-lsh.fr

Lucia M. Tovena
Université Paris VII
tovena@linguist.jussieu.fr

Abstract

In this chapter, we pursue the hypothesis that *quelque* is an indefinite that relies on inference and ignorance, elaborating on our previous work. The form *quelque* N P, in which P is a property, means that the existence of an entity of type N satisfying P is a piece of information at which the epistemic agent got by inference (evidential aspect) and that the exact identity of such an entity remains unknown (epistemic aspect). The main points discussed are the following. Intuitively, *quelque* may seem to belong to the group of free choice determiners, together with *n'importe quel* and *un quelconque*. We show that such an association is plausible, provided one includes the evidential aspect. Moreover, we propose that the limited tolerance of *quelque* to occurring in the immediate scope of negation should be analysed as a manifestation of its inner semantic organisation, composed of a main content—constituted by an existential value typical of indefinites—and a conventional implicature—constituted by its inferential and epistemic values. This analysis leads us to set aside a characterisation of *quelque* as positive polarity item, which would be an ad hoc stipulation. Finally, we set up some lines of analysis concerning the origin and the development of *quelque*. This gives us the opportunity to identify several important issues, among which we can recall the question of whether the concessive use is a byproduct of the ignorance component or the reverse, and the question of whether and how to reconcile the concessive meaning with the existential interpretation.

keywords: *quelque*, epistemic determiner, evidentiality, positive polarity items, diachronic study

1 Introduction

French speakers have a host of *free choice* items (FCIs) at their disposal, e.g. *n'importe quel* (no matter which), *un quelconque* (one whichever), *tout* (all), *quiconque* (whoever), Pronoun/NP + *que ce soit* (-ever), etc. (Jayez and Tovena, 2005, 2006). How close to each other are they and how strong are their similarities? In this paper, we are going to discuss the determiner *quelque*. This determiner has attracted interest from semanticists due to its particular combination of properties (see Culioli, 1982; Van de Velde, 2000; Jayez and Tovena, 2002,

*Thanks to Christiane Marchello-Nizia and Donka Farkas for commenting on a draft version.

2006, 2008a; Corblin, 2004; Paillard, 2006), although it might be rather marginal in the group because it is felt to be somewhat literary or formal in many of its uses in modern French.

In short, three properties of *quelque* immediately bring a linguist beyond the zone of expected behaviour for a plain indefinite like *un* (a). First, *quelque* obeys a constraint of ignorance that shapes it as an anti-specific determiner. Broadly speaking, specificity corresponds to the possibility of identifying a particular individual as satisfying a given property. Specificity is a crucial feature in the typology of determiners (cf. Farkas, 2002a,b,c; Haspelmath, 1997), where it interact with the notion of free choice. In the case in hand, the NP formed by *quelque* N can be referential in the sense defined by Dekker (1998) and Jayez and Tovena (2005), but the speaker must not be able to identify the individual to whom the NP refers, which means that readings that contain reference and identification of the referent are barred.

Second, in their analysis, Jayez and Tovena (2008a) have shown that the determiner *quelque* implement a form of evidentiality in the nominal domain. The existence of the referent is not directly asserted, rather it is an interpretation that results from an *inferential* operation from the clausal content, see (1). This type of interpretation corresponds to a preference that may vary depending on the speaker, and presumably the variation is due to the fact that this determiner is not frequently used.[1] The contrast between (1b) and (2) illustrates the relevance of the role played by the source of information.

(1) a. ?? Hier, j'ai rencontré quelque amie
        yesterday, I met QUELQUE friend
    b. Hier, Yolande a dû rencontrer quelque amie
        yesterday, Yolande must have met QUELQUE friend

(2) ? Yolande m'a dit qu'elle avait rencontré quelque amie
    Yolande told me she met QUELQUE friend

This aspect cannot be predicted simply by characterising *quelque* as anti-specific, i.e. by imposing that the referent is not identified, see the contrast in (3). The sentence in (3a) is more natural if *commentaire* is in the plural, but the plural form *quelques* has a much more liberal distribution and will not be discussed in this paper.

(3) a. ? Il a fait quelque commentaire, dont je ne me souviens plus
        he made QUELQUE comment I no longer remember
    b. Il a fait un commentaire quelconque, dont je ne me souviens plus
        he made some comment or other I no longer remember

Finally, *quelque* is (very) marginal in the scope of clausemate negation, but not under higher

---

[1] This reason is hinted at also by Culioli in his paper.

clause negation nor when another downward monotone operator intervenes between negation and determiner. This behaviour suggests an analogy with *some* in English, see Farkas (2002c), and relates it to the issue of the interaction of negation with so-called *positive* polarity, see Szabolcsi (2004) on this point.

In this chapter, we carry on with the analysis of the epistemic properties of *quelque* primarily in two directions, on the one hand, we endeavour to clarify the impact that the conventional implicature of ignorance has on the distribution of the determiner in negative sentences; on the other hand, we initiate the study of its diachronic evolution. The text is organised as follows. We start by recalling the components of the base meaning of *quelque*, which is subject to two constraints, in section 2. Next, by comparing the properties we highlighted in this section with the notion of *free choiceness*[2], we can put the debate concerning *quelque* in the broader frame of a discussion about forms of epistemic determination that involve degrees of ignorance. The conclusion we reach in section 3 is less clearcut than in our previous work (Jayez and Tovena, 2008a,b), where we had rejected a characterisation of *quelque* as an FC item. The reason we are revising our position is due to our current attempt to take into consideration the variation among judgements and their instability, and to account for it via the constraint of evidentiality that is the specificity of *quelque*. The opening towards the general theme of determiners sensitives to their environnment is continued in section 4, where we present *quelque* in negative environnment and we discuss of the relevance of the notion of positive polarity sensitivity that could be associated to it. In alternative to this type of association, we put forth an explanation that draws uniquely on the general constraints relative to the computation of conventional implicatures. In particular, we show that a conventional implicature introduced by a quantifier is treated at a level that is different from the level where a conventional implicature introduced by a sentential adverb is computed, and this has consequences for the interaction with operators such as negation. This concludes the synchronic part of the description of *quelque*. The second part of the chapter covers a number of features and issues concerning the diachronic evolution of *quelque*. Section 5 is much more exploratory than what precedes it, and it is also much richer in empirical data. These data are presented following the trace of the questions debated in the preceding sections.

2 The base meaning of *quelque*: the epistemic properties

This section presents the core analysis and the main constraints that *quelque* obeys, the Ignorance Constraint and the Inference Constraint introduced in (Jayez and Tovena, 2008a). They are independent from each other, and have the status of conventional implicatures attached to the at issue content.

---

[2]The definition of 'free choice' item is still in dispute in the community, although linguists tend to agree on the set of contexts that caracterise its distribution. In this paper, we work under the hypothesis that a constraint requiring equivalence along one dimension can provide a minimal suitable characterisation for its semantic core.

2.1   The Ignorance Constraint

The Ignorance Constraint *C-Ignorance* is the first of two constraints used for characterising the behaviour of *quelque*. It is recalled in (4) in an intuitive version.[3] In the following, we use the term *epistemic agent* to talk about the bearer of some form of belief, who coincides with the speaker in the default case.

(4)   **C-Ignorance**
       Quelque is appropriate only if the epistemic agent does not know which individual satisfies the description contributed by the sentence.

Recall that the agent is ignorant about the identity of the referent, and this is not incompatible with being certain about its existence, as clearly shown by example (5), where the speaker is sure that a dumb people locked the door.

(5)   Le verrou ne coulisse pas; quelque idiot a fermé la porte avec un cadenas
       The bolt does not slide; QUELQUE dumb people locked the door

The Ignorance Constraint *C-Ignorance* enables us to explain the marginality of example (1a), because it says that the epistemic agent *a* must in principle ignore which individual has the property of 'being a friend of *a* and having been met by *a* yesterday'. This is not very probable, because the very same individual is presented as a friend of the speaker, who is the default epistemic agent in this sentence.

2.2   The evidential constraint of Inference

The second constraint is the Inference Constraint *C-Inference* and it is about the nature of information that there exists a referent for the noun phrase *quelque* N. This issue belongs to the domain of evidentiality, but the content associated with this term is a delicate matter. We follow Aikhenvald, who considers evidentiality to be the linguistic marking of the *information source*. In her view, evidentiality 'does not imply any reference to validity or reliability of knowledge or information' (Aikhenvald, 2005, p. 5) in itself.

The hypothesis put forth by Jayez and Tovena (2008a) consists in assuming that *quelque* provides some indication on the source of information and, moreover, marks it as being of the *inferential* type. By her choice of using the determiner *quelque*, the speaker makes it plain that the proposition expressed is not grounded on knowledge obtained by direct perception or by hearsay. It is important to keep separate the sources of information and the processing

---

[3]For a detailed definition of ignorance the reader is referred to (Jayez and Tovena, 2006).

of such information. In some cases, the type of processing constrains the type of source, for instance visual integration can work only on visual stimuli. On the contrary, inferential processing can apply to the output of other processes, for instance an agent may infer a proposition from what she 'sees', that is to say to the output of a previous application of visual integration to some visual stimuli. This is to say that the agent can use perceptual information or hearsay information to feed an inferential process that results in her asserting the proposition. In all these cases, *quelque* marks the fact that (at least) the last ring in a chain of sources of information, or the only source deemed to be relevant, is an inferential process put in by the agent.

The task of capturing the costraints that rule the behaviour of *quelque* is somewhat complicated by the fact that the sentence does not have to contain overt evidential information independently marked for this determiner to be acceptable. Its use is appropriate whenever it is possible to build an evidential inferential interpretation—see example (6) that is interpreted as meaning 'some idiot or other must have forgotten to switch off'—but does not require that a modal marker be overtly present, be it a verb, an adverb or a mood marker.

(6)   Il y a de la lumière dans le bureau; quelque idiot a oublié d'éteindre
        The light is on in the office. QUELQUE idiot forgot to switch it off.

The Inference Constraint *C-Inference* captures the intuition that one must get at the existential proposition that corresponds to the clause that hosts *quelque* via an inferential process, see (Jayez and Tovena, 2008a). We write R for the restriction (N' in *quelque* N') and S for the scope, i.e. the property expressed by the rest of the sentence.

(7)   **C-Inference**
        A form [*quelque x*] [*R*] [*S*] is appropriate only under interpretations where the epistemic agent *infers* that $\exists x(R(x) \& P(x))$.

Last, let's mention the well known issue of the relation between evidentiality and modality. What is relevant for our discussion is the fact that the use of *quelque* does not force the speaker to confine herself to a specific modal force. The lack of difference in acceptability between a sentence containing an existential modality, cf. (8a), or a universal modality, cf. (8b), vouches for it.

(8)   a.   Yolande a peut-être rencontré quelque ami
              Yolande may have met QUELQUE friend
        b.   Yolande a nécessairement rencontré quelque ami
              Yolande must have met QUELQUE friend

In both cases, the epistemic reading is the only modal reading that matters. The deontic one is never relevant.

2.3 On the link between the constraints

As we stated overtly, the issue of the existence of a referent should be kept apart from the issue of its identification. Ignorance and evidentiality, *C-Ignorance* and *C-Inference* presented in (4) and (7) respectively, are about the identification of an entity. This observation may prompt the question of whether there is a connection between these constraints, for instance an equivalence or an entailment. Let's examine the issue taking *C-Ignorance* as our starting point first. If an agent *a* ignores which individual satisfies a property, generally she cannot have direct access to this piece of information. However, she could have indirect access to it, in a non-inferential way, for instance by hearsay. It follows that *C-Ignorance* does not entail *C-Inference*. Next, let's now consider the same situation but starting from *C-Inference*. If *a* is in a position to infer that some individual satisfies a property, she could also be able to infer *who* is such an individual in which case, the constraint *C-Ignorance* would be violated. Therefore, it is also the case that there is no entailment from *C-Inference* to *C-Ignorance*. The unavoidable conclusion is that there is no logical relation linking *C-Ignorance* and *C-Inference*.

However, there is a pragmatic relationship between the two constraints. Using an indefinite in a situation that conforms to *C-Inference* makes the ignorance interpretation most plausible, as evidenced by the contrast in (9). Sentence (9b) is not impossible, yet it is more difficult to interpret than (9a), that contains the run-of-the-mill indefinite *un*. The sentence in (9c) gives confirmation that inference and identification of the referent are not incompatible per se.

(9)   a.   Yolande a rencontré une amie, Louise
                Yolande met a friend, Louise
        b.   # Yolande a dû rencontrer une amie, Louise
                Yolande must have met a friend, Louise
        c.   Yolande a dû rencontrer son amie, Louise
                Yolande must have met her friend, Louise

One can guess that the inferential interpretation adds plausibility to an interpretation whereby the agent ignores the identity of the referent, and that the semantic configuration of *quelque* can be explained by supposing that the basic interpretation of this determiner is inferential and that this triggers an ignorance interpretation that dominates and subsequently grammaticises. At this stage, this is just a supposition. Furthermore, were one to take it up, she should also explain the interpretive preferences recorded in (9). At this stage of our research, we accept that ignorance is the default interpretation under an epistemic operator, but we do not venture down the slippery slope of a discussion on the scope of indefinites.

2.4 Extensions

Our analysis, based on the combination of the *C-Ignorance* and *C-Inference* constraints, allowed us in (Jayez and Tovena, 2008a) to cover two cases that, prima facie, are exceptions when the distribution of *quelque* is restricted to modal contexts.

The first case concerns habitual sentences. We have shown that such sentences satisfy *C-Inference* because the habituality qualification is a regularity which is not directly perceived (unlike a standard event or object). Rather, habituality is inferred by the speaker through a repetition of outcomes presented as non-accidental, see (10a). Habitual sentences still have to satisfy *C-Ignorance*, as evidenced by (10b), where the identity of the friend is made precise.

(10)   a.   A l'époque, je voyais toujours Yolande avec quelque amie
                'At that time, I always saw Yolande with QUELQUE friend'
    b.   ?? A l'époque, je voyais toujours Yolande avec quelque amie, Marie
                'At that time, I always saw Yolande with QUELQUE friend, Mary'

The second case concerns the fact that, when *quelque* combines with an abstract mass noun in episodic non-inferential sentences, the result is much better than with a count or mass concrete noun, see (11)[4].

(11)   a.   Yolande a montré quelque courage
                'Yolande showed QUELQUE courage'
    b.   *Yolande a bu quelque eau [quantité d'eau]
                'Yolande drank QUELQUE water' [quantity of water]
    c.   ? Yolande a quelque beauté
                'Yolande has QUELQUE beauty'

The abstract mass nouns that fit with *quelque* denote particularised properties, which have specific spatio-temporal manifestations and are often analysed as *tropes* (Williams, 1953; Campbell, 1990) in the philosophical literature. In order to account for the contrast in (11), Jayez and Tovena (2008a) introduce a distinction between *internal* tropes, like *courage* or *hesitation*, which can combine with *quelque*, and *external* tropes, like *beauty* or *slowness*. Internal tropes correspond to internal states or events and can be observed only through their

---

[4]The taxonomic reading of concrete mass nouns–the preferred one in examples like (i)–is not relevant, because this use is similar to a form of count discretisation.
(i) # Yolande a bu quelque eau [type d'eau]
    'Yolande drank QUELQUE water' [kind of water]

effects, which implies some sort of inference—a required ingredient in *C-Inference*. The satisfaction of *C-Ignorance* can more generally be explained by the properties of mass nouns, which allow for degrees or types, with some indeterminacy about which degree/type is referred to.

When *quelque* combines with an internal trope, it also triggers a 'downplaying' effect, see (Van de Velde, 2000; Jayez and Tovena, 2002). For example, (11a) indicates that the speaker is not certain that Yolande showed great courage. This effect, which is also found with *un certain* ('a certain'), see (12), corresponds to a Q-implicature (Horn, 1989) triggered by the indefinite.

(12)   a.   Yolande a montré un certain courage
                'Yolande showed some courage'
        b.   Il y a une certaine hypocrisie à prétendre cela
                'There is some hypocrisy to alleging this'

The nature of the effect has to be clarified. The contexts where *quelque* has a downplaying interpretation are episodic sentences which often convey an existential scale (Hoeksema and Rullmann, 2000; Tovena, 2003). Two points deserve to be mentioned. First, *quelque* and *un certain* underspecify the degree of the trope. This underspecification can be decreased by choosing some interval of the degree scale, either an inferior (13a,14a) or a superior one (13b,14b).

(13)   a.   Yolande a montré quelque courage, mais pas tant que ça
                'Yolande showed QUELQUE courage, but no THAT much'
        b.   Yolande a montré quelque courage, et même beaucoup de courage
                'Yolande showed QUELQUE courage, and even much courage'

(14)   a.   Yolande a montré un certain courage, mais pas tant que ça
                'Yolande showed some courage, but no THAT much'
        b.   Yolande a montré un certain courage, et même beaucoup de courage
                'Yolande showed some courage, and even much courage'

Second, since we assume that underspecification concerns the whole scale, including its median and higher regions, we must explain why we have a *downplaying* effect rather than a reinforcement effect and why the interpretation does not simply depend on context. In fact, we observe here a general phenomenon, intuited by Ducrot (1972). In his terminology, existential judgements have a positive 'argumentative force'. More precisely, with scales, they facilitate inferences about the possibility of a specification with the median or higher region and render more difficult similar inferences using the lower region (see Jayez (2005), Jayez and Tovena (2008c) on this point). This accounts for contrasts like those in (15). For (15a), introducing the proposition that Paul graded some papers eliminates all cases where Paul graded no paper, which automatically renders more probable the proposition that Paul graded more papers than a certain numeric threshold t, whatever it could be. *Mais* ('but') expects an opposite orientation[5] (the direction of variation of the probability) and is thereby compatible with 'Paul did not grade many papers'. However, *mais* cannot invert the opposite argumentative direction, according to which the proposition that Paul graded some papers would render *less* probable the proposition that Paul graded a number of papers superior to some t. This orientation simply does not exist and (15b) remains opaque.

(15)   a.   Paul a corrigé quelques copies, mais pas beaucoup
                'Paul graded some papers, but not many'
        b.   ?? Paul a corrigé quelques copies, mais beaucoup
                'Paul graded some papers, but many'

This general configuration accounts for the presence of *mais* in (13a) and (14a), in order to signal the argumentative orientation. So, the downplay effect is a side-effect of inference facilitation ('argumentation' in Ducrot's parlance), while underspecification derives from the ignorance implicature conveyed by *quelque* and *un certain*.

The final point we discuss is the *approximation* value that it is tempting to associate with *quelque* in view of examples like (16). One might assume that, in such examples, the speaker does not want to commit herself to a precise evaluation and only gives some rough indication. This is consonant with remarks by Farkas (2002c) about *some* and with the analysis proposed by Kagan and Spector (2008) for the Hebrew determiner *eyze*.

(16)   a.   Dans la soirée, quelque deux cents personnes se sont réunies devant Spandau
                [*Le Monde*, août 1987]
                'In the evening, QUELQUE two hundred persons gathered in front of Spandau'
        b.   Villeneuve et les centres d'appels : quelque mille emplois au bout du fil [Internet]
                'Villeneuve and the call centers: QUELQUE one thousand jobs at the end of the (phone) line'

However, examples like (17) suggest that the situation is more complex. In some cases, *quelque* can be found with precise quantities. For instance, for (17a), there might exist a list counting the HBM lodgings and giving the sum of two hundred and twenty three.[6]

---

[5]Argumentative orientation corresponds to the fact that the proposition 'Paul graded some papers' renders more probable every proposition of the form 'Paul graded a number of papers superior to t' for an arbitrary threshold t.

[6]The usual tests for approximation are not very reliable with *quelque*. For instance, *environ quelque deux cent vingt-trois* ('about QUELQUE two hundred and twenty three') and *exactement quelque deux cent vingt-trois* ('exactly QUELQUE two hundred and twenty three') are out. One can add *environ* and *exactement* as comments

(17)   a.   J'en veux pour preuve les quelque deux cent vingt-trois logements HBM qui vont être remis à la location en 1996 [Internet]
'A proof of that is the QUELQUE two hundred and twenty three lodgings that will be for rent in 1996'

        b.   Sacha Guitry fut renvoyé de onze lycées [...] et réalisa quelque trente trois films [Internet]
'Sacha Guitry was expelled from eleven grammar schools and shot QUELQUE thirty three films'

However, even when there is no approximation, *quelque* does not present the exact quantity as just a measure but as the representative of a property. For instance, the two hundred and twenty three lodgings mentioned in (17a) instantiate a property like 'being a significant number of lodgings'. In this respect, there is some fuzziness since the property admits several representative values and this use appears to be similar to the combination with abstract nouns presented above.[7] When it introduces a numeral, *quelque* does not select a particular region (lower, median or higher), as the continuations for (17a) shown in (18) indicate. It is necessary to use the context in order to decide. In such cases, it is probably more interesting to take into account the argumentative role of *quelque*, in the sense made clear above, than to limit its interpretation to the reference to a particular region on a scale.

(18)   J'en veux pour preuve les quelque deux cent vingt-trois logements HBM qui vont être remis à la location en 1996, ce qui est peu / beaucoup / raisonnable /moyen ... etc.
'A proof of that is the QUELQUE two hundred and twenty three lodgings that will be for rent in 1996, which is not much / much / reasonable / a moderate figure ... etc.'

3   Ignorance and free choiceness

The question arises whether *quelque* is a free choice (FC) item, because its properties are very similar to those of *un quelconque*, which (Jayez and Tovena, 2006) show to be a FC item. This question makes sense only with regard to an explicit definition of FC items. Following Jayez and Tovena (2005), we define an element to be FC whenever it satisfies the constraints in (19).[8]

---

or rectifications: *Sacha Guitry ...fut renvoyé de onze lycées et réalisa quelques trente trois films, ou à peu près / très exactement* ('Sacha Guitry was expelled from eleven grammar schools and shot QUELQUE thirty three films, or so/exactly').

   [7]Kagan and Spector (2008) also discuss the relationship between the Hebrew determiner *eyze* and properties.

   [8](Jayez and Tovena, 2008d) contains a recent presentation of the debate on FC items with numerous pointers to the literature.

(19)   **Equity** A tripartite form [FC item] [*R*] [*S*] is compatible with an interpretation *I* only if :

    A. *every* member of *R* can be *S* under *I* (NO LOSER)

    B. *every* member of *S* can be $\neg S$ under *I* (NO WINNER)

Constraint (19A) says that no member of the restriction is excluded. Constraint (19B) says that no member of the restriction is imposed. The joint effect of both constraints, metaphorically subsumed under the term *Equity*, accounts for the contrast in (20)–(23), for the FC item *un quelconque*.

(20)   Yolande a probablement rencontré une amie quelconque

       'Yolande probably met some friend or other'

       NO LOSER: Yolande may have met any one of her friends

       NO WINNER: no friend of Yolande's must necessarily have been
                  met by her

Let us start with constraint (19A). If an element that cannot be the referent of the NP is made precise, this violates NO LOSER and makes sentences like (21) awkward.

(21)   a. ? Yolande a probablement rencontré une amie quelconque, qui n'était pas Marie

         'Yolande probably met some friend or other, who was not Mary'

         NO LOSER is violated

    b. ? Prend une carte quelconque, mais pas celle du milieu

         'Pick some card or other but not the one in the middle'

         NO LOSER is violated

However, testing NO LOSER by expanding the sentence is not always a reliable method, because the added material may trigger an accommodation of a new, larger, restriction domain, *before* the application of NO LOSER. A safer strategy is to juxtapose two elements sensitive to NO LOSER but with two opposite indications. It can then be noted that sentences like (22a) sound contradictory or hardly interpretable when compared to sentences like (22b), which are fine. If *un quelconque* was not sensitive to NO LOSER, we should be able to restrict the freedom of choice without problem.

(22)   a. ?? Tu peux prendre une carte quelconque mais pas n'importe laquelle

         'You may pick some card or other but not (just) any card'

         NO LOSER is violated

    b. Tu peux prendre une carte mais pas n'importe laquelle

         'You may pick a card but not (just) any card'

Next, indicating an obligatory referent entails that NO WINNER is violated. *Un quelconque* is also sensitive to this constraint, as shown by (23).[9]

(23)   ? Yolande a probablement rencontré une amie quelconque, Marie
         'Yolande probably met some friend or other, Mary'
         NO WINNER is violated

With examples like those in (24), we can check that non-FC indefinites are not subject to the two constraints. For instance, the *un* ('a') indefinite accepts that a particular individual is explicitly excluded or imposed.

(24)   a.   Yolande a probablement rencontré une amie, qui n'était pas Marie
                'Yolande probably met a friend, who was not Mary'
         b.   Prend une carte, mais pas celle du milieu
                'Pick a card, but not the one in the middle'
         c.   Yolande a probablement rencontré une amie, Marie
                'Yolande probably met a friend, Mary'

As for *quelque*, while the NO WINNER constraint is clearly satisfied, as illustrated in (25), the observations are less clear for NO LOSER, see (26).[10]

(25)   ? Il y aura bien quelque raison / une raison quelconque, le chômage, pour justifier une grève ou deux
         'People will certainly find some reason or other–the unemployment–to justify a couple of strikes'
         NO WINNER is violated

(26)   a.   ? Il y a une raison quelconque, et je sais que ce n'est pas le chômage, qui explique la grève
                'There is some reason or other–and I know it's not unemployment–that explains the strike'
         b.   % Il y a probablement une raison quelconque, et je sais que ce n'est pas le chômage, qui explique la grève
                'There is probably some reason or other–and I know it's not unemployment–that explains the strike'
         c.   % Il y a probablement quelque raison, et je sais que ce n'est pas le chômage, qui explique la grève

---

[9]If the indication of an obligatory referent is weakened, for instance by adding *par exemple* ('for example') after *Marie*, the violation of NO WINNER is not longer guaranteed.

[10]The '%' notation signals that acceptability varies across speakers.

'There is probably QUELQUE reason–and I know it's not unemployment–that explains the strike'

Before deciding on the status of *quelque*, we need to clarify the possible reasons why judgements on free choiceness constraints are fuzzy in some cases. We hypothesise that the inferential evidentiality attached to *quelque* is a perturbing factor. From a set-theoretic point of view, there is no apparent difference between (26a) and (26b-c): in both cases, the proposition that unemployment is not the cause of the strike cuts down the possibilities opened by the proposition that there is probably some reason for the strike. In fact, there *is* a difference, which concerns the evidential status of propositions. On the one hand, with (26a), the speaker believes that there is some reason for the strike, that is, every possibility compatible with her beliefs satisfies the proposition that there is some reason for the strike. Using *un quelconque* favours an interpretation under which every conceivable reason holds in at least one possibility (NO LOSER). Moreover, the speaker believes that the reason in question is not unemployment, that is, no possibility compatible with her beliefs satisfies the proposition that unemployment accounts for the strike. As a result, the no-unemployment restriction concerns the same possibilities as the existential proposition (there is some reason for the strike) subject to NO LOSER. A contradiction follows, since unemployment is considered both as a possible and an impossible explanation.

On the other hand, with (26b-c), this kind of contradiction does not arise. The speaker believes through some inference that some reason probably explains the strike, that is, every possibility compatible with what she believes probable through some inference satisfies the proposition that the strike has an explanation. Moreover, the speaker believes that unemployment is not an explanation, that is, no possibility compatible with what she believes satisfies the proposition that unemployment is the cause of the strike. This situation does *not* entail that the no-unemployment restriction concerns the same possibilities as those which define what she believes. What the speaker thinks probable by way of inference does not necessarily include what she believes tout court, because modal strength and information source (evidentiality) do not necessarily coincide. A belief that p does not entail that p is the result of an inference. For instance, the speaker may believe that unemployment is not a possible reason but remain unable to derive the same conclusion only by way of inference, because, say, she just accepted what she read in some usually well-informed newspaper. Under this perspective, the behaviour of *quelque* with respect to NO LOSER is a reflex of its evidentiality.

We conclude that the question whether *quelque* is an FC item or not deserves a complex answer: *quelque* can be considered as an FC item, but one whose evidentiality blocks or weakens the effect of NO LOSER.

4 Negative contexts and positive polarity

The last aspect of *quelque* that we are going to take into account is illustrated by example (27). When (27) is accepted, its most natural reading is that there is a file that Yolande probably did not find. In other terms, it is a reading where *quelque* has scope over negation. The other scoping hierarchy, leading to paraphrase the sentence by 'Yolande did not find any file' is hardly possible.

(27)   Yolande n'a   pas dû trouver quelque fichier
         Yolande expletive-neg has neg must   find   QUELQUE file
         Yolande probably missed QUELQUE file
         ?? [neg > *quelque*] vs. [*quelque* > neg]

So, *quelque* is not natural in the immediate scope of a negation under a narrow scope interpretation.

4.1   Licensing and anti-licensing

Examples like (27) can be seen as a case of anti-licensing similar to those described for the English determiner *some* in terms of sensitivity to positive polarity (see Baker, 1970; Szabolcsi, 2004). For items traditionally categorised as Positive Polarity Items (PPIs), the anomaly illustrated in (27) can be traced to an incompatibility between narrow scope and antiadditive operators, that is operators that obey de Morgan's law that $\neg(p \lor q) = \neg p \,\&\, \neg q$.

The parallel between PPIs and *quelque* extends to the acceptability of *quelque* in cases like (28), where negation is in the matrix clause, or like (28b), where there is an 'intervener'[11] like *toujours* ('always'). Baker (1970) had noted that the combination of an anti-licenser and a licenser rescues *some* (29a) and his observation can be replicated for *quelque* (29b).

(28)   a.   Je ne pense pas que Yolande ait trouvé quelque fichier
             'I don't think Yolande found QUELQUE file'
        b.   Yolande ne trouvait pas toujours quelque excuse
             'Yolande didn't always find QUELQUE excuse'

(29)   a.   It's impossible that Yolanda didn't find some file
        b.   Il est impossible que Yolande n'ait pas trouvé quelque fichier

Although this empirical parallel is interesting, one can wonder whether the notions it relies on

---

[11] We borrow the term from Szabolcsi, who applies it to elements that seem to undo the anti-licensing relation.

are really explanatory. At the moment, there is no accepted theory about how anti-licensing can be defeated or about why anti-licensing is driven by negation alone and can be cancelled by a simple intervener. Moreover, the PPI label itself refers to the (partly) common behaviour of elements which remain highly heterogeneous with respect to their category (adverbs, determiners, verbs) and their semantic content. The situation is similar for Negative Polarity Items (NPIs). The strategy we follow here consists in trying to derive the PPI profile from semantic properties whenever it is possible.

4.2 A matter of implicature

In (Jayez and Tovena, 2008a), we proposed that the sensitivity to the status of information (evidentiality and ignorance) of *quelque* is a conventional implicature. Equivalently, it is not the result of a contextual inference (conversational implicature) or a presupposition, but a conventional part of the meaning of *quelque*, along with its main content, which is just existential quantification like *un* ('a'). By using the quantification structure [*quelque*] [*R*] [*S*], the speaker signals that she has only indirect inferential information about the fact that an unknown individual satisfies the restriction and the scope. The meaning is divided into two parts, as shown in (30), as proposed by Potts (2005) in the spirit of Grice.

(30)   [*quelque*] [*R*] [*S*]:
       a.   Main content = there is at least one individual x satisfying the restriction and the scope.
       b.   Implicature = x remains unidentified and the fact that x satisfies the restriction and the scope is only inferred.

Before elaborating, let us show that the pattern we are going to analyse is not isolated. It is well-known that presuppositions tend to *project*, that is, are not cancelled by certain operators like negation or interrogation, see (Geurts, 1999) for a general introduction. For instance, (31a) presupposes that Paul smoked at some point in time and this presupposition survives in (31b,c).

(31)   a.   Paul stopped smoking
       b.   Paul didn't stop smoking
       c.   Did Paul stop smoking?

We do not pretend to introduce here a specific proposal for representing presuppositions, but we can provide a minimal description that will suffice for our needs in the paper. Intuitively, a sentence like (31a) communicates that, for a certain point in the past, say t, Paul did not smoke after t and smoked before t, see (32).

(32) $\exists t(past(t)$ & $\neg Paul$ smokes after t & Paul smokes before t)

The general form of this expression is $Qx(MC(x)$ & $PP(x))$, where MC is the main content and PP the presupposition. One can assume that the presupposition is 'protected', meaning that, if Q is existential, $\exists x PP(x)$ must be satisfied by any interpretation. For (31b), this constraint entails that (31b) is true if and only if there exists a point in the past such that Paul smoked before this point (the presupposition is protected) but no point in the past after which Paul did not smoke, which entails that there is a point in the past before which Paul smoked and after which he still smoked.[12]

Potts (2005) shows that, in many cases, conventional implicatures behave like presuppositions. One would therefore expect to observe an analogous result for *quelque*. In other terms, negating [*quelque*] [R] [S] would mean that there is not individual that satisfies R and S (negation of the main content) and, simultaneously, that some unknown individual satisfies R and S, which is contradictory.[13]

Why don't we observe a systematic anomaly with negation in *every* sentence conveying a presupposition or an implicature? A detailed and principled answer is beyond the scope of this paper, but one can reasonably hypothesise that the end result, that is, our intuition of normalcy or anomaly, depends on the distribution of information within the sentence. In order to illustrate the problem, we consider two different cases. With aspectual verbs like *begin* or *stop*, we have a transition between states and the quantificational structure is unlike that for *quelque*, because the two pieces of information are independent. The fact that Paul has smoked (or does not smoke) does not entail that he does not smoke or continues smoking (or has been smoking or not). In contrast, the fact that some individual remains unidentified does not make sense for a non-existing individual.

Let us now compare with evaluative adverbs, which provide a well-known case of conventional implicature. For instance, *Unfortunately, Paul failed his exam* implicates that Paul's failure is unfortunate. The negated version, *Unfortunately, Paul didn't fail his exam*, cannot mean that Paul's failure—a non-existing event—is unfortunate. Clearly, our intuition is that the adverb 'sees' the negation and bears on the proposition that Paul did not fail his exam. In contrast, in a tripartite structure where *quelque* acts as the quantifier, it cannot operate on

---

[12]Quite generally, we have $\neg \exists x(MC(x)$ & $PP(x)), \exists x PP(x) \models \exists x(PP(x)$ & $\neg MC(x))$. The possibility of deriving just one formula and, as a result, to bind all the variables with just one existential quantifier is a model-theoretic property, independent from the treatment of presuppositions. The relevant point is that the existence of an entity that satisfies the presupposition is jeopardised by negation.

[13]An additional problem is the status of evidentiality. It should probably concern the negation of the main content, not the main content itself, because, otherwise, we would face a case of illocutionary suicide, the same proposition, i.e. the main content, say ϕ, being presented as false by the speaker in the main content of the negated form, i.e. $\neg\phi$, and presented as inferred in the implicature introduced by the very same speaker. A different possibility is that the implicature concerns $\neg\phi$, which leads to another kind of problem: the implicature then concerns both ϕ and $\neg\phi$ in two distinct dimensions (ignorance and evidentiality). Although this is not logically impossible, it remains to be shown whether an addressee can make sense of such a complicated situation.

the negation applied to the rest of the sentence unless it takes wide scope, a configuration that corresponds precisely to the non-problematic interpretation that some unknown object satisfies the restriction but not the scope.

Our analysis leads to four conclusions. First, it allows us to account for the remarkable parallelism between *quelque* and the complex determiner *je ne sais quel* ('I don't know which/what') (Jayez and Tovena, 2008a). The data in (33) show that *je ne sais quel* is awkward when in the scope of a clausemate negation, whereas the negation has no effect when it is in the matrix clause.

(33)   a.   # Yolande n'a pas trouvé je ne sais quel fichier
                 'Yolande didn't find I don't know what file'
        b.   Marie ne pense pas que Yolande ait trouvé je ne sais quel fichier
                 'Mary doesn't think that Yolanda found I don't know what file'
                 = *Mary doesn't think that Yolanda found some unknown file*

This contrast is interesting because *je ne sais quel* is not mentioned in the list of PPIs or NPIs. If we assume that *je ne sais quel* has the same semantic structure as *quelque* and conveys an ignorance implicature, we have a simple explanation for their similarity. Moreover, this proximity between the two items lends support to our central intuition that it is difficult to imagine that a non-existing entity is 'unknown'.

Second, when the implicature is interpreted in situ, that is, independently from the application of an operator to the main content, no particular problem arises, even when this operator is negative. This is the case when the syntactic hierarchy allows one to construct a clear distinction between the clause containing *quelque* and a negative operator in some higher clause. In such cases, we recognise a standard configuration pointed out by Baker. This kind of situation echoes Chierchia's (2004) proposal that conversational implicatures are processed locally. In the present case, we have a *conventional* implicature of ignorance and we propose to extend Chierchia's idea in the following way. In a first stage, the tripartite form [*quelque*] [*R*] [*S*] is processed normally, without any contradiction coming from the interaction between ignorance and negation. Next, negation is applied, which amounts to negating the existence of a situation where some unknown individual satisfies *R* and *S*.

Third, the compatibility of interrogation with *quelque* is explained by the fact that interrogation scopes over the entire clause that hosts *quelque*, exactly like a negative operator in a higher clause. This can be shown by comparing to other conventional implicatures, which are not effected by interrogation. For example, (34a) and (34b) mean 'Did Paul fail his exam, which would be unfortunate/surprising', but not 'It is unfortunate/surprising that one wonders whether Paul failed his exam'. The scope of negation, which is an independent property, is convergent with our hypothesis: whenever an operator can embed the whole *quelque*-clause, the implicature of the determiner can be interpreted locally, without semantic conflict.

(34)   a.   Est-ce que, malheureusement, Paul a échoué à son examen?
           'Did Paul–unfortunately–fail his exam?'
        b.   Est-ce que, bizarrement, Paul a échoué à son examen?
           'Did Paul–surprisingly–fail his exam?'

Finally, the strong similarity between *some* (Farkas, 2002c) and *quelque* is now less mysterious. Both determiners exploit a central epistemic value (ignorance). Given that they are not morphologically related, it would be strange that they happen to show very similar PPI empirical properties by pure chance.

One might object that *quelque chose* and *something* or *quelqu'un* and *somebody/someone* have, strictly speaking, no ignorance value, (see 35a), but still obey the same restrictions with respect to negation. However, all these pronouns exploit a form of ignorance since they cannot be used to refer to an individual that would be categorised and identified by all the participants. For instance, (35a) is not natural if the speaker believes that the addressee has a precise idea about which lorry was unloading. Similarly, (35b) is not to be used if the participants mutually know who is coming, unless the speaker tries to be ironical.

(35)   a.   J'ai vu quelque chose, un camion qui déchargeait des caisses
           'I saw something, a lorry which was unloading crates'
        b.   Tiens, voilà quelqu'un
           'Look, someone is coming'

5   The evolution of *quelque*

The goal of the second part is to present a number of observations and questions related to the evolution of *quelque* in Old French (OF) and Middle French (MF). OF is considered to span the 11th-14th centuries and MF the 15th and 16th. The first occurrences of *quelque* are to be found at the beginning of the 12th century, about 1120.[14] We used texts between 1100 to 1550, from the *Base du Français Médiéval* (http://bfm.ens-lyon.fr/), from the ELICO project quotation set (http://elico.linguist.jussieu.fr/) and from FRANTEXT (http://www.frantext.fr/). We will comment only examples from the BFM.

5.1   The origin of *quelque*

Quelque can be analysed as the result of merging the two elements of the *quel* N *que* construction. According to Buridant (2000, § 572, p. 670), the *quel* + *que* combination had initially two properties.

---

[14] We thank Christiane Marchello-Nizia for this precision.

1. It belonged to a general system of relative-paired expressions (and it is called *relatif en emploi couplé* 'relative in a paired usage' by Buridant), where a relative pronoun has an indefinite-like form as antecedent. Together, they constitute an indefinite relative clause that tends to freeze into a fixed form (called *locution couplée à antécédent en 'quel'* 'paired expression with *quel* as antecedent' by Buridant).

2. It had a concessive reading.

The structure Buridant assigns to *quel que* is as in (36).

(36)   quel N   que S
        antecedent rel. clause

The reason why *quelque* is categorised as a relative pronoun rather than as a complementiser in (36) is the existence of several forms in the texts, corresponding to the subject, direct complement and locative functions, see (37).

(37)   et en quel lieu ou   il soit   en   avroit   il molt grant duel, s'il
        and in QUEL place where he be-subj of that have-cond he very deep grief, if he
        le   savoit
        that knew
        'and, in whatever place he could be, he would be deeply sorry if he knew that'
        et, en quelque lieu qu'il puisse être, il en serait fort chagriné s'il le savait
        [BFM, Lancelot-Graal ou Lancelot en prose, unknown author, early 13th century]

The mode of presentation and the examples chosen by Buridant suggest that the *quel* N *que* structure has a universal interpretation. In *quel* N, *quel* is an interrogative or correlative element, which introduces a variable over a set of N-individuals.[15]

The *que* + S element is normally in the subjunctive, like in other similar constructions (Buridant, 2000, § 279, p. 350). This is not obligatory, though, as illustrated by examples (38) and (39), which were brought to our attention by Marchello-Nizia.

(38)   Quel   part que la pucelle vet, Arranz est toz   tens an agait, et   toz garniz
        Which place that the virgin goes, Arranz is every time on watch, and all ready
        de li   ferir
        of her strike-inf
        'Wherever the virgin goes, Arranz is watching her and all ready to strike her'

---

[15]Foulet (1919) notes that combining interrogative words with *quel* in order to convey indeterminacy was very frequent in OF.

Où que la vierge aille, Arranz la surveille et se tient prêt à la frapper
[Eneas 7157-8, 12e siècle]

(39)   Il li dit : "Or choisissiez des deus le quel que il vos plest"
He him said : "Now choose of the two the which that it you pleases"
'He told him "Now, choose which one of the two you prefer"'
Il lui dit: "à présent choisissez celui des deux qui vous plaît"
[Le chevalier de la charrette, v. 289, Chrétien de Troyes, written ca. 1180]

Quer (1998, p. 202) proposes that the subjunctive in free relatives can express domain widening, like FC items. Although the comparison with FC items remains an issue (see section 3), we keep the general idea that the subjunctive indicates that the set of N-individuals under consideration includes members that occupy an extreme position on a scale of typicality, relevance or appropriateness. One may conjecture that the concession interpretation is facilitated by the subjunctive mood.[16]

The last point to note is that OF has at least three structures containing *quel* or *quelque*.
a. *quel* + *qui/que/où* relative pronoun, as in (37) repeated below,
b. *quelque* + N + *qu-* relative pronouns, as in (40),
c. *quelque* N, as in (41).

(37)   et en quel lieu ou il soit en avroit il molt grant duel, s'il
and in QUEL place where he be-subj of that have-cond he very deep grief, if he
le savoit
that knew
'and, in whatever place he could be, he would be deeply sorry if he knew that'
et, en quelque lieu qu'il puisse être, il en serait fort chagriné s'il le savait
[BFM, Lancelot-Graal ou Lancelot en prose, unknown author, early 13th century]

(40)   qui tant a meffait que jamais n'est digne de estre amé, quelque
who so much has misdone that never deserves of be-inf loved, QUELQUE
vaillance qui soit en lui
courage that be-subj in him
'who has done so much wrong that he does not deserve any love, no matter how
valiant he might be'
qui a tellement mal agi qu'il ne mérite pas d'amour quel que soit son courage
[BFM, Chroniques et conquêtes de Charlemagne, David Aubert, 1458]

(41)   car il n est pas hon qui ne peche, tourjorz a chascuns quelque teche
for there is no man who not sins, always has each one some stain

---

[16]Whether the concession interpretation was grammaticized or felt as an implicature in OF is still an open question.

'for there is no man without sin, everybody has always some stain'
car il n'est d'homme qui ne pêche, chacun a toujours quelque souillure
[BFM, Roman de la rose, Jean de Meun, entre 1269 et 1278]

Concerning the direction of the scale, the *quel que* et *quelque que* forms are compatible with high or low values.

5.1.1 Intermediate conclusion

It is highly probable that *quelque* and *quel + que* have similar meanings, but the details of their evolution are somewhat unclear. Combettes (2004), agreeing with Foulet (1919), mentions for *quelque* an analogy with *qui que*, *que que*, etc. However, as noted by Foulet, the reasons why a correlative construction evolved into a regular determiner like *quelque*, like in (41), remain to be understood.

According to Foulet, *quelque* as a determiner originated in an idiom *à quelque paine* (lit. with QUELQUE pain) = *à quelle peine que ce soit* (lit. with what pain that it be-subj) = 'whatever pain it might cause', 'with much pain'.[17]

An evolution along these lines is indeed possible in view of the high frequency of *à quelque paine* in our corpus, at a period (before 1350) where *quelque* does not seem to exist as a determiner. Still, the reasons why the expression itself emerged and became so frequent are not known.

Under the hypothesis of a transition from concession to indetermination, and given that *quelque* as a determiner appears as 'weaker' in a sense, since it is neither concessive nor universal, as explained in the next section, expressions such as *à quelque paine* might have undergone a form of weakening themselves and come to mean 'with some pain', rather than 'with much pain'.

More generally, it is not always possible, in particular in the older texts, to decide whether *quelque* is concessive and intensive rather than epistemic or affective. For instance, how should one paraphrase *à quelque paine*: 'with much pain', 'with some, undetermined, degree of pain', 'with some, irrelevant, degree of pain'? Should one assume that the three interpretations were simultaneously available at some point in time? Combettes (2004) clearly defends the first (intensive) interpretation, which he sees as the most probable in a number of contexts. However, the intuitions are sometimes difficult to justify and it is not clear that one

---

[17]This paraphrase is not a retrospective fantasy, since an equivalent expression can be found in OF texts, for instance, *Non obstant Helsis se sauva, a quelque paine que ce fust, et entra dedens Brunebier* ('In spite of that Helsis escaped, however difficult it was, and entered Brunebier') (BFM, Chroniques et conquêtes de Charlemagne, David Aubert, 1458). Other similar expressions can also be found, but occur much less frequently, for example *à quelque ennui* (lit. with QUELQUE worry) or *à quelque meschief* (lit. with QUELQUE misfortune).

131

must assign a unique and constant meaning to the expression.

5.2 Main uses

In the present section, we try to convey a feel of the role of *quelque* between 1200 and 1550, by listing its main uses.[18] We mention five points, which echo the questions raised in the previous sections.

Concession use It is well represented and is not very different from what is to be found in subsequent stages of the French language, including the present one. Occurrences are more frequent after 1450, but can be found also in older texts, as in this excerpt from Joinville.

(42)　et　encore ferons　nous pis　se nous ne　tuons le　roy,　quelque
　　　　And even　do-future we　worse if we　not kill　the king, QUELQUE
　　　　asseurement que nous li　aions　　donné
　　　　assurance　that we　him have-subj given
　　　　'And we will do even worse if we do not kill the king, whatever assurance we gave
　　　　to him'
　　　　Et nous ferons encore pire si nous ne tuons pas le roi, quelque assurance que nous
　　　　ayons donnée
　　　　[BFM, Mémoires ou Vie de saint Louis, Jean de Joinville, 1307].

Use as a determiner *Quelque* as a determiner is more and more frequent as time goes by but is already present in older texts. Interpretations are usually habitual, generic, or intensional (under the scope of a modal operator).

(43)　Male Bouche qui　riens　n'　esperne trueve a chascune quelque　herne
　　　　Bad　Mouth　who nothing neg spares　finds　to each one QUELQUE fault
　　　　'Bad Mouth, who pardons nothing, finds a weakness in everybody'
　　　　Mauvaise Bouche, qui ne pardonne rien, trouve à chacun quelque défaut
　　　　[BFM, Roman de la rose, Guillaume de Lorris, 1227].
　　　　Iteration and habituality

(44)　au　temps que Fortune est amie　de quelque　homme et　qu' elle l'　a　mis
　　　　at the time　that Fortune is　friend of QUELQUE man　　and that she him has put

---

[18]Within this time span, there is no significant grammatical change for *quelque*, apart from the emergence of the new morpheme *quelqu'un* (lit. QUELQUE + indefinite determiner, 'somebody'), in the 13th century, with a raise in frequency in the 15th. In contrast, the determination system undergoes major changes, including the loss of specificity for *un* ('a'). We are grateful to Marchello-Nizia for this precision.

en aucun estat, alors il   trouvera   de faulz amis   sans   nombre
in some   state, then he find-future of false friends without number
'As soon as Fortune makes friend with some man and establishes him in some social
position, he will find innumerable false friends'
Lorsque le sort prend quelque homme en amitié et le place dans une certaine position,
alors il trouvera de faux amis sans nombre
[BFM, Jean de Saintré, Antoine de la Sale, 1456].
Interprétation générique

(45)   Qant ce vint au   quatrime jour, et   que euls et   lors cevaus furent tout
        When it came to the fourth   day and that them and their horses were all
        rafresqi et en grant volenté de ceminer avant   pour   trouver quelque
        refreshed and in strong will   to travel   forward in order to find   QUELQUE
        aventure, il   se departirent
        adventure, they left
        'When the fourth day came and they and their horses had rested and they desired to
        move forward in order to go through some adventure, they left'
        Quand le quatrième jour arriva et qu'eux et leurs chevaux furent reposés et très
        désireux d'avancer pour trouver quleque aventure, ils se mirent en route
        [BFM, Chroniques, Jean Froissart, 1385]
        Purpose clause

(46)   a.   et   fault   que malgré   moi je me tiengne en ce lieu jusquez j'
              And is necessary that in spite of me I remain-subj in this place until   I
              aye   quelque   bonne nouvelle
              have-subj QUELQUE good   new
              'And, unwillingly, I have to remain here until I have some good news'
              et je dois malgré moi rester en ce lieu jusqu'a ce que je reçoive quelque bonne
              nouvelle
              [BFM, Chevalier de la Charrette ou Lancelot, Chrétien de Troyes, 1176]
        b.   Encores   veul et   vous commande que tous les jours de quelque   Pater
              Moreover want and you order   that all the days of QUELQUE Pater
              noster ou autre oroison vous servez
              Noster or other prayer you use
              'Moreover, I want and command that you say some Pater Noster or some other
              prayer everyday'
              De plus je désire et ordonne que vous disiez quelque Pater Noster ou autre prière
              chaque jour
              [BFM, Jean de Saintré, Antoine de la Sale, 1456].
              Future possibilities

(47)   si vous l' apportez en quelque   lieu
        If you it bring   to QUELQUE place
        'If you bring it somewhere'
        si vous l'apportez en quelque lieu
        [BFM, *Cent nouvelles nouvelles*, auteur inconnu, 1462]
        Conditionals

In view of these and many similar examples, already available around mid-12th century, *quelque* N was not necessarily concessive but rather anti-specific, i.e. used to refer to an indeterminate individual satisfying the description expressed by N. If the concession use was really prior in time, one can plausibly conjecture that anti-specificity is based on the equivalence associated with concession. In a concession use, the individuals that satisfy a given property P are ordered along a scale according to their probability of causing or facilitating some particular effect. So, their equivalence derives from a pragmatic implicature: if the P-individual that is the less likely to trigger the effect triggers it anyway, the other individuals probably trigger it too.

Anti-specificity entails presenting all the P-individuals as equivalent with respect to a property or a proposition. For equivalence, one needs a modal structure, consisting of a set of equivalent possibilities containing one individual per possibility.[19] Some examples show that, from the 1400 period on, the ignorance value is salient, which amounts to using the epistemic states of an agent as nodes for the modal structure. (48) illustrates this value.

(48)   Si   s'en va   et fait   mauvese chiere, dont   sa femme cognoist
        However goes away and makes bad   face,   from which his wife   knows
        bien qu' il y a   quelque chose
        well that there is some   thing
        'However, he goes away and makes a face, hence his wife realises that there is something wrong'
        Mais il s'en va en faisant la tête, ce qui fait que sa femme se rend bien compte qu'il y a quelque chose
        [BFM, Quinze joies de mariage, unknown author, 1400].

The epistemic reading If one assumes a transition from concession to ignorance, it remains to explain why the endpoint of the evolution is rather epistemic than referential or affective (indifference, etc.).

The existential value Why is the determiner mainly existential? The concession structure allowed for a universal interpretation. For instance, in (49), the preferred interpretation is clearly a universal one.

---

[19]This is not a strictly necessary assumption, but it simplifies the presentation.

(49) Franceis   furent mult orgueillos, mult cruels e   mult damagos, par
      Frenchmen were   much proud,   much cruel and much obnoxious, by
      quel que   leu   que il   passoent
      QUELQUE place that they passed
      'Frenchmen were very arrogant, cruel and obnoxious, whatever place they went
      through'
      Les français se montrèrent extrêmement arrogants, cruels et nuisibles, en quelque
      lieu qu'ils traversaient
      [BFM, Roman de Rou, Wace, ca. 1170]

This interpretation does not seem to be available for the determiner without a modal operator. For instance, a sentence like *Fortune est amie de quelque homme* ('Fortune is friendly to
QUELQUE man'), adapted from (44), cannot mean that chance is friendly to every man. In
(44), one finds a conditional modal operator, which is known to give rise to a universal reading for wide-scope indefinites, as in donkey sentences and similar structures. For example,
*If chance favours a man and establishes him in some social position, he will find innumer-
able false friends* can be paraphrased by 'for every man, if chance favours him and …etc.'.
Assuming an ignorance value, the absence of a universal interpretation is expected, since the
truth of the generic sentence would entail the truth of the sentence for each individual, an
interpretation which conflicts with ignorance.

However, one can also observe that it is difficult to find a universal interpretation with the
quelque N *que ce soit* construction. This points to a general problem. The literature on FC
items shows some variation as to the existential or universal status of those items, see (Dayal,
2005; Giannakidou, 2001; Horn, 2001; Jayez and Tovena, 2005). In the case of *quelque*, it
seems that, for the universal value to be salient, an iteration is needed, that is, a sequence of
similar situations that each host a particular individual.[20] There is no example of a generic
or episodic use in our corpus, which suggests that *quelque* is an existential indefinite, even in
the concessive construction *quelque* N *que*.

Summarising, our hypothesis is that *quelque* probably originated as a concessive item signalling that all the degrees or modes of a property have to be considered, and that it evolved
into an existential epistemic indefinite signalling the epistemic equivalence (ignorance interpretation) of all the individuals in a domain.

Negative environments At this stage, the problem of negative environments resurfaces. In
a number of examples, *quelque* combines with negation as a standard existential indefinites
($\neg\exists \Rightarrow \forall\neg$). The concessive examples (50a) illustrate this possibility and have exact counterparts in modern French (50b).

---

[20]It is precisely the interpretation of (49), where *passoent* has an imperfective morphology.

(50) a. sans   estre empeschiés, arestés ou molestés en quelque   manière que ce
         Without be   held,   delayed or troubled in QUELQUE way   that it
         soit
         be-subj
         'Without being held, delayed or troubled in whatever way'
         [BFM, Chronique, Enguerrand de Monstrelet, 1441]
     b.   sans être retenus, retardés ou importunés de quelque manière que ce soit

One can also find examples with *quelque* alone (51) and they also have modern counterparts in French (52).

(51) a. onques en nul sens ce   n' avint   qu' en si biau   vergier n' eûst
         never   in any way this neg happened that in so beautiful orchard neg was
         huis ou eschiele ou quelque pertuis
         door or ladder   or some   opening
         'It absolutely never happened that so beautiful a garden had no door, no ladder
         or no opening whatsoever'.
         [BFM, Roman de la rose, Guillaume de Lorris, 1227]
     b.   adviser   que ne soiés   devant quelque   seigneur ou dame
         to take care that neg be-subj before QUELQUE lord   or lady
         'to avoid putting oneself before any lord or lady'
         [BFM, Jean de Saintré, Antoine de la Sale, 1456]

(52) a. il n'est absolument jamais arrivé que, dans un si beau jardin, on ne trouve (pas)
         quelque porte, ou quelque échelle ou quelque ouverture
     b.   veiller à ne pas se placer devant quelque seigneur ou quelque dame

(52a) is not problematic if we assume that analyses such as Baker's (1970) or Szabolcsi's (2004) for *some* can be extended to *quelque*, since both authors predict that the simultaneous presence of two antilicensers—two negations in (51a) and (52a)—rescues *some*. The situation is different in (51b) and (52b), where we have only one negation and *quelque* has narrow scope. Our intuition on examples of this kind is that they get a semantic structure that can be roughly paraphrased by 'make sure that one is not in a situation where one stands before some lord or lady'. In this respect, *quelque* ('some') is not in the immediate scope of negation. However, we have no explanation to offer as to how to derive such a licensing semantic structure.

Finally, one can find examples which cannot be directly adapted for modern French.

(53) a. il se   trouva tout sain et   haittié de son corpz, sans   avoir
         He himself found all   sound and healthy of his body, without have-inf

         quelque   essomte
         QUELQUE injure
         He realised that he was entirely untouched and in good health, without any injure
         [BFM, Roman du Comte d'Artois, auteur inconnu, 1460]

    b.   *Il s'aperçut qu'il était entièrement intact et en bonne santé, sans avoir quelque blessure

Such examples raise several questions, for which we cannot provide answers in our present state of knowledge. Should we interpret (53) as concessive, in which case *sans quelque essomte* means 'without having any injure, whatever it is'? If this interpretation is correct, why did this interpretive option disappear at subsequent stages, since *quelque* became incompatible with clausemate negation? Should we separate more sharply *quelque* as an epistemic determiner and as a concessive item? Should we consider that *quelque* is epistemic but is not a PPI in cases like (53a), which entails under our approach that it did not convey an ignorance implicature.

6 Concluding remarks

The work presented in this chapter develops our hypothesis (Jayez and Tovena, 2008a) that the form *quelque* N P, in which P is a property, means that the existence of an entity of type N satisfying P is a piece of information at which the epistemic agent got by inference (evidential aspect) and that the exact identity of such an entity remains unknown (epistemic aspect). The epistemic component of meaning, and the concessive component that can be associated to it, tell us to put *quelque* in the family of FC and epistemic items, provided one includes the evidential aspect. We have clarified the impact that the conventional implicature of ignorance has on the distribution of the determiner in negative sentences. Finally, we have laid the foundations for the study of the origin and the development of *quelque*. This has given us the opportunity to identify several important issues, among which we can recall the question of whether the concessive use is a byproduct of the ignorance component or the reverse, and the question of whether and how to reconcile the concessive meaning with the existential interpretation.

References

Aikhenvald, A. (2005). *Evidentiality*. Oxford, Oxford University Press.
Baker, C. L. (1970). Double negatives. *Linguistic Inquiry 1*, pp. 169–186.
Buridant, C. (2000). *Grammaire Nouvelle de l'Ancien Français*. Paris, Sedes.
Campbell, K. (1990). *Abstract Particulars*. Oxford, Blackwell.

Chierchia, G. (2004). Scalar implicatures, polarity phenomena, and the syntax/pragmatics interface. In A. Belletti (ed.), *Structures and Beyond: The Cartography of Syntactic Structures, vol. 3*, pp. 39-103, New York, Oxford University Press.

Combettes, B. (2004). La grammaticalisation d'un déterminant indéfini: *quelque* en Moyen Français. *Scolia 18*, pp. 9–40.

Corblin, F. (2004). Quelque. In F. Corblin and H. de Swart (eds.), *The Handbook of French Semantics*, pp. 99–107. Stanford, CSLI.

Culioli, A. (1982). A propos de *quelque*. In *Actes du Colloque franco-bulgare de linguistique. Contrastive Linguistics*, reprinted in Culioli, A. Ed.) (1999), *Pour une linguistique de l'énonciation, T.3*, pp. 49–58, Paris, Ophrys.

Dayal, V. (1995). Quantification in correlatives. In E. Bach, E. Jelinek, A. Kratzer, and B. Partee H. (Eds.), *Quantification in Natural Languages*, pp. 179–205. Dordrecht, Kluwer.

Dayal, V. (2005). The universal force of free choice *any*. In *Linguistic Variation Yearbook*, pp. 5–40. Amsterdam, John Benjamins.

Defrancq, B. and D. Willems (1997). *Quelque chose*: un objet pas comme les autres. *Travaux de Linguistique 35*, pp. 91-102.

Dekker, P. (1998). Speaker's reference, description and information structure. *Journal of Semantics 15*, pp. 305–334.

Ducrot, O. (1972). *Dire et ne pas dire*. Paris, Hermann.

Farkas, D. (2002a). Extreme non-specificity in Romanian. In C. Beyssade and al. (Eds.), *Romance Languages and Linguistic Theory 2000*, pp. 127–151. Amsterdam: John Benjamins.

Farkas, D. (2002b). Specificity distinctions. *Journal of Semantics 19*, 213–243.

Farkas, D. (2002c). Varieties of indefinites. In B. Jackson (Ed.), *Proceedings of Semantics and Linguistic Theory XII*, Cornell University, CLC, pp. 59-84.

Foulet, L. (1919). Quelque. *Romania 45*, pp. 220–249.

Geurts, B. (1999). *Presuppositions and Pronouns*. Amsterdam, Elsevier.

Giannakidou, A. (2001). The meaning of free choice. *Linguistics and Philosophy 24*, pp. 659–735.

Haspelmath, M. (1997). *Indefinite Pronouns*. Oxford: Oxford University Press.

Hoeksema, J. and H. Rullmann (2000). Scalarity and polarity. In J. Hoeksema, H. Rullmann, V. Sánchez Valencia, and T. van der Wouden (Eds.), *Perspectives on Negation and polarity items*, pp. 129–171. Amsterdam, John Benjamins.

Horn, L. R. (1989). *The natural history of negation*. Chicago, Chicago University Press.

Horn, L. R. (2001). *Any* and (-)*ever*: Free choice and free relatives. In *Proceedings of the 15th Annual Conference of the Israeli Association for Theoretical Linguistics*, pp. 71–111.

Jayez, J. (2005). How many are 'several'? *Belgian Journal of Linguistics 19*, special issue directed by S. Vogeleer on *Bare plurals, indefinites and weak-strong distinction*, pp. 187-209.

Jayez, J. and L. M. Tovena (2002). Determiners and (Un)certainty. In B. Jackson (Ed.), *Proceedings of Semantics and Linguistic Theory XII*, Cornell University, CLC, pp. 164–

183.

Jayez, J. and L. M. Tovena (2005). Free–Choiceness and Non Individuation. *Linguistics and Philosophy 28*, pp. 1–71.

Jayez, J. and L. M. Tovena (2006). Epistemic determiners. *Journal of Semantics 23*, pp. 217–250.

Jayez, J. and L. M. Tovena (2008a). Evidentiality and determination. In *Proceedings of Sinn und Bedeutung 12*, pp. 271–286.

Jayez, J. and L. M. Tovena (2008b). Scenarios of equivalence - The case of *quelque*. (submitted for the volume *Funny Indefinites*) ms. ENS-LSH and Université Paris VII.

Jayez, J. and L. M. Tovena (2008c). *Presque* and *almost* : how argumentation derives from comparative meaning. In O. Bonami and P. Cabredo (Eds), *Proceedings of Empirical Issues in Syntax and Semantics 7*, pp. 217-240.

Jayez, J. and L. M. Tovena (2008d). Facts, models and problems concerning free choiceness. Handout of the talk delivered at the Workshop *Free choiceness: facts, models and problems, 20th ESSLLI* Hamburg D, available at http://elico.linguist.jussieu.fr/fc-esslli08.html.

Kagan, O. and I. Spector (2008). Alternative semantics for the Hebrew determiner *eyze*. In *Twentyseventh West Coast Conference on Formal Linguistics*, pp. 247–255.

Paillard, D. (2006). *quelque* N / *quelques* N. In F. Corblin, S. Ferrando, and L. Kupferman (Eds.), *Indéfinis and prédication*, pp. 417–428. Paris, Presses Universitaires de la Sorbonne.

Potts, C. (2005). *The Logic of Conventional Implicatures*. Oxford, Oxford University Press.

Quer, J. (1998). *Mood at the Interface*. Ph. D. thesis, University of Utrecht.

Srivastav, V. (1991). The syntax and semantics of correlatives. *Natural Language and Linguistic Theory 9*, pp. 637–686.

Szabolcsi, A. (2004). Positive polarity – negative polarity. *Natural Language and Linguistic Theory 22*, pp. 409–452.

Tovena, L. M. (2003). In the complement of *deny*. In *Working papers in Linguistics*, pp. 171–186. University of Pennsylvania.

Van de Velde, D. (2000). Les indéfinis comme adjectifs. In L. Bosveld, M. Van Peteghem, and D. Van de Velde (Eds.), *De l'indétermination à la qualification. Les indéfinis*, pp. 203–272. Arras, Artois Presses Université.

Williams, D. C. (1953). On the elements of being. *Review of Metaphysics 7*, pp. 3–18.

Some "PPIs" are just Hyper-existentials

Francis Corblin
Université Paris-Sorbonne
& Institut Jean Nicod (CNRS-ENS-EHESS)

Francis.Corblin@paris-sorbonne.fr

Abstract

This paper shows that the French indefinite pronouns (*quelqu'un, quelque chose)* are neither PPIs (Baker 1970), nor double NPIs (Szabolcsi 2004).

It claims that the scope restrictions involving negation and the impossibility to get a generic interpretation of these items, can only be explained by assuming that they have a strong vocation for existential readings, which can be seen as a qualified come-back to Russell's (1905) view. The paper establishes that this preference is a lexical property of the French determiner *quelqu-*.

B. Russell (1905) introduces a semantic analysis of English *some* as an existential quantifier. A sentence like "Some man is being obnoxious" would be analyzed under this view as :

1. There is an *x* such that *x* is a man, and *x* is being obnoxious.

Russell extends this proposal to English *a* and claims that a sentence including an indefinite description like *an F is G* translates in formal logic as the formula : " $\exists$ x Fx $\wedge$ Gx".

This analysis has been widely accepted as the classical semantic analysis of indefinites, but the main problem it raises is that it cannot be generalized to every context, as shown by the work of Kamp and Heim in the 80s. They have shown that there are contexts (e.g. *donkey sentences*) in which an indefinite NP *cannot* translate as an existential quantifier. A rather common wisdom since then is to assume that indefinites have no quantifying force of their own, that they are mere variable-introducers to be bound by operators provided by the linguistic context.

In the present work on the French semantic pronouns *quelqu'un, quelque chose,* we make some sort of qualified come-back to the classical view of Russell by establishing that the constraints on the use and interpretation of these indefinite pronouns cannot be captured without assuming that they have a strong vocation for existential readings. I will establish that this analysis is the best way for explaining the very special behavior of these items with negation, a well-known data which motivates their analysis as *positive polarity items* since Baker (1970). In addition, I will show that this vocation for existential readings can also cover the observation, rarely signaled and discussed in the literature, that indefinite pronouns do not accept true generic readings (in contrast to indefinite determiners).

By considering in some details the contexts in which French indefinite pronouns are licit/illicit in the close vicinity of a negation, I will try to show that these pronouns are neither *positive polarity items,* nor *double negative polarity items* (as proposed by Szabolcsi 2004) but just variable place-holders having a strong aversion for contexts asserting the non-existence of satisfiers for the variable.

Since in French indefinite pronouns are based on the determiner *quelque,* I will collect some arguments for establishing that this existential preference can be considered as a lexical property of this specific determiner, a somewhat paradoxical conclusion, since the singular determiner *quelque* is no longer used in modern French except in the scope of modal operators (Corblin 2004), so in contexts to the antipodes of existential binding. A way of dissolving the paradox will be suggested.

1   Some differences between *quelque chose/ quelqu'un* and *un N*

Let us take as an observation-grid the following map due to Haspelmath (1997) :

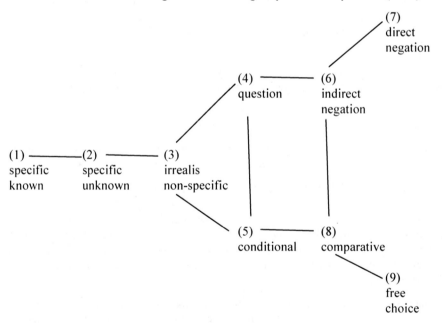

Figure 1 : *Implicational map of indefinite pronouns uses, from Haspelmath (1997 : 4).*

Haspelmath distinguishes some contexts (questions, conditionals, etc.), some kinds of interpretations (specific, irrealis, free-choice etc.), and introduces a typological generalization according to which, if a given language has different indefinite pronouns, a given form can only be used in connected sites of this map. We have nothing to say about this typological generalization here, and we are just taking this map as an observation grid for capturing the main relevant contexts for documenting the constraints on indefinite pronouns and indefinite determiners.

French indefinite pronouns[1] and indefinite determiners as well, have no "free-choice" reading, as illustrated by (1) and (2). The preferred form for expressing free-choice in French is *n'importe qu-*. By free-choice reading is meant the reading of the English *any* in sentences like *Pick any card.* (1) and (2) can be considered as tests that a given form has no free-choice reading : one can take the sentence with the indefinites as true without accepting the validity of the sentence with the unambiguous free choice *n'importe qu-* as true.

(1)   Tu peux inviter un ami, mais pas n'importe qui.
        You can invite a friend, but not anyone.

(2)   Tu peux inviter quelqu'un, mais pas n'importe qui.
        You can invite someone, but not anyone.

But it is well known that *un N* and *quelqu'un* behave very differently when in the syntactic scope of a clause-mate negation ("direct negation" for Haspelmath):

(3)   Je n'ai pas dit un mot.
        I did not say a word.

(4)   Je n'ai pas dit quelque chose.
        I did not say something.

The difference is as follows: in (3) *un mot* can be interpreted in the semantic scope of the negation, and the sentence will convey the meaning :"I did not say anything"; but in (4) *quelque chose* cannot be interpreted in the semantic scope of the negation, and (4) cannot convey the meaning : " I dit not say anything". The only accessible meaning is : "There is something I did not say".

Should we, then, characterize such expressions as "PPIs" as suggested by Baker (1970)?

Note that it has often be observed that although the terminology conveys that such "PPI's" would be the symmetrical counterpart of NPIs, there are very important asymmetries between true NPIs and these expressions. An NPI has to be "licensed" by an overt part of its context, which means that if the form is placed in a context deprived of the required properties, the result is agrammatical. But for indefinite pronouns, all one can observe is not

---

[1] Up to now, we use *"indefinite pronouns"* as a convenient terminology restricted to pronominal expressions based on *quelque : quelque chose, quelqu'un, quelque part.*

agrammaticality, but a constraint on scope hierarchy: in (4) *quelque chose* must have scope over the negation, but we have a perfect grammatical sentence.

One can imagine to extend the notion of licensing, or more exactly of anti-licensing, to the logical form, or to any form of semantic representation: grammar would count terms not allowed to sit in the scope of a clause-mate negation. This purely semantic notion of PPI would explain that such PPIs cannot be used in site [7] of Haspelmath's map. Although very different in nature from the syntactic notion of NPI commonly accepted in the literature, this semantic notion of PPI might have a chance to capture the fact and to give a good picture of the singularities of the expressions under consideration.

But there at least two problems:

1. It is not always true that a clause-mate negation refuses to take in its immediate scope the variable introduced by an indefinite pronoun. This has been repeatedly noted (a.o.) by Baker (1970), Jespersen (1917), Szabocsi (2004) and Corblin (2004).

2. There are other phenomena independent of negation, but manifesting themselves as preferred/prohibited scope hierarchies which contrast in the same way indefinite pronouns and indefinite determiners, namely the capacity to be interpreted in the scope of the generic covert operator *Gen* (Cf. Corblin 2009a).

It is of the utmost utility, then, first to get a panoramic view of the distributions of the two kinds of expressions (i.e. regular indefinite determiners and indefinite pronouns) with relation to other quantifiers of their context, and second, to go into more details regarding the constraints involving negation and indefinite pronouns.

Haspelmath's map provides an useful tool for a survey of the distribution of indefinite pronouns/indefinite determiners.

Figure (2) represents the sites and kind of interpretations accessible to each expression.

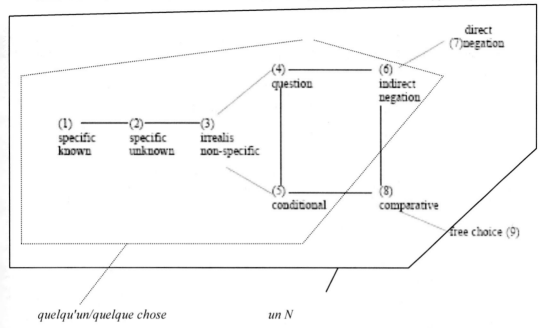

quelqu'un/quelque chose   *un N*

Figure 2 : interpretations of indefinite pronouns and determiners

Figure 2 notes that in contrast to the indefinite NP *un N*, the indefinite pronouns *quelqu'un, quelque chose* cannot be interpreted as the argument of a comparative construction. (5) is correct (and ambiguous), although (6) can only be interpreted by an existential binding of the variable associated to the indefinite pronoun:

(5)   Ce singe est plus intelligent qu'un homme.
        This monkey is more intelligent than a man.

(6)   Ce singe est plus intelligent que quelqu'un.
        This monkey is more intelligent than someone.

Sentence (5) has two interpretations:

        (i) For any man x, this monkey is more intelligent than x.

        (ii) There is a man x, such that this monkey is more intelligent than x.

Sentence (6) can only have the interpretation (ii).

This fact, which, to my knowledge, has remained unnoticed in the literature, is not easy to explain at face value.

What we know for sure about the argument of comparative constructions is that it is a licensing context for NPIs. But it is not the case that in general, NPI licensors cannot take indefinite pronouns in their semantic scope. Interrogatives, for instance are also NPI licensors, as (7) illustrates:

(7) Est-ce-que vous avez la moindre idée de ce qu'il a pu faire?
     Int. particle-you have the slightest idea of what he did?

le moindre is considered as the prototypical NPI in French, and it is , as expected, licensed by interrogatives.

Placed in such a context, indefinite NPs and indefinite pronouns behave exactly alike: they can be interpreted either by existential closure (out-scoping the interrogative operator) but they can be interpreted in the scope of the interrogative operator as well:

(8) Est-ce que vous avez vu quelqu'un?
     Int. particle-you have seen someone.

Sentence (8) means either (i) or (ii), "?" being a notation for the interrogative operator associated to the interpretation : "I wonder if ()" :

      (i) ? (There is a person x such that you have seen x).

      (ii) There is a person x such that ? (you have seen x)

And this duality of interpretation is preserved once *quelqu'un* is replaced by *a person.*

The relevant property of comparative constructions might be that they allow the variable introduced by an indefinite determiner to be interpreted in the scope of a *generic* quantifier. If one accepts to analyze generic reading via an invisible quantifier GEN, in the spirit of Krifka and al. (1995), one will interpret (9) as (10):

(9) Pierre est plus malin qu'un singe.
     Pierre is more clever than a monkey.

(10) GEN x [(monkey (x) → (Pierre is more clever than x)]

To be more precise, (9) is ambiguous, and allows both existential closure and the generic reading represented in (10).

Once admitted than (9) admits a generic reading, one has to make a more general observation : it is a striking fact that in general, indefinite pronouns (by contrast to indefinite determiners) do *not* accept true generic readings. By "true" generic reading, I mean a generic reading arising in the absence of any linguistic expression that one would be inclined to translate as some sort of (possibly weak) universal quantifier. This observation is illustrated by (11-16):

(11) Un homme est difficile à convaincre.   Generic reading possible
      A man is difficult to convince.

(12)   Quelqu'un est difficile à convaincre.   No generic reading
            Someone is difficult to convince.

(13)   Une chose n'a pas d'âme.   Generic reading possible
            A thing has no soul.

(14)   Quelque chose n'a pas d'âme.   No generic reading
            Something has no soul.

(15)   Une chose n'a pas de prix.   Generic reading possible
            A thing has no price.

(16)   Quelque chose n'a pas de prix.   No generic reading
            Something has no price.

In contrast, as soon as an explicit quantifier is introduced, the indefinite pronoun can be interpreted in the scope of this quantifier.

(17)   Quelqu'un *peut* être difficile à convaincre.
            Someone can be difficult to convince.

(18)   Quelque chose peut avoir une âme.
            Something may have a soul.

(19)   Quelque chose a *en général* un prix.
            Something in general has a price.

Even for very well-known generic sentences like (20), and for very large extension terms like *man* (interpreted in such generic sentences as "human being"), if the indefinite NP is replaced by an indefinite pronoun (although its domain restriction is also "human being"), the sentence is awkward:

(20)   Un homme est mortel.
            A man is mortal.

(21)   Quelqu'un est mortel.
            Someone is mortal.

The empirical generalization emerging from these observations is:

Empirical generalization 1:

The French indefinite pronouns cannot be interpreted in the scope of the invisible generic operator GEN in contexts open to generic readings of indefinite determiners.

To my knowledge this empirical generalization has not been explicitly made in the literature, and it makes the landscape of indefinite pronouns distributions even more complex. The notion of PPI, whatever difficulties it encounters, has at least the merit to unify the identity of indefinite pronouns by a special relation to negation. And the same is true for the notion of double NPI introduced by Sczabolcsi (2004). In both analyses indefinite pronouns are just variable introducers with special requirements on their context having to do with negation. If we are correct, negation or more generally monotonicity, is not the only contextual feature relevant for characterizing their special behavior. Genericity, a feature at first glance unrelated to negation is also relevant.

2   More about the constraints on negation scope

As already recalled, formulating correctly the constraints on negation scope is far from being an easy matter.

In simple sentences, it is enough to say that indefinite pronouns cannot be interpreted in the scope of a clause-mate negation. But this is valid only for simple sentences, since it has been noticed repeatedly that it is possible to do so (to interpret an indefinite pronoun in the scope of a clause-mate negation) in some configurations involving more complex environments embedding this simple context.

Szabolcsi (2004) claims that in English, if a negation with an indefinite pronoun in its immediate syntactic scope is itself in the scope of an anti-additive operator, it is possible to interpret the indefinite variable in the scope of its clause-mate negation.

For French, the "anti-additive" operators of Szabolcsi (2004) are exactly the operators called "négatifs" in Corblin & de Swart (2004): verbal negation (*ne...pas*), negative quantifiers (*personne, rien, aucun...*), and the preposition *sans*.

These operators are identified by a set of properties listed in Corblin & de Swart (2004). Two of them, as a matter of illustration are:

a) the licensing of a *de* direct object:

(22)   Pierre n'a pas de pain.
        Pierre has not *de-bread.*

(23)   Pierre est resté deux jours sans manger de pain.
        Pierre stay two days without eating *de*-bread.

b) the licensing of *du tout.*

(24)   Pierre ne mange pas du tout.
        Pierre do not eat-*du-tout.*

(25)   Personne du tout n'est venu
        Nobody -*du-tout* came.

None of these operators can take an indefinite pronoun in its "immediate" scope in simple sentences:

(26)   Personne n'a mangé quelque chose.   Only existential binding
        Nobody ate something.

(27)   Il est parti sans dire quelque chose.   id.
        He left without saying something.

By "immediate scope" is meant that if there is an intervening operator between the negation and the indefinite pronoun, the indefinite variable can be interpreted in the scope of the operator, which is itself outscoped by the negation :

(28)   Pierre n'a pas toujours quelque chose à faire.   neg> toujours > indefinite
         Pierre has not always something to do.

The relevant empirical generalization is formulated as follows by Szablocsi (2004):

> "*Some*-type PPIs do not occur within the immediate scope of a clause-mate anti-additive operator [negation, FC]".

But it is known that this constraint disappears when the negative operator itself is in the scope of another operator, as illustrated by (29)-(31).

(29)   Je ne crois pas que Jean n'a pas dit quelque chose.
         I do not believe Jean did not say something.

(30)   Je suis surpris que Jean n'ait pas appelé quelqu'un.
         I am surprised Jean dit not call for someone.

(31)   Si Jean n'a pas appelé quelqu'un, il a eu tort.
         If Jean did not call for someone, he was wrong.

Szabolcsi's claim is that all the operators which license NPIs have this "by-pass" role, and are what she calls "rescuers": they will make accessible the interpretation of the pronoun in the immediate scope of the negative operator:

> "*Some*-type PPIs do not occur within the immediate scope of a clause-mate anti-additive operator [negation, FC] unless this anti-additive operator itself is in an NPI licensing context."

It seems that this generalization holds for French as well. Consider a NPI licensor like *Je ne crois pas que...* as in (32):

(32)   *Je ne crois pas* qu'il ait la moindre chance.   Licensor of NPI
         I do not think he has the slightest chance.

If, in this context, one embeds a sentence otherwise awkward or obligatorily existential, the whole sentence is grammatical and admits, without any problem, an interpretation of the variable in the immediate scope of the clause-mate negation, as illustrated by (33):

(33)   Je ne crois pas qu'il n'a pas invité quelqu'un.
         I do not think he did not invite someone.

But, and on this I part with Szabolcsi's claim, at least for French data, it seems that *any operator* taking the negation in its scope will have the same effect, with no special privilege for NPI licensors. Consider (34):

(34) Pierre ne mange pas quelque chose le matin.
      Pierre does not eat something in the morning.

This sentence is not acceptable, unless the indefinite pronoun *quelque chose* is interpreted by existential closure, giving: "there is something Pierre does not eat in the morning."

If this sentence is embedded under "Il est fréquent que...", the resulting sentence is grammatical, and licenses the interpretation of the indefinite pronoun in the immediate scope of the clause-mate negation in (35):

(35) Il est fréquent que Pierre ne mange pas quelque chose le matin.
      It is frequent that Pierre does not eat something in the morning.

The sentence (35) can easily be interpreted as: it is frequent that Pierre does not eat anything in the morning. And the same is true for the indefinite pronoun *quelqu'un* in (36) :

(36) Il est fréquent que Pierre ne passe pas ses vacances avec quelqu'un.
      It is frequent that Pierre does not spend his holydays with someone.

But the context "Il est fréquent que ..." is not a NPI licensor as shown by (37):

(37)   Il est fréquent que Pierre ait *la moindre idée.
      It is frequent that Pierre has the slightest idea.

And it it easy to find a huge set of such contexts, unable to license NPIs and nevertheless perfect "rescuers" for the "no clause-mate negation scope" constraint. I give in what follows some of them:

(38) Je suis certain que Jean n'a pas appelé quelqu'un.
      I am sure that Jean did not call someone.

(39) Je sais que Jean n'a pas appelé quelqu'un.
      I know that Jean did not call someone.

(40) Je suis certain que personne n'avait pris quelque chose pour diner.
      I am sure that nobody had had something for dinner.

(41) Je suis certain que Pierre n'avait pas pris quelqu'un dans sa voiture.
      I am sure that Pierre had not taken something in his car.

(42) Il y a beaucoup de gens qui ne vivent pas avec quelqu'un.
      There are lots of people who does not leave with someone.

(43) Je suis persuadé que Pierre n'a pas dit quelque chose contre moi.
      I am convinced that Pierre did not say something against me.

(44) Je suis convaincu que Pierre ne dîne pas avec quelqu'un ce soir.
      I am convinced that Pierre does not have someone for dinner at night.

(45) Pierre pourrait ne pas inviter quelqu'un.
      Pierre might not invite someone.

If I am correct about the data, the conclusion to be drawn is that Szabolczi's generalization is just a part of the picture: it is true that NPI's licensors help to by-pass the constraint "not in the scope of a clause-mate negation", but they are far from being alone to do that. Almost any operator out-scoping the negation is also a rescuer.

We have then to replace Szabolcsi's generalization by the following one:

Empirical generalization 2.

Indefinite pronouns cannot be interpreted as a variable in the immediate scope of a clause mate negation in the context : #NEG ∃ (x), NEG being the higher operator of the sentence.

This generalization has been previously made in Corblin (2004: 106) for the *quelqu-* paradigm in French :"The *quelqu-* paradigm contributes a variable which cannot be interpreted in the scope of widest scope negation" .

This generalization derives correctly that nested negative propositions in general, will be much more acceptable with the indefinite pronoun interpreted in the scope of a clause-mate negation than simple propositions.

For simple propositions, it is necessary as well to add some extra-constraints which does not concern specifically indefinite pronouns, but more generally indefinite NPs.

It is a common observation that indefinites (in general) cannot be interpreted in the scope of a clause-mate negation in the context of a universal quantifier. Consider the following couple of sentences :

(46)   Tout le monde n'a pas dit un mot.
         Everyone does not say a word.

(47)   Tout le monde n'a pas dit quelque chose.
         Everyone does not say something.

Although the indefinite *un mot* can, in general, be interpreted in the semantic scope of a clause-mate negation, this is no longer the case, when both are in the syntactic scope of a universal quantifier. It looks actually impossible to interpret *un mot* in the scope of the negation in (46), and to get the meaning :" Everyone says nothing". And this is triggered by universal quantification, since in the parallel sentence (48), the interpretation in the scope of negation is accessible:

(48)   Une personne n'a pas dit un mot.
         A person did not say a word.

So in order to predict that sentence (47) cannot be equivalent to "Every one says nothing", nothing specific to the theory of indefinite *pronouns* is required: the fact must be a prediction of the theory of *indefinites* (in general), and the discussion is far beyond the scope of this paper.[2]

Let us focus on the theory of indefinite pronouns. If any kind of out-scoping operator is a rescuer, the thesis of Szabolcsi which sees PPIs as doube NPIs cannot capture their specific properties, because there are licensing contexts which are not NPI licensors.

As a whole, we are left with two empirical generalization regarding the so-called PPIs in which the relation to negation plays a role less crucial than what most theories assume:

1. These items have specific scope constraints with relation to the generic operator GEN.

This property has nothing to do with negation.

2. These items prohibits an interpretation in the scope of a clause-mate negation iff this negation is the topmost operator of the sentence.

This strange-looking association of constraints on the very same lexical item in French does not seem to be a mere accident. I do not want to get involved here in the detailed analysis of other languages, but from the literature, it looks clear that French is not an isolated case in this respect.

No existing category gives a good idea of the singularity of these items.

If to be a PPI means that they cannot be interpreted in the scope of a clause mate negation, they are not PPIs.

The thesis that they are double NPIs is a try for giving them a nature more in accordance with their complex properties with relation to negation. But we have seen above that they can be licensed in the scope of a negation by an out-scoping operator, irrespective of this operator being a NPI licensor, or not.

Last but not least, neither the notion of PPI nor the notion of double NPI can predict that these items cannot give rise to generic quantification of their associated variable.

3 A proposal for deriving the empirical generalizations

What is decisive for allowing the interpretation of *quelqu'un, quelque chose* in the scope of a negation is only the fact that another explicit operator takes the negation in its scope.

---

[2] I do not know if this fact has been noticed and discussed in the literature. Note that the impossibility to outscope a regular indefinite interpreted in the scope of the clause mate negation looks a property of the sole universal quantifier, since all other quantifiers can outscope such an indefinite: *Moins de dix personnes n'ont pas dit un mot, plus de dix personnes n'ont pas dit un mot* (less than ten persons/more than ten persons did not say a word) accept an interpretation of the indefinite in the scope of the clause-mate negation.

If we are correct, this operator can be a modal operator, which makes the embedded proposition part of some possible world, but this operator can also be any kind of epistemic operator, even those which reinforce the validity of the embedded proposition. There is no difference in acceptability between (49) and (50), and in both sentences the interpretation in the scope of the negation is licensed:

(49)   Il est possible que Pierre n'ait pas téléphoné à quelqu'un.
        It is possible that Pierre did not phone to somebody.

(50)   Il est prouvé que Pierre n'a pas téléphoné à quelqu'un.
        It is proved that Pierre did not phone to somebody.

For generic interpretations, what is prohibited is only the interpretation in the scope of what is commonly analyzed as the invisible quantifier GEN, that is to say the generic interpretations deprived of any explicit quantifier. As already said, indefinite pronouns can be used in general sentences, if they are in the scope of an explicit quantifier like in (51) and (52) :

(51)   Si quelqu'un vit longtemps, il risque d'être malade.
        If someone lives for a long time, someone riks to be ill.

(52)   Si un singe est plus malin que quelqu'un, il le domine.
        If a monkey is more clever than someone, it will dominate him/her.

It is very difficult, at first glance, to perceive a relation between these two constraints.

Do GEN and (topmost) NEG have some semantic property in common which would explain the behavior of indefinite pronouns? On this track, one is looking for something comparable to decreasing monotonicity as an explanation for licensing NPIs.

Or is there a specific property of indefinite pronouns which would explain, as a result, that, maybe for different reasons, both GEN and topmost NEG are disliked by indefinite pronouns?

In what follows, I will make a proposal along the lines of the second view. I will claim that it is for different reasons, both in direct opposition to the properties of indefinite pronouns that the constraints regarding NEG and GEN apply for the very same lexical expression.

3.1 Existential closure revisited

The notion of "existential closure" was introduced by Heim (1982) and a similar notion (interpretation at the top-level of the DRS) is used by Kamp (1981).

The notion is called for by the treatment of indefinites (mostly indefinite determiners, indefinite pronouns are considered more rarely in these works). The initial problem is that Russell's thesis (indefinites *are* existential quantifiers) is incompatible with some linguistic data, especially with the so-called "donkey-sentences". The proposed solution is that indefinites are not quantifiers, but only variable introducers, this introduction being made very often in the scope of unselective quantifiers which ends as binders of the variable.

But these approaches must add something special for connecting indefinites and existential quantification, since many indefinites end up as existentially quantified variables, even if no lexical quantifier of the context can be charged for this existential quantification. This is what "existential closure" does. It produces, in Kamp's system, a top-level quantification of indefinite variables if these variables are not interpreted in the scope of contextual binders.

In some sense, this may look as a revenge for Russell: indefinites may not *be* existential quantifiers, but indefinites are associated to a device that take them as existentially quantified if nothing else happens; and the considered existential quantifier is not lexically expressed, which means that this quantifier is so to speak "triggered" by indefinite expressions.

But this is not the full picture, since indefinites determiners have also *generic* interpretations. It has been proposed, in Corblin (2009b) to consider the invisible generic quantifier GEN as another closure device. As existential closure, GEN produces a quantified interpretation without any intervention of a lexical quantifier, and as existential closure, it is triggered by indefinites.[3]

A way of deriving the observed facts is to assume that regular indefinite determiners accept generic closure (in some special contexts), but that indefinite pronouns have a strong preference for existential closure, and do not accept to be bound by GEN. This view can be maintained even if one does not want to consider the binding by GEN as a closure. Even in that case, a theory-independent point must be conceded: in contexts where no explicit binder (lexical quantifiers) takes them in their scope, there is a strong difference between regular indefinites (possibly interpreted as generic) and indefinite pronouns (only interpreted by existential closure). The present assumption is not much more than a way of accommodating the facts. The underlying theoretical view is that indefinites can be seen as mere variable introducers, although they may not be completely unspecified about their "quantificational destiny"; in other words, it might be the case that indefinites have a less strong association to existential quantification than Russell thought, but a less negligible relationship to existential quantification than dynamic semantics suggests.

This approach assumes that in the scope of a lexical binder, there is no difference between the indefinite pronoun and the indefinite determiner: both have a dependent reading when interpreted in the scope of the quantifier, and a marked reading when interpreted by existential closure. This is illustrated by (53) and (54):

(53)   Si vous voyez quelqu'un appelez-moi.
         If you see someone, call me.

(54)   Si vous voyez un étudiant appelez-moi.
         If you see a student, call me.

---

[3] There is no consensus that GEN operates only for indefinites, or for some other linguistic categories like bare plurals.

The preferred interpretation of (53) and (54) is the dependent interpretation of the indefinite variable *(si>quelqu'un/un étudiant)*. The interpretation by existential closure *(there is someone/a student, such that, if you see her, call me)* is less accessible, probably because it is not likely to prefer an invisible quantification device to the local binding offered by a lexical quantifier.

I asked native speakers if one of the existential readings is more natural than the other, and I did not get very neat preferences. In cataphoric contexts, speakers tend to prefer strongly the determiner to the pronoun as (55)/(56) shows:

(55)   Si vous voyez quelqu'un, Pierre, appelez-moi.
        If you see someone, Pierre, call me.

(56)   Si vous voyez un étudiant, Pierre, appelez-moi.
        If you see a student, Pierre, Appelez-moi.

But it is not very easy to interpret this preference.

The biggest difference, as already said, is that the sole indefinite *determiner* allows a generic interpretation. See the contrasts (11)-(16) supra. Considering that both existential closure and generic binding are general options offered by the grammar, it should not be surprising that different linguistic categories be defined by relation to these options: for instance a given expression accepts one option, but not the other. This might seems strange if the relevant categories are determiner/pronoun, but, as we will see later, the so-called French indefinite pronoun is actually a form of the *quelqu-* paradigm, that is to say, an expression based on an other indefinite determiner than the regular *a, an*.

Once considering that we have two different determiners, the regular, or "basic" one, *a*, and the determiner *quelque*, it becomes more natural to assume that this lexical difference supports semantic differences, like, for instance, a difference in the kind of implicit quantification process they select.

To prove that all the lexical forms of the singular determiner *quelqu-* are allergic to GEN might be a real work, in particular because the singular form of the determiner *(quelque)* is restricted to modal contexts in modern French (see for instance Corblin 2004) and is a determiner much less used in ordinary language than *some* in English, for instance. So we cannot offer simple examples showing that the only interpretation of a given occurrence of *quelque N* cannot be generic and is interpreted by existential binding. But we can give examples establishing that *quelque* can never be interpreted as a generic taking scope over the modal. Consider (57) and (58):

(57)   Pierre pensait qu'un singe pouvait escalader ce mur.
        Pierre thought that a monkey could climb up this wall.

(58)   Pierre pensait que quelque singe pouvait escalader ce mur.
        Pierre thought that some monkey could climb up this wall.

In (57) it is possible to interpret: for any monkey, Pierre thought that it can climb up the wall. But it is impossible to interpret this way (58); which can only mean : Pierre thought that there can be a monkey such that it can climb up the wall.

This is a confirmation that *quelque* cannot be interpreted in the scope of GEN and comfort the assumption that the access to the scope of GEN is a lexical property attached to the quantifier *quelqu*.

Up to now, the analysis is rather stipulative. It notes a fact, that indefinite pronouns cannot be interpreted in the scope of GEN, and derives it by assuming that indefinite pronouns, with relation to implicit binders, have a strong preference for existential binding, and no access to the scope of GEN.

I will try to show now, that this view offers a way of understanding the apparently very complicated constraints on the possibility of interpreting the indefinite pronoun in the scope of a topmost clause-mate negation.

3.2 Constraints on negation scope revisited

The crucial fact to explain is the following contrast:

(59) Personne ne déclare quelque chose.   *ill-formed except if existential*
      Nobody declares something

(60) Pierre ne dit pas quelque chose.   *ill-formed except if existential*
      Pierre does not say something.

vs

(61) Tout le monde déclare quelque chose.   *existential or dependent*
      Everyone declares something.

(62) Si quelqu'un ne déclare pas quelque chose…   *existential or dependent*
      If someone does not declare something…

This contrast establishes that negation, as compared to other logical operators (universal quantifiers, *if*, etc…) cannot take an indefinite pronoun in its scope if the negation is the topmost logical operator.

It looks like a very bizarre constraint, as compared to what happens more generally about scope hierarchy. If it were a mere constraint of relative hierarchy (prohibition, preference) with a quantifier of the context, we would be in a well-known situation. Indefinite pronouns would just have the property of imposing a reverse hierarchy when in the syntactic scope of a negation.

But once taken into account the so-numerous exceptions to this rule documented in the literature, it becomes even controversial that there is such a rule at all. If, as we have tried to show in the previous section, the out-scoping of *any* operator over the negation removes any constraint, it becomes even questionable that it is worth mentioning that indefinite pronouns have special problems with negation as such.

A simple solution would be to assume that the existential preference of indefinite pronouns for existential binding is strictly antagonist to what a topmost negation achieves, namely the strong assertion that there is no such individual. In effect, if one tries to find out what is the distinctive property of "to be interpreted as a variable in the scope of a topmost negation", as compared to "being interpreted is the scope of an embedded negation", it seems that one has to conclude that the considered case is the only one which strongly asserts that there is no such individual.

Any other context in which an indefinite pronoun is interpreted in the scope of a negation will leave open the possibility that there are such individuals.

This is uncontroversial if the outscoping operator makes the negative proposition part not of the real world, but part of a possible world, for instance if this operator itself is a negation, or a modal operator, as in (63) and (64):

(63)   Il n'est pas vrai Pierre n'a pas mangé quelque chose.
        It is not true that Pierre did not eat something.

(64)   Il se pourrait que Pierre ne rencontre pas quelqu'un avant ce soir.
        It might be the case that Pierre does not meet someone before nitgh.

But this is also the case if the operator *asserts* the validity of the proposition, as illustrated by (65)-(67), which looks more problematic:

(65)   Il est certain que Pierre n'a pas vu quelqu'un.
        It is sure that Pierre did not see someone.

(66)   Il est évident que Pierre n'a pas vu quelqu'un.
        It is evident that Pierre did not see someone.

(67)   Il est vrai que Pierre n'a pas vu quelqu'un.
        It is true that Pierre did not see someone.

And this even true for operators which *presuppose* the valididy of their argument as factive verbs:

(68)   Je sais que Pierre n'a pas vu quelqu'un.
        I know that Pierre did not see someone.

My intuition is that the non-existence is not a problem if it is explicitly presented as the object of an attitude or an evaluation (even positive). In these cases, so to speak, the non-existence is not merely asserted, but remains something which is under discussion, evaluated, something like an object of though, not a bare assertion of non-existence as a topmost negation would achieve.

The general fact underlying this assumption is that any "indirect" presentation of an assertion weakens its strength. For instance, there is a difference between (69) and (70)-(71):

(69)   John is here

(70)   There is no doubt that John is here

(71)   It is certain that John is here.

The first sentence is associated to a stronger commitment of the speaker, maybe because the assertion is not in the scope of any attitude and presented as a mere fact.

In this view, the so-called PPIs have actually nothing against being interpreted in the scope of a clause-mate negation, but they have something against their use in the direct assertion of non-existence of individuals making true the sentence.

And it is possible to see this behavior as a manifestation of their strong vocation for existential readings: the interpretation in the scope of a top-most negation can be seen as the more antagonist option w.r.t. the preference for existential readings.

This proposal has some advantages compared to analyses one can find in the literature :

1. It proposes a single analysis for two different and otherwise unrelated constraints (no generic reading, no interpretation in the scope of a topmost negation).

3. It addresses new questions about the nature of such constraints, since the notion of PPI, as a reverse image of the notion of NPI is no longer a key for deriving the properties of indefinite pronouns.

The proposal assumes that lexically distinguished variable place-holders (i.e. indefinites in the dynamic semantic sense) come with preference/exclusions regarding their semantic representation. An indefinite pronoun is used only when the existence of particular individuals of a class is considered in the sentence: this excludes both cases in which it can be "implicitly" assumed that any member of the class is considered, and cases in which the sentence declare that no member of the class can be considered because the class is empty.

The contrast between indefinite pronouns and determiners is worth discussing in this perspective.

A first opposition is between a "regular indefinite" almost deprived of any constraint regarding the contexts in which it can be used as a variable place-holder[4], and an indefinite pronoun, not accessible to generic binding and to readings in the scope of a top-most negation.

But obviously, it is not the contrast determiner/pronoun which is relevant: it is a matter of contrast between two lexically distinguished determiners, *un* and *quelque,* since the so-called French indefinite pronouns are morphologically based on the determiner *quelque.*

In French, as in many other languages, an "indefinite pronoun" is actually an indefinite determiner, which is not the regular indefinite but a lexically distinct form, associated to a

---

[4] The relation between existential closure and generic binding interpretations of indefinite determiners is discussed as a preference "issue" in Corblin, 2009b.

small set of lexical nominal heads marking semantic basic sorts (persons, things, localization).

quelque   *un*

                chose

                part

Although the association of these two components is lexicalized (it is impossible to introduce modifiers), a natural assumption is that the special properties of these expressions are inherited from the determiner (*quelque* in French, and *some* in English).

In French, I have shown in Corblin (2004) that the constraints regarding *negation* hold for the singular determiner *quelque,* and even for the plural determiner *quelques* although they are not as strict as they are for the singular form. It is reasonable then, to take the aversion for the interpretation in the scope of the topmost negation as a property of the determiner *quelqu-*.

As for constraints regarding *genericity*, they are strict for the singular determiner *quelque.*

(72)   Quelque animal vit longtemps.   No generic reading
        Some animal lives a long time.

As a reminder, note that the relevant constraint concerns genericity obtained without any visible quantifier, as in (18). If there is an explicit operator, generic readings are easily obtained.

For the plural *quelques,* things are more complicated. Corblin (1987) notes that there are generic readings of *quelques,* especially in comparative or contrastive contexts, and provides the following example :

(73) Quelques dessins valent mieux qu'un long discours.   Corblin 1987
        Some drawings are better than long discourses.

But in the vast majority of cases there is a neat contrast between a sentence using the regular indefinite *des,* which is easily interpreted as a generic sentence, and the same sentence using *quelques* which is not, as illustrated by (74)/(75):

(74)   Des vaches mangent du foin.   generic
        Des-cows eat hay.

(75)   Quelques vaches mangent du foin.   not a generic sentence
        Some cows eat hay.

It can be claimed, then, that what we analyze as a vocation for existential binding (no generic reading, no interpretation in the scope of a top-most negation) is a property of the French determiner *quelqu-* and is inherited by the indefinite pronoun based on this determiner.

The French singular *quelque* is an interesting case in this perspective. If we are right, it must be characterized as an expression associated to a preference for existential interpretation, as the other members of the *quelqu-* paradigm. And it is true that it cannot be interpreted in the scope of a topmost negation, and has no generic reading.

But this determiner is also characterized as a modal or epistemic determiner (cf. Corblin 2004, Jayez & Tovena 2005, Jayez & Tovena *forthcoming*) in contrast to the indefinite pronouns *quelqu'un, quelque chose*, and to the plural form *quelques.*

In episodic contexts, for instance, *quelqu'un* is natural:

(76)   J'ai invité quelqu'un à dîner ce soir.
         I invited someone for diner at night.

But in the same context, *quelque* is not acceptable:

(77)   J'ai invité quelque collègue à dîner ce soir.
         I invited some colleague for diner at night.

Quelque is associated to epistemic ignorance or indifference, and can only be interpreted in modal contexts. This makes almost impossible to interpret it by existential closure.

I do not think that this fact can be interpreted as an argument against the present view.

A theory independent observation is that the epistemic value is not a lexical property of the determiner *quelqu-* in all its realizations, but only of the singular form of the determiner. The relevant notion of lexicalization for such a case might be : specialize a given form of the paradigm (e.g. singular) to modal contexts, or, equivalently, ban it from existential closure readings.

But as a member of a given lexical paradigm, the lexicalized form does not acquire a capacity that other forms do not have. In this case, the singular *quelque* remains unable to be interpreted in the scope of a topmost negation, or as a variable in the scope of the invisible generic operator.

This special case leads to remind that the wording "existential preference", or "existential vocation" that we use for short can be misleading. We do not assume that the forms of the paradigm prefer to be interpreted by existential closure (over being interpreted in the scope of some other quantifier of their context). It is in that case that the existence of a form having the properties of the singular *quelque* would be a blatant counter example. What we do assume is that *quelqu-* can only be used when the existence of particular individuals of a class is considered in the sentence, which excludes both interpretation in the scope if a topmost negation (existence denied) and generic readings (no particular individual considered). Under this conception, the existence of a member of the paradigm behaving as the epistemic *quelque* is perfectly compatible with the analysis.

4   Conclusion

4.1 A short summary of the proposal

Indefinite French pronouns (*quelqu'un, quelque chose*) are neither PPIs, nor double NPIs. They are indefinites (variable introducers) with a distinctive property defined as their "existential vocation", which is the source of two constraints:

1) In the absence of any lexical quantifier, they do not accept to be interpreted in the scope of the invisible operator GEN.

2) They cannot be interpreted in the scope of a top-most negation, which would boil-down to assert the non-existence of satisfiers for the variable.

4.2 Open issues

The parallel between what is commonly given as the semantics of *quelque* and the specific constraints on its behaviour w.r.t. other operators of its context discussed in this paper is very striking.

Quelque is defined in Generalized Quantifier Theory as an existential determiner, a determiner asserting that the intersection of two sets is not empty. And moreover, it is commonly associated with *quelque* an implicature that not all the elements of the restrictor are members of its scope. This mirrors quite well the constraints we subsume, rather imperfectly, under the heading "existential vocation". Structures strongly asserting the non-existence of satisfiers are ruled out by the constraints on negation : no interpretation in the scope of a top-most negation. The constraint regarding genericity can be reworded as follows: when interpreting *quelque*, never assume that *all* the individuals of the class are concerned (no binding by an invisible GEN). The ban on GEN can be though of as an image of the "not all" implicature invoked in the analysis of the expression meaning.

It looks as if these parts of the meaning of *quelque* were not just contents to freely combine with other operators, and possibly to cancel in the scope of the relevant contents (e.g. negation or GEN) but were features that the behavior of the expression w.r.t. other operators should preserve in any licit combination.

Suppose the meaning of *quelque N* be defined as: "there are such Ns (existential in the TQG sense), and assume by default that not all Ns are such" (the result of the classical "scalar implicature"). What is striking when one considers what is licit and what is not in terms of interaction between *quelque* and operators of its context, is that combinations which would blatantly produce opposite results are just ruled out.

The theoretical import of this case study, if we are correct in the case analysis, would remain to be considered.

References

Baker, C. L. (1970). Double negatives, *Linguistic Inquiry*, 1:169–186.

Corblin, F. & de Swart, H. eds. (2004). *Handbook of French Semantics*, CSLI Publications, Standord.

Corblin, F. (1987) *Indéfini, défini et démonstratif,* Droz.

Corblin, F.(2002). *Représentation du discours et sémantique formelle,* P.U.F.

Corblin, F. (2004). *Quelque.* In *Handbook of French Semantics*, CSLI Publications, 99-109.

Corblin, F. (2009 a). La vocation existentielle des pronoms indéfinis, *Revue française de philologie*, Université de Belgrade.

Corblin F. (2009 b). The roots of genericity: plural definites and singular indefinites, Communication au colloque Genericity : meaning and uses, ENS, mai 2009.

Haspelmath, M. (1997). *Indefinite pronouns*, Oxford, Oxford University Press.

Heim, I. (1982). *The semantics of definite and indefinite noun phrases.* Doctoral Dissertation, University of Massachussetts at Amherst, Published in 1989 by Garland, New York.

Jayez, J. et L. M. Tovena. (2002). Determiners and uncertainty. In *Proceedings of SALT 12*, 71–111.

Jayez, J. & Tovena, L. (2005). Free-choiceness and Non Individuation, *Linguistics and Philosophy* 28, 1-71.

Jayez, J. & Tovena, L. (forthcoming). Scenarios of equivalence -- The case of `quelque' in Hinterwimmer Stefan, Hendriss Cornelia (eds.) Funny Indefinites, Springer.

Jespersen, O. (1917). *Negation in English and other languages*, reprinted in Selected Writings of Otto Jespersen 1962, George Allen and Unwin Ldt.

Kamp, H. (1981). A Theory of Truth and Semantic Representation, Dans J. Groenendijk, T. Janssen, M. Stokhof (eds.). *Formal Methods in the Study of Language.* Amsterdam: Amsterdam Center, 277-322.

Krifka, M., Pelletier, F.J., Carlson, G., ter Meulen A., Chierchia, G., Link, G. (1995). *Genericity: an introduction.* Dans *The Generic Book, U. of Chicago Press.* 1-124.

Lewis, D. (1975). Adverbs of quantification, Dans E.L. Keenan (ed.), *Formal Semantics of Natural Language*, Cambridge, Cambridge University Press.

Russell, B. (1905). On Denoting, *Mind* 14, 479-493.

Russell, B. (1919). *Introduction to Mathematical Philosophy*, London, George Allen and Unwin.

Szabolcsi, A. (2004). Positive polarity -- negative polarity, *Natural Language and Linguistic Theory*. 22/2, 409-452.

N'IMPORTE QUEL IN A DIACHRONIC PERSPECTIVE[1]

S. Pescarini

Université Nancy 2 / ATILF-CNRS (UMR 7118)

Sandrine.pescarini@atilf.fr

Abstract

The aim of his paper is to present the construction process and the development of indefinites based on the verb *importer*. Elements of this family are regularly used since the beginning of the 19th century. The compositionality principle played a major role to get to the current forms of these determiners. We will focus our attention on *n'importe quel*.

We argue that *n'importe quel* can have three interpretative values: (i) widening, (ii) indifference and (iii) low-level.

1   Introduction

N'importe quel has recently entered in the French lexicon and his use has progressed in Modern French. It is a Free Choice item (FCi) as it allows random selection of a referent from a set of possible individuals. We assume that *n'importe quel* is a determiner because it occurs in initial position of the noun phrase (NP) and it shows gender and number[2] agreement with the related name.

Muller (2007) notices that *n'importe qu-* constructions can have three possible interpretations. The first and the second ones are similar to widening and low-level. We define these notions in the next section of this paper. The third interpretation is based on the notion of scale with a low-level direction (*ex* : On nous fait manger n'importe quoi ! (Muller, 2006)). In this example, a scale is conceivable. The endpoints could be on one side *the best for the health* and on the other side *the worst*. Reed (2000) also argues that *n'importe qu-* implies a scale notion.

According to Vlachou (2007), each FCi is associated to one or more of the following readings: widening, ignorance, indifference, indiscriminacy, indistinguishability and low-level. Four of these six values have been assigned by Vlachou to *n'importe qu-* constructions: widening, indiscriminacy, indistinguishability and low-level.

In Contemporary French, we consider that *n'importe quel* can have three interpretative values, namely widening, indifference and indiscrimination. On the basis of examples from Frantext, we show that these values could be expressed by *n'importe quel* from the

1 We would like to offer our most sincere thanks for the reviewers' comments.
2 There is no general consensus on this point among linguists. We provide some syntactic arguments in support of our analysis.

beginning of its use as a determiner. Because we use Frantext, our analysis is based on literary French.

In our paper, we detail in section 2 the semantic values *n'importe quel* can bear. Then, we describe the process leading to the formation of *n'importe quel* (section 3). In section 4, we pay attention to other constructions based on the verb *importer*. Section 5 concludes our article.

2   The interpretative values of *n'importe quel*

2.1   In Contemporary French

As mentioned above, Vlachou (2007) argues that *n'importe qu-* can express widening, indiscriminacy, indistinguishability and low-level.

Consider first the notion of widening. Widening was introduced by Kadmon and Landman (1993) for the analysis of *any* as both FCi and Polarity Negative item (NPi).

(1)   "In an NP of the form *any CN*, *any* widens the interpretation of the common noun phrase (CN) along a contextual dimension." (Kadmon and Landman, 1993: 361)

This value involves the consideration of more entities in the domain of quantification that it would be the case for a NP introduced by an indefinite determiner like *a*.

In (2), *n'importe quel* allows the widening of the set of times: all moments can be considered, even those we don't think of.

(2)   [...] à l'inverse de l'igname, le taro est périssable et doit être mangé aussitôt déterré. Il peut être planté **à n'importe quel moment** [...] (J. W. Page, *Les Derniers Peuples Primitifs*, 1941)
       '[…] unlike yam, taro is perishable and should be eaten soon unearthed. It can be planted **at any time**.'

If we turn towards indiscriminacy, Vlachou (2007: 348) notices that this value "implies the random selection by an agent of an entity out of a set of alternatives. Consider a set A of alternatives $\{a_1, a_2,..., a_n\}$. An agent chooses randomly out of this set if the probability of the agent to choose an alternative a_n is $1/n$, where *n* is the amount of alternatives".

The indiscriminacy value is Horn's notion (2000b) applied to *any* when the latter was preceded by *just*. In this use, there is no ambiguity; *any* is an FCi even if it is in the scope of negation.

(3)   a. A whale is not **any fish**. (NPi) (Horn, 2000a)
       b. A trout is not **any fish**. (FCi) (Horn, 2000a)

(4)   a.* A whale is not **just any fish**. (NPi) (Horn, 2000a)
       b.   A trout is not **just any fish**. (FCi) (Horn, 2000a)

Possible ambiguity is cleared up by our encyclopaedic knowledge. In fact, we know that a whale is a mammal and that a trout is a fish. There is just one possible interpretation. Therefore, *just* can't be employed in (4a) because of our world knowledge.

According to Vlachou, indiscriminacy is expressed in (5), where *n'importe comment* can be paraphrased by *au hasard*.

(5)   Le choix n'a pas été fait **n'importe comment** mais conformément à ce que laissaient prévoir les caractères sociologiques de ces indécis : niveau de vie, résidence, religion. (Vlachou, 2007: 149)
'The choice was not made **randomly** but in accordance to the sociological profile of these indecisive persons: living standards, residency, religion.'

Consider now indistinguishability. This interpretation is available if and only if the pragmatics of the context is compatible with the fact that the entity can be characterized as being average or common (Vlachou, 2007). Indistinguishability has common points with indiscriminacy. The difference between these two values is that indiscriminacy FCI describes a choice made by an agent.

(6)   Her illness is not **just any illness**. Mary suffers from HIV. (Vlachou, 2007: 135)

In this example, as Mary did not choose randomly her illness, there isn't indiscriminacy. However, different levels of illness exist, some being more serious than others. Therfore, example (6) expresses indistinguishability. In this example, the illness that is referred to is more serious than the average.

Let's turn finally to the low-level value. Vlachou (2007) considers that low-level implies that an entity is below the norm in a given context.

(7)   Did you hear the news ? John found something in the street. It is not **just anything**. He found an extremely expensive golden ring. (Vlachou, 2007: 138)

The value expressed by *anything* in (7) is low-level. Indeed, what can be picked up from the pavements of our streets is usually not very valuable. Therefore, these things are below a norm, which could be a utility or a novelty norm. In (7), it is not the case: John found something with of great value.

Our analysis of *n'importe quel* shows that two of Vlachou's values can be expressed by the French determiner: widening and low-level. A third one must be added: indifference[3].

Two conditions need to be fulfilled for the indifference value to obtain: (i) the speaker must be explicitly mentioned and (ii) it must be possible to infer a value's scale. This notion is in accordance with the etymology of *n'importe quel* (section 3). The term "speaker" is to be understood in a broad way as also possibly referring to a character in the text, who expresses himself or who has an attitude of the type *think* or *consider*. In other words, the speaker must be able to feel an emotion.

In (8), there is no mention of a speaker with feeling's capacity. The first condition fails; indifference is not a possible value.

(8)   **N'importe quelle règle, écrite ou coutumière**, touchant à l'organisation des pouvoirs publics ou aux droits des citoyens peut être abrogée ou modifiée par une loi ordinaire. (Georges Vedel, *Manuel Elémentaire de Droit Constitutionnel*, 1949)
"**Any rule, written or usual one**, connected with government or Citizens' Rights can be repealed or modified by an ordinary rule."

---

[3] We have to note that the term of *indifference* was also used by Vlachou (2007) but in a different way. According to Vlachou, indifference describes a special type of FCi, i.e. constructions with free relative: indifference implies that the agent chooses an entity just because it satisfies the properties described by the free relative's referent.

(9)   [...] elle avait mangé de la vache enragée, elle se serait fait couper un bras et même hacher menu pour nous, elle aurait pris **n'importe quel travail** pour s'en sortir, elle aurait fait des ménages. (Anne-Marie Garat, *Dans la pente du toit*, 1998)
        "She went through lean times, she would have her arm cut by anyone, and even have mincemeat made of her for us, she would have taken **any job** to struggle, she would have worked as a cleaning woman."

Unlike the previous example, *n'importe quel* expresses indifference in (9). In this example, the two conditions are fulfilled: there is an explicit manifestation of the speaker and the scale of hardness can be inferred.

We have to point out that widening is a purely semantic notion, whereas indifference and low-level are semantic-pragmatics ones.

The basic notion of *n'importe quel* is widening. We adopt a different point of view from that of Vlachou (2007), who considers that widening appears in some particular contexts. For us, *n'importe quel* always expresses widening and all FCi share this value. This explains our characterisation of widening as a semantic value.

But semantics isn't enough to propose a complete analysis. We cannot exclude the meaning the speaker wants to give to his utterance. Context of the sentence has to be taken into account, and so, the pragmatics. Including the pragmatics in the characterization of *n'importe quel* enables us to put forward two different values: indifference and low-level.

Following Vlachou (2007), we consider that *n'importe quel* expresses low-level when the pragmatics of context is compatible with the characterization of an entity which is below a norm. The type of norm is defined by the context. For example, in (10), the norm is of aesthetic nature or concern the quality of work. A non-aesthetic work can't be considered, so the domain of work among which it is possible to find a referent is restricted.

(10)   Elle travaillerait dans le fin. Elle ne se chargerait pas, bien entendu, de **n'importe quel bricolage**. Du joli travail, qu'elle ferait. Il ne fallait pas oublier qu'elle s'y connaissait, et même sans parler de machine à coudre, qu'elle était une brodeuse hors ligne. (Louis Guilloux, *Le Pain des Rêves*, 1942)
        "She would work in delicacy. Of course, she wouldn't do **any do-it-yourself.** Nice work, she would do. We didn't forget that she is a connoisseur. Even without a sewing machine, she was an excellent embroiderer."

The interpretation of (10) is the following: "she doesn't do any do-it-yourself, she doesn't do rough works."

In fact, the presence of negation items in a sentence is responsible for low-level interpretation. The negation excludes individuals below a norm defined by the context, and widening occurs only on one part of the domain of quantification. In (10), individuals in the do-it-yourself domain are excluded. In negation items, we include negative prefix:

(11)   Il est en particulier **inutile** de chercher à établir des vignes dans **n'importe quel terrain** ; le fait que ce terrain était jadis planté en vigne n'est pas suffisant pour que l'on puisse y établir à coup sûr des vignes greffées. (Louis Levadoux, *La Vigne et sa Culture*, 1961)
        "There is no point to plant some vines in **any ground**; the fact that this ground have before vine stock isn't enough to grafted vines sprout."

However, low-level can also appear in an affirmative sentence. In this case, low-level can result from the association of *n'importe quel* to a lexical item with negative connotation (12) or from an enumeration of *n'importe qu-* constructions like in (13).

(12)   Il ferait bien mieux, crois-moi, de se dépêcher de finir sa thèse et de se faire nommer n'importe où, dans **n'importe quel trou**… (Nathalie Sarraute, *Le Planétarium*, 1959)
"He should better end his PhD thesis quickly, trust me, and find a work anywhere, in **any dump**…"

(13)   Je suis prête à répondre à tous les noms qu'on me donnera, à faire de moi **n'importe quoi**, à m'en aller vivre **n'importe où**, dans **n' importe quelle maison**, **n' importe quel pays**. (Irène Monesi, *Nature Morte devant la Fenêtre*, 1966)
"I'm ready to take any name that anybody wants to give me, to do **anything**, to leave **anywhere**, in **any house**, in **any country**."

Such as negation, a lexical item with a negative connotation allows a restriction of the domain of quantification, like *trou* ('dump') in (12). In fact, all places cannot be qualified as dump. Moreover, low-level is strengthened by the fact that another *n'importe qu*-construction, *n'importe où* ('anywhere'), is employed in the sentence just before *trou*.

In (13), the nouns introduced by *n'importe quel* (*maison* 'house', *pays* 'country') have no negative connotation. Despite this fact, this sentence is interpreted as expressing some low-level value. This suggests that low-level is not dependant of the context only. Both the context in which *n'importe quel* is used and the semantic content of *n'importe quel* are relevant facts to account for low-level interpretation. We can refer to the definition of widening proposed by Kadmon and Landman (1993), in which they indicate that the interpretation of the noun is widened by *any* "along a contextual dimension".

Notice that the contextual dimension is not always explicit and shared by all speakers. Native speakers of French have generally the common feeling that *n'importe quel* is not as neutral as some other indefinites. *N'importe quel* is more expressive (cf. Pescarini, 2008). As a matter of fact, if we replace *n'importe quel N* by another indefinite NP, like *un N quelconque* ('*just any N*') in (14), the utterance can be ambiguous. The expression of widening and / or low-level appears with *n'importe quel*, but not with *un N quelconque*. The interpretation of (14a) depends of the contextual dimension chosen: work or hard work.

(14)   a. Elle fera **n'importe quel travail**.
        'She will do **any work**'
    b. Elle fera **un travail quelconque**.
        'She will do just any work, **no matter what this work is**.'

The impression that (14a) isn't neutral results of the use of the term *travail* ('*work*'), but not only. In (14a), we feel that the work in question will be below a norm, at the difference of (14b). If we now consider (15) where the noun introduced by *n'importe quel* has no negative connotation, it appears that several interpretations can be distinguished.

(15)   Marie pourrait porter **n'importe quelle robe** pour aller à la soirée.
    'Mary could wear **any dress** to go to the party.'

The expression of (15) leads us to include more entities in the domain of quantification, entities usually not considered as part of it. However, depending on the point of view of the speaker, the worst or the best can be included. So, the example (15) can have at least two different interpretations:

(15')   a. Marie pourrait porter **n'importe quelle robe** pour aller à la soirée, même la plus moche, la plus mal taillée, car de toute façon, elle a une silhouette parfaite.
        'Mary could wear **any dress** to go to the party, even the most horrible dress, badly tailored; it's not a problem, because she's a perfect body.'

b. Marie pourrait porter **n'importe quelle robe** pour aller à la soirée, même la plus somptueuse, avec le décolleté le plus plongeant, car de toute façon, elle a une silhouette parfaite.
'Mary could wear **any dress** to go to the party, even the most sumptuous dress, with a plunging neckline; it's not a problem, because she's a perfect body.'

In both cases, *n'importe quel* is not neutral. The example (9), repeated below, is similar to example (14a):

(9)   [...] elle avait mangé de la vache enragée, elle se serait fait couper un bras et même hacher menu pour nous, elle aurait pris **n'importe quel travail** pour s'en sortir, elle aurait fait des ménages. (Anne-Marie Garat, *Dans la pente du toit*, 1998)
"[...] she had gone through lean times, she would have had her arm cut and even have mincemeat made of her for us, she would have taken **any job** to struggle through it, she would have worked as a cleaning woman."

The work that she will do will probably not be very interesting or fulfilling. The addition of *même* ('*even*') in the sentence reinforces the low-level value: *elle aurait pris **n'importe quel travail** pour s'en sortir, elle aurait même fait des ménages ('she even would have worked as a cleaning woman')*. In this example, *un N quelconque* can replace *n'importe quel N*.

Note that variations can be observed in the expression of *n'importe qu-* constructions' values. For example, low-level seems more important when expressed by *n'importe qui* ('*anybody*') *n'importe quoi* ('*anything*') than by *n'importe quel* ('*no matter which*'):

(16)   Mais si, tu verras, ai-je murmuré. Ne sois pas jaloux de **n'importe quoi** tout le temps. (Geneviève Brisac, *Week-End de Chasse à la Mère*, 1996)
'You will see that is the case, I have murmured. Stop being jealous of **anything** all the time.'

Negation, which makes it possible to trigger the expression of low-level, narrows the domain of quantification and has an impact on indifference and widening. That is the case in (10), for example. In fact, indifference and widening are connected values: the first one follows from the second one. Since the exact constitution of the domain of quantification doesn't affect the interpretation of *n'importe quel*, one is allowed to infer that the identity of the chosen element isn't important. Indifference would be a notion close to the one of Non-Individuation (NI) introduced by Jayez and Tovena (2005). According to the authors, the identity of the NP's referent containing the FCi is not relevant for the truth of the sentence when NI, i.e. non-specification in Muller's terminology (2006), is expressed. Non-specification is a close synonym of non-individuation, but can be applied to cardinal quantifiers (Muller, 2006: 24)[4].

Indifference is implied by the *random feature*, defined by Kleiber and Martin (1977). It can be summarized as follows: the constituents are all on the same level and one of them can be chosen randomly[5].

---

[4] « c'est ce que Jayez & Tovena nomment non-individuation, et que je préfère nommer non-spécification parce que le même phénomène peut toucher des quantifieurs de cardinalité diverse » Muller (2006).
"this is what Jayez & Tovena qualify as non-individuation, and what i would rather qualify as non-specification because quantifiers of varied cardinal types can be concerned by the same phenomenon"
[5] We can establish a parallel between NI and the *random feature* if we consider that, in both notions, all elements are of the same level.

In this study, we put aside indiscriminacy and indistinguishability, these notions being irrelevant for our analysis. The main difference between them holds in the absence of any possible choice as far as indistinguishability is concerned. But we do not consider this as a real distinction. Indeed, in Vlachou's example (cf. 5), the agent has to make a choice.

To sum up, in our corpus, we observe three different interpretative values of the French determiner *n'importe quel*: widening, which is a semantic value, and indifference and low-level, which are semantic-pragmatics ones.

2.2   The interpretive values of *n'importe quel* at its creation

N'importe quel is an FCi first employed at the end of the 18th century. The widening value, correlated to the notion of FCi, was expressed from the beginning.

(17)   Cependant, partout où j'allais, au Prado, au Buen Retiro, dans **n'importe quel autre lieu public,** un homme me suivait, dont les yeux vifs et perçants semblaient lire dans mon âme. (Jean Potocki, *Manuscrit trouvé à Saragosse*, 1815)
'However, wherever I went, to Prado, to Buen Retiro, to **any other public place**, a man followed me. His eagle eyes seemed to read into my soul.'

In the previous example, the FCi conveys only one value: widening. But widening isn't complete, as two places are excluded (Prado and Buen Retiro). The adjective *autre* ('other') is responsible of the exclusion and its use results in a geographic restriction. However, exclusion does not block widening. In (17), except from Prado and Buen Retiro, the domain of quantification includes all possible places, even most improbable ones.

Since the beginning of its use, *n'importe quel* can be used to express the others interpretative values detailed in section 2.1. Consider examples (18) and (19), which convey indifference:

(18)   Mais quel besoin aurais-je eu de m'inquiéter de la lenteur de **n'importe quel travail** ; je sentais tout le temps que j'avais devant moi, et que cet ouvrage une fois achevé je n'aurais aucune autre occupation, (Pétrus Borel, *Vie et aventures de Robinson Crusoé* [trad.], 1836)
'Why should I worry of the slowness of **any work**; I feel that I have plenty of time and when I would have this work done, I will not have any other occupation.'

(19)   Duvernet a demandé à jouer **n'importe quel rôle**, et il entre en scène au 3me acte, en disant : les lampes sont-elles à l'heure ? (George Sand, *Correspondance : 1851*, 1851)
'Duvernet asked to play **any role**, and came on stage at the 3rd act, saying: are lights in time?"

In (18) and (19), the two conditions required to allow indifference are fulfilled by the presence of an overt speaker and an underlying value's scale, respectively a scale of hardness of work in (18) and one of the importance of the role in (19). What is suggested in (19) is *even the least important*.

From the middle of the 19th century, some examples in which native speakers could feel low-level are attested:

(20) mais j'ai toujours cru "qu'un amour comme le mien ne pouvait entrer en comparaison". Vous auriez seulement dû élargir[6] la proposition et dire **n'importe quel espèce d'amour**. (Gustave Flaubert, *Correspondance (1846)*, 1847)
'But I have allways believed "that a love like mine couldn't be compared". You should just have to widen the clause and said **any kind of love**.'

(21) Matelote, grosse, ronde, rousse et criarde, ancienne sultane favorite du défunt Hucheloup, était laide plus que **n'importe quel monstre mythologique** (Victor Hugo, *Les Misérables*, 1862)
'Matelote, fat, chunky, redheaded and screaming, formerly favourite of the late Hucheloup, was uglier than **any mythologic monster**.'

For low-level value, the choice of the noun modified by *n'importe quel* can be a determining factor, as shown by the previous examples (20-21). In fact, the term *kind of* (20) can be considered as pejorative; we can add, for example, *even the most destructive*. In (21), the syntagm *mythologic monster* is a depreciative one, even more so if the beauty of a woman is compared to this NP.

This value appears more often as we move forward the century. The kind of sentences used also plays a role in the expression of low-level. In fact, a sentence seems more expressive when it isn't an affirmative one, like interrogative or exclamative clauses in (22) and (23) Moreover, as we noticed previously, a repetition of *n'importe qu-* constructions has influence on low-level, as in example (23).

(22) Et les caractères de Mlle De Varandeuil, de Germinie, de Jupillon, vous les trouvez, n'est-ce pas ? Inférieurs aux caractères de **n'importe quel mélodrame du boulevard**. (Edmond & Jules de Goncourt, *Journal : mémoires de la vie littéraire : t. 3*, 1890)
'And the natures of Mlle De Varandeuil, de Germinie, de Jupillon, you find them lower than those of **any melodrama farce**, isn't it?'

(23) Sotte ! Est-ce que tu aimes ton bien ? Mais que quelqu'un te demande n'importe quoi, tu le lui donnes avant qu'il ait fini ; n'importe qui, oui, **n'importe quel galvaudeux**, je t'ai vue ! (Paul Claudel, *La Jeune fille Violaine*, 1892)
'Silly girl! Do you like your possession? But if anyone asks you anything, you give it to him before he finishes his request; anybody, yes, **any sully**, I saw you!'

As we have shown, *n'importe quel* could express its three interpretative values from the beginning, i.e. when it appeared in the French lexicon. In our corpus, we can note that widening and indifference are present from the beginning of the century, whereas low-level appears a bit later, in the middle of 19th century. However, this doesn't prove that this value didn't exist before, but only that our corpus doesn't contain occurrences of low-level before 1850.

After this description of the possible interpretative values of *n'importe quel*, we will now consider in detail its formation.

3   The formation of *n'importe quel*

N'importe quel is a complex expression build out of several constituents. The main one is the verb *importer*. This verb means "être important, compter" ('*to be important, to matter*')

---

[6] In this extract, Flaubert put together the terms *widen* and *n'importe quel*. He unintentionally noted that *n'importe quel* expressed widening.

in modern French, according to the Trésor de la Langue Française (TLF). The first occurrence of *importer* was noted in 1536 with the meaning "exiger, nécessiter, comporter" (*'to require'*). In 1543, its meaning changed in "concerner, être de conséquence pour quelqu'un, pour quelque chose" (*'to concern, to have consequence for someone, something'*).

Whereas *n'importe quel* was attested in our corpus from the beginning of the 19th century, there is no mention of it in the main old French dictionaries before the 8th edition of the *Dictionnaire de l'Académie française* (1932-35). However, in its 6th edition, several constructions from the verb *importer* already appeared, like *n'importe qui, n'importe quoi, n'importe lequel,* or *n'importe comment. N'importe quel* is mentioned, but not in its current form. It appears with a preposition between *n'importe* and *quel*, as in the following example: *n'importe par quel moment* (àt no matter which time'). At that time, it looks as if it was a construction not yet lexicalized.

After making an inventory of *n'importe qu-* forms, we tried to understand what construction process was responsible for these forms, relying on data from Frantext corpus.

The first occurrence of *n'importe quel* in our corpus is a plural form and is dated from 1762, the first singular one being dated from 1784:

(24)   Mon ami, en général, n'aime point les chiens ni les autres bêtes, **n'importe quels noms** elles aient, ni comme quoi elles marchent. (Denis Diderot, *Lettres à Sophie Volland : t. 1*, 1762)
'Habitually, my friend doesn't like neither dogs nor others animals, **no matter their name** or the way they walk.'

(25)   Je lui répondis, **n'importe quelle pièce**, toutes iront également au but, dès qu'elle en-verra la représentation. (Nicolas Rétif de La Bretonne, *La Paysanne pervertie, ou les Dangers de la ville*, 1784)
'I answer him **any play**, because all will go to the point, as soon as she will get the performance going.'

However, the use of *n'importe quel* really took off from 1830, as shown in table 1, the number of occurrences of *n'importe quel* increases, whereas the number of texts is roughly the same.

	1750-1779	1780-1809	1810-1838	1839-1869	1870-1900	1901-1925
N'importe quel / quelle		1 (1784)	9	73	157	312
N'importe quels / quelles	1 (1762)[7]		2	4	4	5

Table 1: number of *n'importe quel(le)(s)* occurrences in Frantext

---

[7] The dates in parentheses correspond to the first example of the form found in our corpus.

Period	1750 - 1779	1780 - 1809	1810 - 1838	1839- 1869	1870 - 1900	1901 - 1925
Number of texts	232	150	240	400	307	336

Table 2: number of texts in Frantext

The evolution is similar for the other constructions based on the verb *importer*, such as *n'importe* + pronoun (*qui, quoi*). We noticed however that *n'importe qui* appeared earlier in our corpus, as it is attested in Frantext since 1630. Nevertheless, Béguelin (2002:7) indicates that the interpretation is ambiguous with these first constructions.

(26)   Pauvre frère ! vois-tu, ton silence t'abuse,
         De la langue ou des yeux, **n'importe qui** t'accuse, (Pierre Corneille, *Mélite ou les fausses lettres*, 1633)
         'Poor brother ! Do you see that your silence fools you;
         With the tongue or eyes, anybody points to you'

For Béguelin, the syntactic analysis of [*n'importe qui*] as one constituent is an anachronism, *n'importe* being at this time just employed as a governing verb. The analysis should be the following: [n'importe]$_V$ [qui t'accuse] $_{wh-P}$. The context seems to reinforce this idea, because it is difficult to analyse *n'importe qui* as a lexicalized form in this example. But Béguelin's analysis seems problematic with other examples (see 27), where it is not so easy to consider *importe* like a governing verb.

(27)   cotteray icy les livres que j'ay de luy, affin que Msrs les Elzevirs ou Msr Le Maire,
         à qui j'en parlé aussy et qui me promit de me les envoyer, me les envoyent,
         n'importe qui, pourveu qu' ilz ne les envoyent deux fois, à quoy vous prendrez,
         s'il vous plaist, garde. (Le Père Marin Mersenne, *Correspondance : t. 2 : 1628-1630*, 1630)
         'I have some books of him. I talked about it to Mr les Elzevirs or Mr Le Maire,
         who promises to send me these books, send them to me, **whoever**. Let's hope they
         just don't send them twice, you will pay attention, please.'

In a footnote, Béguelin analyses this example and asserts that *importe* is a governing verb. But *n'importe qui* being in apposition, it is difficult, on a syntactic perspective, to adopt his point of view.

All occurrences of *n'importe qui* and *n'importe quoi* in Frantext are taken into account in the following table:

	1630- 1659	1660- 1689	1690- 1719	1720- 1749	1750- 1779	1780- 1809	1810- 1838	1839- 1869	1870- 1900	1901- 1925

N'importe qui	3 [8] (1630)			1				3	41	68	92
N'importe quoi								6 (1823)	70	142	184

Table 3: number of occurrences of *n'importe qui/quoi* in Frantext

Looking at table 3, it appears that the use of *n'importe qui* and *n'importe quoi* became regular at the same period than *n'importe quel*.

The evolution of *n'importe lequel* is similar: the first occurrence in our corpus is dated from 1779 but it was regularly employed from 1839.

We can mention at least two reasons for the late apparition of *n'importe quel*:

On one hand, *n'importe quel* is built on the verb *importer*, a loan word from Italian (*importare*). *Importer* recently entered in the French lexicon in 1536. Previously, the verb employed and semantically equivalent was *chaloir*[9]:

(28)   Il li   enortet, dont   lei   nonque chielt
        Il lui ordonna, ce dont à elle jamais   chaut
        Il lui ordonna, mais peu lui chaut (*La Cantilène De Sainte Eulalie*, 881)
        'He ordered him, but it doesn't **matter** to him.'

On the other hand, we postulate that four main stages succeeded one another to get to the current form of *n'importe quel*. The distinction made between these different stages came from the evolution of the form observed in our corpus.

The first stage corresponds to the verb *importer* conjugated at the third person of singular, in the present tense: ***importe***. This conjugated form is the central component in the construction of *n'importe quel*. The verbal form chosen was the most employed one. In fact, *importer* appears mostly at the third person of singular. There are only a few exceptions, even when the subject isn't impersonal: on forty-three occurrences of *importer* in the 16th century, just two of them are at the third person of plural. One example is given under (29). We can add that on these forty-three occurrences, seven are not employed in present tense, such as example (30).

(29)   Comme j'ay opinion que la robbe longue et le bonnet carré est le propre et plus
        honneste acoustrement d'un prestre ou d'un magistrat, jaçoit que ces acoustremens
        n'**importent** rien à l'honesteté, (Guy de Brués, *Les Dialogues de Guy de Brués
        contre les nouveaux académiciens*, 1557)
        'As I think that the long dress and the square cap are the most appropriate dress for
        a priest or for a magistrate, I believe the dress doesn't **matter** with regards to
        honesty.'

---

[8] No real occurrences of *n'importe qui* exists before 1720 if we adopt Béguelin's analysis, and just one if (27) is a real form of *n'importe qui*.

[9] *Chaloir* was ambiguous in Old French. Apart from "importer", it could mean: "chauffer", "préocupper" ('*to warm, to preoccupy*').

(30)   hyer apres disner le Roy me fist appeler, et estant devant luy, avec tresinstante et pitoyable priere me requist, tout bagné de larmes, de faire chose pour luy qui luy **importoit** de la vie. (Pierre Boaistuau, *Histoires tragiques,* 1559)
'Yesterday, after diner, the King called me and beseeched me to do something for him. A thing which really **matter** for him.'

Few years later, in 1592, the negative particle *n'* appeared in front of *importe*. This form, ***n'importe***, which can appear with an impersonal subject, is the second stage in the construction of *n'importe quel*. *N'importe* is employed like an idiom which expresses the indifference of the speaker towards the fact enunciated (cf. 31). The impersonal subject is not part of the selected form for the construction of the determiner, because it was an optional element.

(31)   S'il me messied à moy, comme je le croy, **n'importe** : il peut estre utile à quelque autre. (Michel de Montaigne, *Essais : t. 2 (livre 3),* 1592)
'If it doesn't suit me, like I think it, **no matter**.'

The third stage is of the form: ***n'importe + preposition + quel + N***. This construction appears in our corpus in 1604.

(32)   Andromache : - Qu'il se reserve encore à leur donner la chasse.
Priam . - Peut estre à coüardise il soroit imputé.
Andromache : - **N'importe par quel prix**, mais qu'il soit racheté.
Priam : - Mais quel esprit constant consentira de faire
Un vray mal pour un bien à peine imaginaire ? (Antoine de Montchrestien, *Hector,* 1604)
'Andromache : - He sets aside to chase them.
Priam : - Maybe he would attribute by cowardise.
Andromache : **It doesn't matter how**, but he has to reedem himself.'

In (32), the preposition *par* ('*by*') is used, but this construction accepts other prepositions. It can be *en* ('*in*') for example (33). We listed all the prepositions we found in this construction in table 4.

(33)   Un jour, dit un auteur, **n'importe en quel chapitre**, deux voyageurs à jeun rencontrerent une huistre. (Nicolas Boileau-Despréaux, *Épistres : 1670-1698,* 1698)
'One day, an author said, **no matter the chapter**, two travellers with an empty stomach met an oyster.'

At third stage, we are still in a verbal construction with the following syntactic division: *[n'importe [en quel chapitre]$_{PP}$]$_{VP}$*. Moreover, we noticed that some similar constructions had built other idioms, such as *qu'importe:*

(34)   Ma vie, à moi, est dans mes deux filles. Si elles s'amusent, si elles sont heureuses, bravement mises, si elles marchent sur des tapis, **qu'importe de quel drap** je sois vêtu, et comment est l'endroit où je me couche ? (Honoré de Balzac, *Le Père Goriot,* 1843)
'My life is my two daughters. If they have fun, if they are happy, well-dressed, if they walk on a carpet, **no matter** how my clothes and the place where I sleep are?'

(il) n'importe	1601 -	1630-	1660-	1690-	1720-	1750-
+ preposition	1629	1659	1689	1719	1749	1779
(il) n'importe	1601 -	1630-	1660-	1690-	1720-	1750-
+ preposition	1629	1659	1689	1719	1749	1779

- par	1 (1604)						2
- en		1 (1646)	1	2			2
- dans ('*into*')							
- sur ('*on*')						1 (1734)	
- à ('*at*')			1 (1675)			4	1
- de ('*from*')						2 (1742)	1
- avec ('*with*')							
- chez							1 (1776)
- pour ('*for*')							
- vers ('*to*')							
- sous ('*under*')							

(il) n'importe + preposition + quel N :	1780 - 1809	1810 - 1838	1839 - 1869	1870 - 1900	1901 - 1925	1926 - 2006
- par	4	3	8	3		
- en	1	2	2			
- dans		2 (1833)	4	3		
- sur	1	1	1			
- à	1	5	8	8		2
- de	1	1	3	3		
- avec			1 (1851)			
- chez		1				1
- pour		1 (1831)	1			
- vers		1 (1836)				
- sous		1 (1840)				

Table 4: number of occurrences of (*il*) *n'importe* + *préposition* + *quel* + *N* in Frantext

In table 4, we only recorded the occurrences that can be considered as forms corresponding to the third stage of formation of *n'importe quel*. As a consequence, similar forms introducing free relatives aren't counted. Free relatives are relatives that do not modify a noun. Their structure can be described as follows: *[preposition + quel + N + clause]* preceded by *il n'importe*. The clause contains a null element, a "gap", which has the same reference as N:

(35)   a. N'importoit [de quel trait j'avois l'ame blessée] : Il me falloit plustost bannir de
         la pensée (Jean Desmarets de Saint-Sorlin, *Aspasie*, 1636)
         'No matter how I have the soul hurted: I should rather banish of my mind.'

b. N'importoit [de quel trait] $_{SP}$ j'avois l'ame blessée [-] $_{SP}$]

This example is similar to the previous one:

(36) Il n'importe [de quel endroit vienne la doctrine], pourveu qu'elle soit salutaire (Charles Sorel, *La Bibliothèque françoise de M. C. Sorel, ou le Choix et l'examen des livres françois qui traitent de l'éloquence, de la philosophie, de la dévotion et de la conduite des moeurs*, 1664)
'No matter where the doctrine comes from, provided as it is beneficial.'

The TLF adds that *n'importe quel* was rarely employed until the second half of the 19th century. *N'importe + preposition + quel(le) + noun* was the common construction used in the first half of the 19th century. But it was supplanted by a new construction with a modification of the place of the preposition: the preposition moved in front of *n'importe*. This constitutes the fourth stage that led to the current form of *n'importe quel*: **(préposition) + *n'importe* + *quel* + *N*** (cf. 17).

(17) Cependant, partout où j'allais, au Prado, au Buen Retiro, dans **n'importe quel autre lieu public,** un homme me suivait, dont les yeux vifs et perçants semblaient lire dans mon âme. (Jean Potocki, *Manuscrit trouvé à Saragosse*, 1815)
'However, anywhere I went, to Prado, to Buen Retiro, in **any other public place**, a man followed me. His eagle eyes seemed to read into my soul.'

At the beginning, this construction was only used when the verb had to be followed by a preposition. Then, *n'importe quel* could be employed even if the verb didn't introduce a prepositional phrase (PP), as in (37).

(37) [...] commandé aussi des boutons d'acier fin ciselé pour un gilet de velours noir, sublime invention qui doit me faire plus d'honneur que **n'importe quelle découverte scientifique** (Jules Barbey d'Aurevilly, *Memorandum (Premier)*, 1838)
'[...] placed an order on polished steel buttons too for a velvet-black cardigan, sublime invention that gives me more honour than **any other scientific discovery**.'

The movement of the preposition led to a change of lexical function: [*n'importe* + preposition + *quel* + N] evolved in [preposition + *n'importe* + *quel* + N], so [*n'importe* + [preposition + [*quel* + N]$_{NP}$]$_{PP}$] became [preposition + [*n'importe* + *quel* + N]$_{NP}$]. At this stage, *importe* is no longer the head of a verbal construction, but a component of a complex determiner.

We assume that two steps are necessary to explain the fourth stage of the formation of *n'importe quel*. In fact, it is reasonable to believe that the syntactic representation in (38) is an intermediate step, leading to the representation (39) that account for the analysis of *n'importe quel* as a complex determiner.

(38) DP

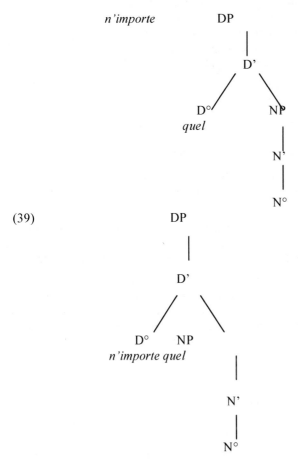

(39)

In contemporary French, the traditional grammars say that *n'importe quel* is not a controversial determiner (cf. Riegel, Pellat et Rioul (1994)). There must have been an intermediate stage between the verbal status and the determiner status. *N'importe quel*, or its previous counterpart, was a verbal form before what we presented as the fourth stage. The construction had already undergone a step of "freezing" as shown by a lot of examples where *n'importe* is in apposition or constitutes a sentence by itself. It seems plausible to imagine that *n'importe* knew a stage without verbal form. This assumption is strengthened by the fact that we know that the same holds for other constructions containing *n'importe*, such as *n'importe qui / n'importe quoi*.

In addition to its change of function lexical, other elements reinforce the idea that *n'importe quel* is a "frozen" form.

First of all, the frequency of use of *n'importe quel* increases over time. Therefore, we can say that *n'importe quel* is well established in usage.

Moreover, *n'importe quel* is a single lemma. Therefore, the insertion of a word between *n'* and *importe*, and between *importe* and *quel* is impossible. In the same way, it's impossible to invert the order of the components.

Furthermore, the meaning of *n'importe quel* isn't compositional. The initial meaning of the different components cannot be found through the actual meaning of the complex determiner. The compositionality principle played a major role to get to the current form of this determiner, but there are no signs of it anymore. For example, *n'* has lost his negative meaning while *n'importe quel* became a determiner. This fact shows that *n'importe quel* is a frozen form. In fact, if we paraphrase the examples that we gave to illustrate the third stage and the fourth one, we show that *n'* isn't a negative item in the last stage anymore.

(33') il n'importe pas en quel chapitre [cela se passe].
'it doesn't matter in which chapter [it happens]'.

(37') sublime invention qui doit me faire plus d'honneur que toute découverte scientifique.
'sublime invention which give me more honour than all scientific discoveries.'

In (33'), the negation is a necessary condition for the sentence to be well-formed. This condition is not needed in example (37'), where *n'importe quel* is quasi-synonymous with *tout* ('*all*').

Originally, the NP [*n'importe quel N*] was constituted by *n'importe* and an embedded NP [*quel N*] (cf. the structure in (40)). At this stage, the denotation of *n'importe quel* was obtained in a way similarly to that of the pronouns and the adverbs of *n'importe qu-* family.

But we can't analyse *n'importe quel* like the other elements of the *n'importe qu-* family anymore. As we have shown, *n'importe quel* has to be analysed as a complex determiner, *n'importe quel*, followed by a noun. Given the current syntax of *n'importe quel N*, especially the absence of an embedded interrogative NP, the semantics of these NP could hardly be compositional.

(40)

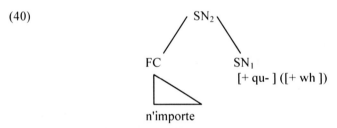

The development of *n'importe quel* is the result of a lexicalization process. *Importe* was first used in affirmative contexts, and then in negative ones (*n'importe*). As the process started during the period in which the impersonal subject and the negative particle *pas* were still optional, the idioms were created without *il* and *pas*. *N'importe* allowed the creation of set constructions. We adopt the following definition of lexicalization, adapted from Prévost and Fagard (2007):

(41) L'émergence de toute nouvelle forme, peu importe son processus de formation au cours de l'histoire et son résultat, est le fruit d'une lexicalisation.
'The emergence of any new form, no matter its process of formation nor its result, is due to a lexicalization.'

We give our definition of lexicalization to clarify our position about the process that applied to the formation of *n'importe quel*: lexicalization or grammaticalization. In fact, we think that it is the result of process of lexicalization, and not grammaticalization.

At first, as a new form is created, we must consider this form and not its components. *N'importe quel* becomes a new word and, as such, a morphosyntactic category is assigned to the latter. To make it clear, we will use the generative grammar terms. Brinton & Traugott (2005) recall that two types of lexical functions have to be distinguished in generative grammar: major categories and minor ones. There are four major syntactic categories, i.e. nouns, verbs, adjectives and prepositions, and two minor categories, i.e. determiners and complementizers. Subsequently, the former were called lexical syntactic categories and the latter functional syntactic categories. *N'importe quel* is part of a functional syntactic category. But being part of a functional category doesn't mean that it results from a grammaticalization process. In fact, a functional feature was assigned to *n'importe quel* from its creation and its syntactic category didn't change.

Moreover, *n'* lost its negative value. As the meaning of the idiom isn't compositional (cf. 33' and 37'), it is a sign of lexicalization.

The same holds for other indefinites built with *n'importe*, such as *n'importe qui* or *n'importe quoi* in particular, which can be employed as a noun:

(42)   Cette réception, c'est un grand **n'importe quoi** !
         'This party is **a** total **nonsense!**'

As nouns are one of the major categories, and because *n'importe quoi* can be used as a noun (42), a lexical category can be assigned to *n'importe quoi*. Therefore, *n'importe quoi* satisfies our definition of lexicalization.

4   Comments on the formation of the *n'importe qu-* set

As we already mentioned, *n'importe* is the main component of a family of indefinites: *n'importe quel / lequel / qui / quoi / où / quand / comment*, which belong to different morphosyntactic categories. In fact, *n'importe quel* is an indefinite determiner, whereas the others are classified as indefinite pronouns or adverbs. Despite this difference, our corpus shows that the process of formation is the same for the whole set. To get to their current forms, all the forms went through at least the two first stages, which we recall below, and some of them went through all four stages.

> (i)*importe*: the verb *importer*, conjugated at the third person of singular, is the main component of the set.
>
> (ii) *n'importe*: from 1592, the negative particule *n'* was used in front of *importe*.
>
> (iii) *n'importe + preposition + qu-*: from 1604, *importer* could introduce a PP; the preposition was placed between the verb and the pronoun. The syntactic analysis is then the following: *[VP n'importe [PP preposition + qu-]]*
>
> (iv) *(preposition) + n'importe + qu- (+ N)*: at the beginning of the 19th century, the preposition moved. It led to the formation of the complex determiner *n'importe quel* and to that of the indefinite complex pronouns *n'importe qui* and *n'importe quoi*.

It is not the case that the whole family of *n'importe qu-* constructions has gone through the four stages of evolution. In fact, we haven't found any occurrences of the third stage for the forms made up of *n'importe* and an adverb. It seems that constructions like *n'importe + preposition + où / quand / comment* haven't been used. It's not surprising because a preposition can't be used to introduce the adverb *comment*. However, it's possible to insert a few prepositions before *où* and *quand*: *jusqu'à* is an example of a heavy one, but others, like *par*, can appear before *où*. Anyway, the number of possible prepositions can't be compared to the one of prepositions introducing *qui* or *quoi*. We assume that the heaviness of *jusqu'à* acted as a brake on the construction process of indefinite pronouns described above.

Therefore, we postulate that the adverbs built on the verb *importer* were formed by analogy with the pronouns. Even if adverbs and pronouns were quoted all at once in the 6th dictionary of the French Academy (1832-1835), this doesn't go against our hypothesis if we argue that the process was fast. We can't find occurrences attesting of the third stage of *n'importe lequel* either. But we think that this is purely accidental, because many prepositions can be used in front of *lequel*. The fact that we used a limited corpus for our analysis can be held responsible for this pieceof data. Another explanation could be suggested, namely that the heaviness of *lequel* blocked the formation process, and *n'importe lequel*, as the adverbs, was built by analogy with *n'importe qui* / *n'importe quoi*.

All the elements of the *n'importe qu-* family are built in a similar way: the third component is always an interrogative element. This fact is not fortuitous and not specific to French. In fact, in others languages, indefinite FCi have, among their components, an interrogative item. For example, in English, there are two sets of FCi, one constructed on *any* and the other on *ever*. Haspelmath (1997) noticed that several indefinites had an interrogative component across languages. According to him, these indefinites can have different interpretative values: (i) ignorance, as *neştine* "*any person*" in dialectical Rumanian, (ii) politeness or volition, as the Italian *qualsivoglia* "*any*", (iii) possibility, as *mi-še-hu* "*someone*" in Hebrew and (iv) indifference, such as *no matter who* in English. Haspelmath called them (i) *I don't know*, (ii) *pleases / want*, (iii) *it may be* and (iv) *no matter* respectively. *N'importe qu-* constructions are parts of the last set. This set, like the others has equivalents in different languages:

(43)   French: n'importe **qui**

(44)   English: no matter **who**

(45)   Dutch: onverschillig **wie**
          'no matter **who**'

(46)   Deutsch: gleich **welcher**
          'no matter **which**'

5   Conclusion

N'importe quel is an indefinite FCi which appeared recently in the French lexicon. The determiner is part of a family of indefinites constructed on the verb *importer* and built compositionally. But further to the lexicalization process, the meaning of *n'importe qu-* constructions is no longer perceived as compositional.

The construction and the development of the members of the *n'importe qu-* family are similar. They were used from the beginning of the 19th century. We have showed that four main stages can be isolated in their evolution. Some of the members of the family went through all these four stages. Others skipped the third stage and reached the fourth by analogy, like *n'importe où* / *quand* / *comment*.

Finally, we have argued that *n'importe quel, n'importe qui* and *n'importe quoi* could take from the beginning of their use the different interpretative values of widening, low-level and indifference. Widening is a purely semantic notion, whereas indifference and low-level are semantic-pragmatics values.

References

Béguelin, M.-J. (2002). Routines syntagmatiques et grammaticalisation : le cas des clauses en *n'importe*. In H.L. Andersen et H. Nølke (éds), *Macro-syntaxe et macro-sémantique*, pp. 43-69. Berne, Peter Lang.

Brinton, L. J. and E. C. Traugott (2005). *Lexicalization and language change.* Cambridge, Cambridge University Press.

Haspelmath, M. (1997). *Indefinite Pronouns.* Oxford, Clarendon Press.

Horn, L. R. (2000a). *Any* and (-) *Ever*: Free choice and free relatives. In *Proceedings of the 15th Annual Conference of the Israeli Association for Theoretical Linguistics*, pp. 71-111.

Horn, L. R. (2000b). Pick a theory (not just any theory): Indiscriminatives and the free choice indefinite. Dans L. Horn et Y. Kato (éds), *Negation and polarity: syntactic and semantic perspectives*, pp. 147–192. Oxford, Oxford University Press.

Jayez, J. and L. M. Tovena (2005). Free-choiceness and Non Individuation. *Linguistics and Philosophy 28*, pp. 1-71.

Kadmon, N. and F. Landman (1993). *Any. Linguistics and Philosophy 4*, pp. 353–422.

Kleiber, G. and R. Martin (1977). La quantification universelle en français. *Semantikos 2*, pp. 19-36.

Muller, C. (2006). Polarité négative et free choice dans les indéfinis de type *que ce soit* et *n'importe. Langages 162*, pp. 7-31.

Muller, C. (2007). Les indéfinis free choice confrontés aux applications scalaires. *Travaux de linguistique 54*, pp. 83-96.

Pescarini, S. (2008). Expressivité et détermination. Communication au Colloque *Ecart et expressivité*, Nancy-Université.

Prévost, S. and B. Fagard (2007). Grammaticalisation et lexicalisation : la formation d'expressions complexes. *Langue française 156*, pp. 3-8.

Reed, P. (2000). *Any* and its French equivalents. *French Language Studies 10*, pp. 101-116.

Riegel, M., Pellat, J.-C. and R. Rioul (1994). *Grammaire méthodique du français.* Paris, PUF.

Vlachou, E. (2007). *Free choice in and out of context: semantics and distribution of French, Greek and English free choice items.* PhD thesis, Université de Sorbonne-Paris IV et Université d'Utrecht.

Lightning Source UK Ltd.
Milton Keynes UK
UKOW051020301112

202963UK00002B/69/P